KEEPING HEART

Ohio University Press
Series in Race, Ethnicity, and Gender in Appalachia

Series editors: Marie Tedesco, Chris Green, and Elizabeth S. D. Engelhardt

Memphis Tennessee Garrison: The Remarkable Story of a Black Appalachian Woman, edited by Ancella R. Bickley and Lynda Ann Ewen

The Tangled Roots of Feminism, Environmentalism, and Appalachian Literature, by Elizabeth S. D. Engelhardt

Red, White, Black, and Blue: A Dual Memoir of Race and Class in Appalachia, by William R. Drennen Jr. and Kojo (William T.) Jones Jr., edited by Dolores M. Johnson

Beyond Hill and Hollow: Original Readings in Appalachian Women's Studies, edited by Elizabeth S. D. Engelhardt

Loving Mountains, Loving Men, by Jeff Mann

Power in the Blood: A Family Narrative, by Linda Tate

Out of the Mountains: Appalachian Stories, by Meredith Sue Willis

Negotiating a Perilous Empowerment: Appalachian Women's Literacies, by Erica Abrams Locklear

Standing Our Ground: Women, Environmental Justice, and the Fight to End Mountaintop Removal, by Joyce M. Barry

Shake Terribly the Earth: Stories from an Appalachian Family, by Sarah Beth Childers

Thinking Outside the Girl Box: Teaming Up with Resilient Youth in Appalachia, by Linda Spatig and Layne Amerikaner

Once I Too Had Wings: The Journals of Emma Bell Miles, 1908–1918, edited by Steven Cox

Women of the Mountain South: Identity, Work, and Activism, edited by Connie Park Rice and Marie Tedesco

Keeping Heart: A Memoir of Family Struggle, Race, and Medicine, by Otis Trotter

Keeping Heart

A MEMOIR OF FAMILY STRUGGLE, RACE, AND MEDICINE

Otis Trotter

Introduction by Joe William Trotter Jr.

OHIO UNIVERSITY PRESS
ATHENS, OHIO

Ohio University Press, Athens, Ohio 45701
ohioswallow.com
© 2015 by Ohio University Press
All rights reserved

Printed in the United States of America
Ohio University Press books are printed on acid-free paper ∞ ™

25 24 23 22 21 20 19 18 17 16 15   5 4 3 2 1

Library of Congress Cataloging-in-Publication Data
Trotter, Otis, 1954–
 Keeping heart : a memoir of family struggle, race, and medicine / Otis Trotter ; introduction by Joe William Trotter Jr.
   pages cm. — (Ohio University Press series in race, ethnicity, and gender in Appalachia)
 Summary: "'After saying our good-byes to friends and neighbors, we all got in the cars and headed up the hill and down the road toward a future in Ohio that we hoped would be brighter,' Otis Trotter writes in Keeping Heart : A Memoir of Family Struggle, Race, and Medicine. Organized around the life histories, medical struggles, and recollections of Trotter and his thirteen siblings, the story begins in 1914 with his parents. By tracing the family's movement northward after the unexpected death of his father, this engaging chronicle illuminates the journeys not only of a black man born with heart disease in the southern Appalachian coalfields, but of his family and community. This testament to the importance of ordinary lives fills a gap in the literature on an underexamined aspect of American experience: the lives of African Americans in rural Appalachia and in the nonurban endpoints of the Great Migration"— Provided by publisher.
 ISBN 978-0-8214-2188-8 (hardback : acid-free paper) — ISBN 978-0-8214-2189-5 (paperback : acid-free paper) — ISBN 978-0-8214-4544-0 (PDF)
 1. Trotter, Otis, 1954– 2. Trotter, Otis, 1954——Family. 3. African Americans—Biography. 4. African American families—Biography. 5. Heart—Diseases—Patients—United States—Biography. 6. West Virginia—Biography. 7. Ohio—Biography. 8. Appalachian Region, Southern—Biography. 9. African Americans—Migrations—History—20th century. 10. Migration, Internal—United States—History—20th century. I. Title.
 E185.97.T745A3 2015
 305.896'073092—dc23
 [B]
                                2015018911

CONTENTS

List of Illustrations — vii

Acknowledgments — ix

Introduction by Joe William Trotter Jr. — xiii

one   Memories of Parents and Places — 1

two   Troubled Waters of Vallscreek — 20

three   The Newcomers — 51

four   New Lease on Life — 68

five   Life on the Avenue / Bitter and Sweet — 103

six   Navigating Heart Disease as a Teenager — 123

seven   College and Career — 147

eight   The Struggle Continues — 174

ILLUSTRATIONS

FOLLOWING PAGE 44

Trotter family tree

Coal mine in southern West Virginia

Coal camp home in southern West Virginia

Miners eating their lunch

My mother and my maternal grandmother with my sister Dee

Rock Elvy Missionary Baptist Church, my father's family church

My brothers and I standing on the spot where our house once stood in Vallscreek, 2010

My brother David, my nephew Carson, my brother Rahmaan, and I standing next to Vallscreek, 2010

My brothers and I in front of the old church in Vallscreek, 2010

Rahmaan reminiscing about our childhood exploration of the railroad trestle, 2010

FOLLOWING PAGE 98

My sister Eva, Ralph Harris, my sister Josie Harris, and a friend, 1956

Josie's and Eva's children with my sister Sakina and me at Cy Young Park in Newcomerstown

My sister Bobbie and my brother Rahmaan dancing in the road by Vallscreek, 1991

My sister Jessie and her son Carson around 1974

Jessie and other students from yearbook pictures of talent show

My sisters Jessie and Mecca as juniors in high school

My sisters Sakina and Mecca in Washington, DC, around 1976

FOLLOWING PAGE 140

My brother David, David Harris, and I

Our Clow Avenue house in Newcomerstown

My sister Voncille on the steps of Trinity Baptist Church,
September 2014

David and I in our school yearbook photos, 1971

My brother James (Rahmaan) in Newcomerstown, 1971

David Trotter, football team photo, 1971

David Trotter, football team photo, 1973

FOLLOWING PAGE 210

7.1 My sister Doris's senior picture, 1967

7.2 My brother David and I at my graduation from
Central State, June 1978

8.1 My sister Dee, back in Vallscreek for the 1991 Excelsior
High School Reunion in War, West Virginia

8.2 A group of former students at the Excelsior High
School Reunion, Homecoming, 1997

8.3 My mother at seventy

8.4 My brother Joe and his wife, LaRue

8.5 My fiancée, Pamela, and I at the Black West Virginians'
recognition dinner, Charleston, 2010

8.6 Voncille and Melvin's wedding

8.7 Trotter 14 reunion, 2012

ACKNOWLEDGMENTS

WRITING THIS BOOK HAS BEEN a long journey of introspection, reflection, and a vicissitude of emotions. At times I felt like abandoning the idea, second-guessed whether or not my story was compelling enough to share in a book, or questioned my ability to complete the work.

Thoughts about the value and uniqueness of my family's story had haunted me for several decades. Not able to ignore this any longer, nearly five years ago I sat down and proceeded to put words to paper.

But this book could not have come to fruition without the many people who assisted with their ideas, suggestions, and reading of different versions of the manuscript; contributions of pictures; information technology support; life-saving medical expertise, which has played a critical role in my life history; and the ongoing spiritual and emotional support of family and friends.

Accordingly, I owe a tremendous debt of gratitude to my brother, Joe William Trotter Jr., Giant Eagle Professor of History and Social Justice at Carnegie Mellon University in Pittsburgh. Throughout the process, from the writing of the introduction to providing expertise, wisdom, insight, and constructive criticism, his assistance has been invaluable in delivering a sense of gravitas and a historical perspective to the story. I am also grateful to my sister-in-law, H. LaRue Trotter, for reinforcing my attention to effective writing style. LaRue read multiple versions of the manuscript and provided positive feedback and suggestions.

My siblings' personal recollections of experiences in West Virginia, Newcomerstown, and Massillon added color and helped greatly to breathe life into the story. For those contributions, I am grateful to Josie, Eva, Dee, Bobbie, Isalene, Doris, Joe, Rahmaan, Mecca, Jessie, Voncille, David, and Sakina. In addition, I am thankful for the gift of a CD, loaded with family pictures, from my nephew, Tyrone Harris, years before I embarked on this venture, not realizing it would later serve such a critical function.

I also owe a debt of appreciation to other loved ones and friends—Deborah Torrence, Bianca Clayton, Sabine Ahmed Wong, Edgar J. Scott, and my former coworker, Sandra Brue, for various suggestions, compliments, and encouragement. Thanks go out to my college friend Steven Mealy for the story about his ancestors escaping from slavery in Kentucky, crossing the Ohio River, and settling in southern Ohio.

Thanks are also in order for Shirley Coker-Kerr, currently of North Carolina, and Geraldine "Gerry" Radcliffe of Canton, Ohio. Shirley provided a wealth of information on the history of the Clow Company and the black community in Newcomerstown. For her part, Gerry provided valuable information on a vanished black community, called Aultman, Ohio, less than a half mile from my Highland Creek home.

No words can express the depth of my appreciation to the staffs of Ohio University Press, the Massillon Public Library, and the Newcomerstown Public Library. These institutions provided generous and diligent assistance in the research and publication of this book. At Ohio University Press, I wish to thank Director Gillian Berchowitz and series editors Chris Green and Marie Tedesco, as well as Kevin Haworth for his astute input. Debts of gratitude also go to Joyce Mason and Sherie Brown of the Massillon Public Library, and to Michelle Cox, Cody Addy, and Margaret Hirschfeld of the Newcomerstown Public Library.

I also wish to extend special thanks to the medical community. None of this could have been possible without the life-sustaining medical care I received at Children's Hospital of Columbus, University Medical Center of Columbus, the Cleveland Clinic, and Aultman Hospital and Mercy Medical Center of Canton, Ohio. I am grateful for these medical institutions and their associated physicians—Donald Hosier and Howard Sirak, Children's Hospital; Charles Wooley, Mary E. Fontana, Charles Love, and James Kilman, University Medical Center; Donald Underwood, Cleveland Clinic; Clifford Johnson and Michael Markel, Mercy Medical

Center and Aultman Hospital—who have served as guardians of my health throughout the years.

I can't forget our family physician, Waldemar Agricola, of Newcomerstown, who set up the initial contact with a congenital heart disease cardiologist in Columbus when I was eight years old. Thanks to the *Columbus Dispatch* and the Columbus Children's Hospital archives for information on the history of Children's Hospital and my childhood cardiologist, Donald Hosier. I'm indebted to the Harvard Medical School Memorial Minutes for illuminating the history and technical dimensions of the surgical procedures to correct one of my heart defects, patent ductus arteriosus. Additionally, I am obliged to the Medical Records staffs of Children's Hospital and University Hospital for retrieving archived information about my diagnosis and treatment.

I owe a very special debt of gratitude to my fiancée, Pamela, for her love, unyielding emotional support, encouragement, and patience as I spent long hours writing and struggling to fashion the story into a logical and readable piece of work. Pamela was more than a cheerleader for me during this endeavor. She took an active role, going far beyond what I would have expected. She read manuscripts, offered suggestions, and volunteered her skills in information technology and graphic design. Without her assistance, things would have been technically more challenging.

Above all, I am grateful to my parents, Joe William Trotter Sr. and Thelma Odell Foster Trotter, for giving me and my siblings the moral, spiritual, and material foundation for survival and development in an often hostile environment. To them, and in memory of the generations before them, I lovingly dedicate this book on behalf of the "Trotter 14."

introduction

JOE WILLIAM TROTTER JR.

KEEPING HEART OFFERS A UNIQUE PERSPECTIVE on the twentieth-century African American experience. This memoir by my brother not only illuminates the personal life and struggles of a black man, born with heart disease in the southern Appalachian coalfields, but also reveals the dynamics of African American family formation and community relations during the era of the Great Migration. Organized around the life history and recollections of Otis Trotter and his thirteen siblings, the story begins in 1914 with our parents, Joe William Trotter Sr. and Thelma Odell Foster Trotter, in rural Pike and Crenshaw Counties, Alabama. Joe and Thelma were born, raised, and married in Jim Crow Alabama. In 1936 the oldest of their fourteen children was also born in Alabama, but within a year after her birth the family moved to Vallscreek, McDowell County, in southern West Virginia. Joe secured a job in the coal mines and Thelma worked exclusively inside the home. Most of the Trotter children were born at home, but the youngest three siblings, beginning with Otis, were born in a hospital in nearby Richlands, Virginia.

Following our father's death in 1957, our mother, as a widow with a large family, struggled for four years to make ends meet before moving to northeastern Ohio. As Otis notes in his memoir, it was a "bittersweet" departure: "After saying our good-byes to friends and neighbors, we all got in the cars and headed up the hill and down the road toward a future in Ohio that we hoped would be brighter." The Trotter family joined what some historians call the Second Great Migration of southern blacks to the urban North. The percentage of all blacks living in cities rose from just over 50 percent during the 1940s to over 80 percent by the 1970s. Almost half of the African American population in the United States now lived in the urban North and West.

While millions of southern blacks migrated from farms and fields to the major metropolitan areas of the urban North, other blacks like the Trotter family moved to small communities outside the large centers of black urban migration. Thelma Trotter moved her family to small industrial towns in northeastern Ohio—Newcomerstown, Tuscarawas County, in 1961 and Massillon, Stark County, in 1974. Vallscreek, Newcomerstown, and Massillon provided the setting for most of Otis Trotter's life. Except for his college years at Central State University in Wilberforce, Ohio, Otis lived in these towns until he moved to Highland Creek, an avenue in nearby suburban North Canton, Ohio, in 2007.

Beginning with his birth in West Virginia in 1954, multiple heart operations and procedures to save his life emerge at the center of Otis Trotter's narrative. A careful student of his own health condition, Otis gives close and detailed accounts of his medical history, along with the ways that he coped with life growing up as a young black male in a large, poor family in predominantly white towns. The Modern Black Freedom Movement of the 1950s and 1960s opened up new opportunities for Otis and some members of his family, along with other twentieth-century southern black migrants, to gain access to better education, jobs, housing, and health care than their parents had had. After earning his BS degree in psychology from Central State in 1978, Otis obtained employment as a special education teacher and vocational trainer at the Stark County Board of Developmental Disabilities in Massillon, from which he retired after thirty years of service in 2009.

As newcomers, the Trotter family faced the added difficulties of integrating into sometimes hostile local black as well as white communities. However, by telling his story alongside the experiences of his parents as well as his siblings, Otis in his memoir underscores intrafamilial, generational, and regional diversity in the lives of black people in Deep South Alabama, Upper South West Virginia, and small-town urban Midwest. When the Trotter family moved to northeastern Ohio in 1961, they entered a shifting environment of class and race relations in the northern reserve. Both Newcomerstown and Massillon had their beginnings during the nation's nineteenth-century struggle over the future of slavery, but few blacks lived in either town until the late nineteenth and early twentieth centuries, when both towns experienced the transition from early commercial to industrial capitalism. By the early twentieth century, new industrial firms—including the James B. Clow and Sons Company in Newcomerstown and the Union Drawn Division of Republic Steel in Massillon—were producing for national and international markets.

As Newcomerstown and Massillon made the transition to industrial production, they also gradually turned toward the recruitment of black workers to meet their labor needs. After a Clow Company plant burned down in nearby New Philadelphia in 1895, city officials gave the company 20 acres of land and $30,000 to relocate in Newcomerstown. Between the late 1890s and the early 1920s, the Clow Company recruited a small ethnically and racially diverse workforce, including Italians, Hungarians, and southern African Americans from Kentucky, North Carolina, and particularly the town of Rock Run, Alabama. Massillon industrialists also recruited blacks alongside immigrants from southern, central, and eastern Europe to staff their expanding steel plants.

Like their counterparts from larger urban areas, small-town black midwesterners soon occupied racially segregated neighborhoods and formed their own community-based institutions. In Newcomerstown, southern blacks lived dispersed across several different streets until the early 1920s, when the Clow Company completed the construction of about thirty new company houses. Located on land across the street from the plant, company-owned houses attracted increasing numbers of blacks to Clow Avenue (later renamed Martin Luther King Drive) and parts of adjoining College Street. By the time the Trotter family arrived, most African Americans lived on one street. Massillon's African American population also became spatially concentrated in certain areas. Unlike in Newcomerstown, however, African Americans occupied a broader range of streets, including Erie near the Tuscarawas River, Tremont, and further south; Walnut Avenue down to the railroad tracks on 3rd Street; the Cherry Avenue Warwick area; and Columbia Heights.

Although on a much smaller scale than their brothers and sisters in metropolitan America, blacks in small-town Ohio also transformed their segregated spaces into communities of mutual self-help and institutional support. More than was the case for their urban counterparts, however, their lives revolved almost exclusively around their families, churches, and a few service, mainly home-based, enterprises. Established partly with support from industrial employers, African American churches emerged during the late nineteenth and early twentieth centuries—Saint James African Methodist Episcopal Zion (1884), Shiloh Baptist (1902), and Friendship Missionary Baptist (1919) in Massillon and Trinity Baptist (1908) and St. Paul African Methodist Episcopal Church (1920) in Newcomerstown. In addition to churches, black Massillonians and Newcomerstownians also established a number of businesses, including barber and beauty shops, dance halls, and small candy and soft drink concessions to serve the needs of their own small communities. Massillon produced the most outstanding example of black entrepreneurship. John Henry "Big Jenny" Lowry owned and operated the Vahepa Hotel, later named the Globe. Lowry also operated an ice company, a beverage bottling company, a sanitation business, and a brickyard. When he died in 1936, the city lowered the flag to half mast in his honor.

Despite such vibrant institution-building activities, the small communities the Trotter family entered were undergoing gradual economic and demographic decline. Newcomerstown's total population peaked at 4,500 people in 1940. In 1956, when the Clow Company closed its doors and moved out of town, the city's population began dropping, gradually declining to a total of 4,150 in 1970. The African American population also declined, from 180 in 1940 to 139 in 1960 and to only 106 in 1980. As Newcomerstown's African American population declined, however, Massillon's black population expanded. In 1920 only 2,800 blacks (about 1.5 percent of the total) lived in all of Stark County. By 1950 black Massillonians had increased to 2,100, or 7 percent of the city's total. When the Trotter family arrived in 1973, nearly 3,000 blacks lived in Massillon. At about the same time, between 1970 and 1980, Massillon's total population declined by nearly 2,000 (from 32,500 to 30,550, or by 6 percent), as major industrial firms trimmed their workforces or moved away from the city altogether.

Although the Trotters arrived in Newcomerstown and later Massillon during a period of losses in population and jobs, the moves represented a substantial improvement in the family's well-being. The ten Trotter children who moved to Newcomerstown in 1961—the older siblings having graduated from high school and moved out on their own—for the first time attended racially integrated public schools and participated in a variety of integrated extracurricular activities, including sports, music, and drama. Contrary to widespread stereotypes regarding the capacity of young school-age black migrants to succeed in northern schools, the Trotter children generally performed well in their studies. Most important, however, Otis gained access to life-saving medical care.

As the Trotter family confronted the challenges of making a living—those members not living at home did regularly send money to help ends meet—and integrating into the schools and other aspects of the town's public life, they also struggled to integrate into the established black community. They joined the local Trinity Baptist Church, listened to music and danced at the Chatterbox Club, and patronized the local candy, soft drink, and barber and beauty shops. Nonetheless, in 1973 the family moved to Massillon. Unlike the move to Newcomerstown, the short journey to Massillon, less than an hour away, was "bitter," not "bittersweet." The Trotter family had made friends. They had also received and been given help in times of need. But the intraracial tensions and conflicts that had persisted over the years finally precipitated the family's move, and the newcomer cycle started over again. This time, however, the number of siblings living at home was down to three, including Otis. They were all nearing graduation from high school and looking forward to forging independent lives of their own.

After four years at Central State University, Otis returned to Massillon. He worked briefly as a "district manager" for Massillon's daily newspaper, the *Independent,* before securing employment at the Stark County Board of Developmental Disabilities.

Otis lived in Massillon until his recent retirement. He now lives on Highland Creek Avenue, in a new suburban subdivision that opened with a mix of people from a variety of national, ethnic, and racial backgrounds. But his memoir is more than a tale of three migrations and community and family struggles. It is also literally and figuratively a story about heart—how one man has struggled, lived, and continues to live with heart disease. Otis Trotter found not only a way to survive but a way to educate himself, pursue a professional career, and enrich the lives of his family, friends, and community. At the same time, he developed a profound understanding of and confidence in the efficacy of modern medicine to extend and improve the quality of his life. As his memoir shows, not only has he benefited immensely from innovations in the treatment of heart disease, but he has used his good fortune to improve the lives of others, including thirty years of serving adults with developmental disabilities. *Keeping Heart* thus also reinforces a popular biblical proverb, passed down from generations of African people enslaved in the New World, "Keep thy heart with all diligence; for out of it are the issues of life."

one

<hr>
<hr>

MEMORIES OF PARENTS
AND PLACES

THERE IS NO PHOTOGRAPH of my father. My family and I possess no still images of him, captured in time, which we can cherish as a tangible connection to the past. In the 1940s and 1950s, sitting for an individual or family portrait was often a big event. Photographs were fewer and were treasured, no matter how tattered, as much as gold. Unfortunately, it's not possible to go back in time and capture that special moment. He lives in our hearts and minds, and his impact on our family continues to be felt across the generations.

I can recall several vivid memories of my father. When I was three years old, I would steal honey buns from my dad's lunch bucket, munching on them as I hid in the closet. They were like manna from heaven to me, satisfying my huge appetite for sweets. I had to have been a brave soul to do this, for there seemed to have been an unwritten rule that to steal a coal miner's lunch was an unpardonable sin. (Many years later my oldest brother referred to me as the original HBO—Honey Bun Otis.) But for some reason, I could not seem to resist taking those honey buns. Maybe my congenital heart condition caused my body to exert so much energy that I was always hungry, or perhaps it was because I never suffered any adverse consequences from my dad. I was told that he never wanted to whip me because of my heart.

I would tell the truth when he asked me if I'd stolen his honey bun. I often remember my mother remarking how I told the truth whenever my father asked me if I'd done something. And because of my veracity, I would often escape the dreaded switch. There was one time, however, when I didn't.

My father had bought me a hat, one of those Russian-type hats with the flop ears. I thought it was hideous and hated it, so I burned it in the potbellied stove in the living room. He had always been very hesitant to give me a whipping, but for doing this I got a good one. The whole family seemed to be in a state of shock at this. I remember the house being completely quiet.

I can still remember the regret in Dad's eyes after he punished me, but he had to have felt he'd been justified. With his hard-earned money, he had bought me a good-quality hat that was suitable for the cold winter weather. He'd only been trying to prevent me from catching a cold, which could have had serious consequences for a child whose health was already compromised by a heart problem.

Another of my few memories of my dad is one of his taking me to the doctor, to receive treatment for a cold when I was three years old. I remember us entering a large white building. The waiting area was chilly, with high ceilings and a floor of reddish tiles. I later learned that the doctor's office, in Berwind, West Virginia, about five miles from our home in Vallscreek, was a combination home and office. Our doctor's name was Dr. Emory Lovas. He was employed by the coal company, and is believed by some to have delivered almost all of the babies born in Berwind and the surrounding communities during the 1940s and early 1950s. He had not been the attending physician, however, when I was born.

I remember being examined by the doctor, and being consumed with fear when I saw him preparing what seemed to me to be a huge syringe to administer a shot. I remember that the pain was excruciating as the needle penetrated the muscle in my hip and that my father comforted me as I screamed in agony. And I remember the sucker I got as suitable compensation for my pain.

Not only did our father have a positive effect on our family, he had a great influence on the community as well. He was part of the fabric holding the community together. The significance that my father's life had for us and the local area would become apparent when he died tragically, a victim of homicide.

I was playing in the road with other children on the day it happened. It was a sweltering July afternoon, as is often the case that time of the year in southern West Virginia. It was one of those days so hot that waves of heat could be seen undulating from asphalt roadways. The road we lived on, however, was not asphalt. It was a dirt road, and in the summer heat it became a dust bowl. By the end of the day, children playing in this road would look like dirt daubers. We were black children, and we became even blacker as the coal dust that was mixed in with the dirt of the road covered our clothes and faces.

I was three and a half years old, and my memory of the horrible death of our father is fragmented. I can recall a red ambulance or hearse backed up to the small coal-company house next to ours, the home of my aunt Effie and uncle Josh. The ambulance personnel were loading a body, wrapped in a pure white sheet and on a stretcher, into the back of the vehicle. I was aware that the body was that of my father, but I can't recall having an overwhelming sense of grief. At that early age, children often are not aware of the finality of death. To children the line between life and death is blurred.

The next thing I remember is being at my aunt Effie and uncle Josh's house, where the ambulance had been earlier. I was sitting among family members and neighbors crowded into the small living room. Every available piece of furniture—couches, chairs—was occupied, and seat cushions as well as the arms of chairs were pressed into service. Those who were not sitting were standing around in the living room and on the porch. Wearing sullen expressions, everyone was focused on one of the couches, where my uncle Josh was sitting between the two white sheriff or state police deputies, in their wide-brimmed hats. I could not tell the difference between the two forms of law enforcement officers at the time; they were the same to me.

There was something about those hats the deputies wore that instantly identified them as agents of the law. In fact, they were called "the law." The law then and now engenders a certain emotional response in black people, but especially in 1957 in Jim Crow southern West Virginia, a mere eighty-five years post slavery and reconstruction. The memories of slave catchers, bounty hunters, and racist lawmen tracking down slaves or free black people who dared to challenge Jim Crow laws or were simply defending their dignity were fresh in their minds. Given those experiences, in the minds of many African Americans, white lawmen, right or wrong, had become symbols of the brutal enforcers of the "Dixie" version of apartheid and a system of white privilege. Even I as a child could sense the unpleasant tension that existed in our interactions with the law. Though it is much less the case today, such tension does persist to a degree.

Back then in southern West Virginia, virtually the only times blacks and whites interacted were in the workplace, stores, and other places of business where the only color that mattered was green—and in situations, like the one that day in my uncle and aunt's house, that involved some transgression of the law. My father had worked part time as a barber. He had had black and white patrons, so it was not altogether strange to see a white person at our house. But this was different.

Sitting there on that couch, my uncle looked dazed and puzzled, like someone waking up from a deep sleep, and he seemed to be muttering incoherently. It appeared as though the deputies were asking questions, as one of them was scribbling something on a clipboard, but I can't recall what the questions were. The deputies then stood up, escorted my uncle out of the house, and took him to the county jail. They also took with them the 12-gauge shotgun my uncle had used to shoot my dad three times at point-blank range.

My father's death was foreshadowed by my mother's concerns about our family's living situation. Years later, my older sister Bobbie told me that my mother had been apprehensive about in-laws living so close together. My mother's brother Josh was married to my father's sister Effie—a not-uncommon phenomenon in the South. My mother felt it would have been better to create some physical distance between them and her family. Bobbie quoted my mother as saying, "Familiarity breeds contempt."

When I was older, I learned about the circumstances surrounding my father's death. My uncle, though a gentle and kind man, had a severe problem with alcohol, fueled, it has been suggested, by my aunt Effie's alleged infidelity with a man named Ike Barron, who lived three houses down the road from them. Uncle Josh had been drinking heavily that day, and he started hallucinating about "devils" being in the house.

My grandmother, my mother's and Uncle Josh's mother, Ethel Foster, was living with him and Aunt Effie at the time. Concerned about his extreme agitated and intoxicated state, she hurried over to our house to ask for my father's assistance in calming him down. My dad and Josh got along well, and there was no ongoing dispute between them, according to my aunt Innie—who, with her husband, Thamon, another Foster brother, were also living temporarily with Uncle Josh. Dad went over there to assist, as he had on numerous occasions.

Although this tragedy had an extraordinary impact on my life, it had an even greater impact on my older brother, James, who was eight at the time and had been with my dad right before the incident happened. James had told my dad that he wanted to go over there with him, but Dad had picked him up and "held him tight," then told him to go back to the house. James recalls he and my dad gazing at each other right before Dad entered the house, "seeming as though time momentarily froze." My brother said that no sooner had our father entered the back door than the blasts from the shotgun sounded. James ran into the house, where he witnessed the immediate aftermath of that horrific and traumatic scene. There was nothing he could do as life gradually drained from my dad's body. One can only imagine the lasting impact on the psyche of an eight-year-old child witnessing such a horrendous sight.

I have been told that word spread quicker around Vallscreek than on today's Internet about my father's shooting. "Joe's been shot, Joe's been shot" echoed frantically throughout the hollow. Pandemonium broke out in the streets. Relatives and nonrelatives alike were in a state of shock and grief. My brothers and sisters were literally prostrate in the dusty road, crying, dust turning to mud as their tears hit the road.

While this was going on, my mother was in the hospital, due to complications from the impending birth of my youngest sister. Mom often told the story of how my father came to visit her in the hospital a couple of days before his death. Three times he walked toward the door to go home, only to return to my mother's bedside. The third time my mother said he had tears in his eyes.

The nurse told him, "Joe, go home! We are taking care of your wife," and reluctantly he left.

It was the last time my mother would see her husband and the father of her fourteen children alive. My youngest sister, Ethel Denise, was born eight days later, on July 10, 1957.

The irony of the tragedy is that when my uncle was incarcerated and my aunt returned to Alabama, it opened up the possibility of our moving into our uncle and aunt's house, which at that point was much better than ours. Several weeks before, a group of neighborhood men had been assisting my father in jacking up our house so a basement could be dug. My father and the other men had invested immense physical energy to get the house jacked up to the point they wanted, but unfortunately it collapsed. No one was hurt, but the house was left permanently tilted, with the floors slanted inside. All of their efforts were in vain, and the family's hope of having expanded living space fell further than the house. This was devastating to us, especially since the coal company had not even been willing to help with adding another room to the house before this happened. But shortly after the funeral, we were able to move to the other house.

My memory of the day of the funeral is skimpy, but I do remember a line of shiny 1950s cars, many of them black, parked along the dirt road, which was bounded on one side by a row of small coal-company houses and on the other side by a creek about thirty feet away. On the other side of the creek was a small unpaved parking area where there were more cars. The day was hot and sunny, and the mood was somber. The next thing I remember was arriving at the little country church, and not wanting to get out of the car and go inside. I don't know if I was scared or if I did not want to face the fact that my father was dead. I do remember being inside the church and witnessing everybody's sorrow. Still I was not able to realize the impact that this event would have on my life.

Not yet four years old at the time, I was too young to process hate or vindictiveness. All I knew was that something terrible and seemingly irreversible had happened to my father, and that my uncle Josh had committed a grievous act. I could not hate my uncle for killing my father, I simply had an overwhelming sense of anxiety and concern.

I have been told that when my uncle sobered up in jail, he asked his jailers to get in touch with my dad to come get him out, as he had done on numerous occasions when drunkenness landed Uncle Josh in the slammer. He was not even aware of the terrible act that he had committed.

This was a devastating episode for our family, but it was also a colossal tragedy for the close-knit community of Vallscreek. My father's death resulted in the community losing a valued friend, a trusted coworker in the dangerous coal mines, and a barber who serviced the hair care needs of the area's men and boys. He had also served as a mentor to young men in the community, although most had fathers living in the home. Mentoring young men was a community-wide responsibility, and it was a role my father willingly played.

While the event was a catastrophic one for the family, ironically it may have set us on a course that led to a future brighter than we may otherwise have had. I wonder, had we not eventually moved to Ohio after our father's death, would I have gotten the lifesaving medical attention I needed? Would my brother Joe have become a leading historian of African American and US urban and labor history and chairman of the Department of History at Carnegie Mellon University? Would my sister Voncille have ever worked for the US House of Representatives in Washington, DC, and been involved in community activity in the DC area, through which she has touched the lives of hundreds of people? Would my other siblings have gotten the opportunities to pursue the productive and fulfilling lives that they did?

Notwithstanding our family's ability to adapt to unfortunate circumstances, our father's death thwarted the personal hopes and dreams my parents had for the future of the family. That day constituted another tragedy in the histories, filled with heartache, disappointment, and sorrow, of my mother and father that had commenced in the Deep South state of Alabama.

When several Southern states seceded from the union in 1861, Alabama followed suit; Montgomery hosted the founding convention of the Confederate States of America. It also served as the first capital of the rebellious states. Following the Civil War, Alabama took a leading role in annulling the emancipation and citizenship rights afforded black people after the war, as well as in rolling back other gains made through the Reconstruction Act to improve the condition of blacks in the former Confederate states. In Alabama and elsewhere in the Deep South, African Americans faced the rise of disfranchisement, institutional segregation, and mob violence. Between 1886 and 1895, some ninety blacks died at the hands of lynch mobs in Alabama, the highest number among all states in the Union. As late as the 1930s, only massive and international protests prevented the lynching of nine black men wrongly accused of raping two white women near the town of Scottsboro, Alabama.

The Trotter family had deep roots in Jim Crow–era Alabama. Joe and Thelma Trotter moved from Alabama to West Virginia as the Scottsboro case played out on a global stage. My mother was born in 1919 in Helicon, Alabama, to Willie and Ethel Foster, and she had six brothers. Helicon was in Crenshaw County, adjacent to Pike County to the west. Although it is usually considered one of the so-called Black Belt cotton counties of central and southern Alabama, it became perhaps best known as a timber county. Its land was less rich, and slave labor and sharecropping on cotton units was less extensive, than elsewhere in the Black Belt. My mother's family lived in Helicon for about fourteen years, working on the land of her grandfather, Sherman Foster, raising various crops—corn, beans, watermelon. He also had chickens and hogs, and he owned a plow.

Thelma was about four when her father left Alabama after a conflict with a local store owner. It started with Thelma's father owing the store owner fifty dollars.

The store owner was disrespectful to him, Thelma said. "He [the store owner] would tell my father . . . like when you go buy grocery, go slow boy, like that. Then my father told him he know what he needed. . . . Then he told my father to get all of the money you owe me. . . . My father told him . . . I'll get your damn money."

Her father, refusing to tolerate such treatment, borrowed some money from another white man and paid the store owner off. He then left for Massillon, Ohio, in search of work. After finding a job and a place to stay, he sent for his family. His wife, Ethel, daughter Thelma, and his youngest son, Zack, later went to Ohio to join him; however, his own father, Sherman, would not let his other sons leave. He wanted them to stay and help work the land—in effect, holding them as ransom. Thelma's mother could not bear being separated from the rest of her family, so she, along with Thelma, returned to Alabama. Thelma never saw her father again. It was reported by a family friend who visited them in Alabama that her dad, Willie Foster, had gotten "low sick" and died in 1930 in Cincinnati, Ohio.

Thelma's family sharecropped the land for a white man by the name of Dick Gaddings. The man was probably convinced that the three eldest sons could help produce a good crop. The family worked diligently, raising cotton as the main cash crop. The contract called for working on halves, but the family would come out behind, because the white people kept the books. During the summer, the family received an allowance at the local store and a little money, but when the crops were in, the land owner cheated them out of their share. My mother said, "It wasn't right, because we should have had a profit."

Yet, in spite of the unfair treatment from the land owners and difficult work, life on the farm had its good side. The family grew and canned vegetables for their own table, including beans, greens, sweet potatoes, and corn. They also raised hogs and made syrup for family consumption. Whites were also "sometimes nice in a way." Because the family did not own a cow, the landlord furnished fresh milk and butter.

Thelma reminisced about the happy moments she experienced playing children's games on the farm: "Even though it seemed sometimes there were difficult times . . . I had a happy childhood. . . . I played the games they play today: hopscotch, jacks—all we used were soda tops—jump rope, checkers, cards, old maid, smut, thirty-one, horseshoes, but not as much as they did when we moved to West Virginia."

Around 1933, when Thelma was fourteen years old, the family moved all of their possessions by horse-drawn wagon to Shady Grove, Alabama, less than five miles away. The family moved when her grandfather decided to go live with one of his daughters. Located in Pike County, Shady Grove was in the heart of the rich southern cotton land known as the Black Belt. In Shady Grove, they sharecropped land owned by a man named Zack Crickner. The land in Shady Grove was far better than the land in Helicon. The family continued to grow the same crops, but more of everything.

Yet the family received little more money for their hard labor. Moreover, they all worked harder, including Thelma: "That was terrible, and I worked harder then. That's the two years that I really worked hard on the farm." She recalled not only the difficulty of picking the bolls of cotton in ways to prevent the inevitable pricking of the fingers and hands by the pin-like needles on the cotton plants, but also the necessity of dragging the heavy sacks of cotton around the fields as the pounds mounted over the course of the day's work. She became fully conscious of hard work and the interdependence of the family: "I knew I saw that, you know, how hard my mother was working. . . . I wanted to work as hard as I can to help her out."

During Thelma's last year of farming, in 1935, the family made a "good crop." They harvested ten bales of cotton, weighing about five hundred pounds, and "a crib of corn." She was engaged to be married then, and looked forward to having a nice wedding.

Thelma relates, "That's when the sad time came because we just knew we were going to have a lot of money, and mother had planned to furnish my house. He [the land owner] took all of it [the crop]. That was when I never wanted to work in the field no more. That was Crickner. . . . He seemed like a nice man, but he did something dirty. . . . Then he came to the house, and went to the crib and took our corn. . . . He didn't ask nobody anything. He just went out there and got it."

The entire family was angry over his treatment. Despite that bitter experience, Thelma did get married that fall.

Thelma was sixteen years old when she married Joe William Trotter, who was twenty-one, on October 3, 1935, in Shady Grove, Pike County, Alabama. They were married on the front porch of the bride's mother's house. Guests both invited and uninvited attended the wedding, officiated by the Reverend Gus Pouncy. Reverend Pouncy, a well-known Baptist minister, was also married to Joe's aunt.

Born in Shady Grove, Alabama, in 1914, Joe William Trotter would become my father. He, the eighth child in a family of twelve children born to George William Trotter and Anna Woodson Trotter, attended the Rock Elvy Baptist Church School and worked on his father's land until he married Thelma Odell Foster. Joe's grandfather was George William Trotter Sr., a mulatto. He had many acres of land, which he passed down to his children, including George William Trotter Jr., known simply as William, my father's father.

There was a family story, which no one has been able to verify, that George William Trotter Sr. forced his white father to admit that he was his father. It was said that William Sr. demanded the man own up to the fact or William was going to drown him in a local pond they were swimming in. After being submerged in the water a couple of times, and when he was done coughing up water, the man admitted it.

According to my cousin and my father's niece, Ann Jones Hinson of Tallahassee, Florida, our grandfather William Jr., with whom she and her mother, Selema, lived, was a farmer by profession, managing a very large farm in Pike County, Alabama. It consisted of more than 150 acres, a substantial farm for a black farmer back then. With only a basic elementary education, he relied on his God-given common sense and a good knowledge of the land to run the farm successfully. He raised most of the food they ate—hogs, cows, chickens, greens, peas, corn, onions, Irish potatoes, sweet potatoes, just to name a few. It seemed that something was growing in the garden throughout the year. In the field he grew watermelons, tomatoes, beets, cantaloupes, and cucumbers. He also had fruit trees producing peaches, apples, pears, plums, figs, and mulberries. Pecan trees were on his land, too. The fruit was preserved and the meats were cured to last year-round.

His cash crops were mainly cotton and peanuts, of which he would harvest several bales and tons respectively to take to the market. He would even sometime sell cows. Ann recalls, "Grandfather William would issue money to his family near Big Meeting and Christmas time."

William was both strict and compassionate. As Ann reminisces, "During the Christmas season, he would mail packages to relatives living away in other cities that consisted of pecans, peanuts, sweet potatoes, and other goodies. They would hitch Ola and Dora [two of his mules] to the wagon, and off they would go to the Shady Grove post office to mail those packages."

This tradition was continued by his children. I have fond memories of anticipating an assortment of nuts and other goodies in the mail from Alabama, when our family lived in Vallscreek and later in Newcomerstown, Ohio.

William was stern in the sense that his daughters had to get permission to date, and in most cases a resounding "No!" was expected. Ann indicated that he mellowed out as he got older, allowing his daughter Amanda to move away to Troy, Alabama, to further her education. Ann said, "I had no problem getting him to allow me to visit my brothers in Lakeland, Florida."

Joe and Thelma, like the overwhelming majority of African Americans in the South during that time, did not get any formal education beyond early secondary school. Black males, ironically, attained significantly less education than black females. The opposite was true for white males. Black males had few occupational opportunities beyond agrarian—that is, sharecropping—or a variety of other low-paying industrial jobs, so there was no real incentive to aspire toward greater levels of education.

Women, particularly black women, typically did not progress any higher than the sixth or seventh grade. Although their level of education obtained was relatively low, the roles they filled as child-bearers and nurturers and the duties they performed—preparing meals for their families, cleaning house, washing clothes, doing church work, and even working crops—were invaluable to the stability of the family. More career opportunities would not become available for young African American women—or men—until the 1940s and 1950s.

Upon marriage or shortly before, Joe got a job working in the pulp wood industry, which was booming at the time. His father was not happy about this. He wanted Joe to stay and help work the farm. After living in Shady Grove for a while, Thelma and Joe moved to Bessemer, Alabama, where he got a job in the iron mines. He made five dollars a day, which was good compared to what he made in the sawmill. Joe got the job through a cousin, who worked in the mines in Bessemer, about a hundred miles from Shady Grove. A month or so after getting settled, finding a house and furnishing it, Joe went back to Shady Grove to get Thelma.

About a month after arriving in Bessemer, Thelma contracted typhoid fever. This was a life-threatening illness, but she made a complete recovery.

When my parents moved to Bessemer, they traveled a path charted by earlier blacks from the cotton fields. In the decades before World War I, blacks who had migrated to the Birmingham district returned to their Black Belt homes to recruit other blacks. Through newspapers like the *Christian Hope*, blacks in Birmingham informed relatives of life in the city. They also set up "information bureaus" to assist migrants in finding jobs and housing in the industrial region. Like Joe and Thelma Trotter, large numbers of Black Belt migrants to the industrial district soon departed for the coalfields of West Virginia.

A labor recruiter called "Old Man" Gribble came to Bessemer in late 1935 looking for workers for the West Virginia coal mines.

"Things were booming back in there," Thelma said. "The mines were opening up that hadn't opened in so many years."

Gribble came down to Bessemer with a large empty truck to recruit the men. Before making a decision, several relatives and friends held a meeting at the house of Dave Pouncy. Joe, Thelma, other relatives, and a host of friends, including Fletcher Blackmon, Saul Woodson, and Dave Pouncy, undoubtedly after much prayer and reflection, decided to board the truck, go to West Virginia, and take their chances in the coalfields.

Different forces propelled my mother's and father's families to decide to move or not to move to West Virginia. My father, as suggested before, was motivated by the determination to make a living through an avenue other than farming, even though the opportunity to do well at it was significant. The only relative of his who moved to West Virginia was his cousin, Saul Woodson. On the other hand, since my mother's family—specifically her brothers Josh, Thamon, and Luther—did not own any land but farmed as sharecroppers for landowners who did not treat them right, relocating to West Virginia when the mines were booming was an easy decision.

Subjected to the perpetual indignity of racial oppression, my parents felt the chances of being struck by lightning were greater than the prospects of enjoying a bright future in the Deep South. Growing weary in the face of this reality, they were ready for a change. At this time my mother already had an infant child named Josie, who had been born in Alabama. With this young child in tow, and as the lone female in the group, she dreaded making that long, grueling trip on that crowded truck bed, but she did.

My parents and the rest of the group took with them to the hills of West Virginia those ethical and moral values deeply rooted in their Christian faith, and those beliefs of interdependence within families and between families. They lived by those principles of relying upon each other during unusually difficult times. They understood that no man is an island, that our well-being or destiny is inextricably tied to that of others.

The difficulties they faced in the South, I believe, equipped them to meet future challenges with confidence. They had experienced many trials and tribulations; things could only get better. So they hoped for themselves and their future children.

The Mountain State coal industry offered blacks higher wages and better working and living conditions than rural and industrial Alabama. At a time when most industrial firms in the nation excluded black workers from employment, both the railroad and coal industries hired large numbers of African Americans to open up the bituminous coalfields of southern Appalachia. African Americans helped to lay track for the Chesapeake and Ohio, the Norfolk and Western, and the Virginian. Following the laying of track, large numbers of black men entered the coal mines and eventually started their own families in southern West Virginia and other parts of the coalfields.

My mother and father made their home in Vallscreek, also known as Hartwell, West Virginia. It had been a thriving little hollow in the context of the booming southern West Virginia coal country in the 1920s, but it had started an upswing by the late Depression years and experienced a new boom with the rising energy demands of World War II. Surrounded by hills and forests, and punctuated by a shallow stream, called Vallscreek, this hamlet was a significant distance from Charleston, the state's capital and largest city, but was much closer to the smaller commercial centers of Welch, the county seat, and Bluefield, near the Virginia line. It was even closer to the much smaller town of War, site of the district's white high school, and Excelsior, the all-black high school for the area.

While West Virginia employers restricted blacks to the lower-rung jobs, they paid blacks and whites the same wages for performing the same work. With the coal industry expanding in response to the demands of the steel industry requiring coal to fire its furnaces, the growing auto industry, World War I and declining immigration due to the war, African American workers became more attractive. The black population of West Virginia increased from 64,000 in 1910 to 115,000 in 1930. The bituminous coal–mining counties of southern West Virginia were home to nearly 70 percent of the state's total black population.

While Joe Trotter would find work in the coal mines, Thelma and most wives of black coal miners worked inside the home as well as outside in garden plots used to grow a variety of vegetable crops for home consumption. West Virginia coal mining offered few opportunities for women workers, black or white. Women in coal-mining families had the lowest labor participation rates of women anywhere in the country.

From the outset of its formation during the Civil War, West Virginia provided blacks a greater measure of freedom and opportunities to exercise citizenship rights than their Deep South counterparts. When Virginia seceded from the Union in 1861, western Virginia rejected secession and formed a new state two years later. Nonetheless, the Mountain State entered the Union as a slave state but approved a constitution advocating a gradual abolition of slavery. As most southern states saw an erosion of the brief period of enfranchisement enjoyed during the postbellum period by African Americans, blacks in West Virginia not only retained the right to vote but also organized and exerted considerable political influence through their own McDowell County Colored Republican Organization, local branches of the NAACP, and Marcus Garvey's Universal Negro Improvement Association.

Bucking the expectations of his father, who owned vast quantities of rich land, to follow in his footsteps, my father desired the freedom to choose his own station in life, and that did not include agrarian pursuits as his livelihood. Joe became a coal miner. From the beginning he wore steel-toed shoes, a hard hat with a carbide lamp, and special mining clothes called "bankers" into the mines. He learned how to make his own explosives and dynamite the coal, set timber for his own personal safety, and pace himself in order to minimize damage to his health. He worked at various mines in McDowell County in southern West Virginia during his career, such as the No. 5 Hartwell mine of the New River Consolidated Coal Company and the No. 10 Berwind

My dad was truly a hard worker dedicated to taking care of his family. He dreaded missing work even at times when it could have been easily justified. One time he suffered a fracture to his finger at work. Not wanting to miss the time, he devised his own treatment to stabilize and protect the injury while he continued to work.

My sister Dee said, "He got two sticks, and made a splint for his finger and went back to work. He would take it off every evening, clean and soak his bloodied finger, wrap it, and splint it again."

When Thelma and Joe first came to Vallscreek, they lived with various friends, brothers, uncles, and cousins, until they obtained their own place. My mother and father moved into a four-room house in the lower camp. With the relatively decent income from the mining job, they were eventually able to furnish their house, which included a front and back porch, with more "luxuries" than they ever had before—a radio, wringer washing machine, refrigerator, and electric stove for cooking.

The houses were built by the coal companies, and the furnishings for the most part were purchased from company stores. On the surface, it may appear that the coal companies were extremely benevolent, but the truth is that this was a form of exploitation of the people, who became indebted to the company. The people were granted these things by the company on credit, and they had to pay for them at fairly high interest rates. It turns out that instead of the employees being beneficiaries of a benevolent company, they were victims of economic abuse, with the company owners deriving most of the benefits. That song by Tennessee Ernie Ford—"Sixteen Tons"—comes to mind: "You load sixteen tons, what do you get? Another day older and deeper in debt. Saint Peter, don't you call me . . ." I can remember hearing this song as a little boy in West Virginia. It seemed to be an anthem of sort for coal miners.

The family nevertheless enjoyed things that were rarities for blacks in the rural South at that time. In some ways, however, life was not much better than that they'd experienced in the Deep South. The house for many years still lacked inside running water. They had well water in the back. Later on they acquired a sink in the house with cold running water only. The house did not have an inside toilet but an outhouse behind the house, about two hundred feet up a hill. The house was supplied with two potbellied stoves for heating, one in the living room and the other in one of the bedrooms. Adjacent to the house was a coal bin to supply the stoves with coal. This home would eventually house at its maximum twelve children (the two oldest children had graduated from school and left before the two youngest were born), three adults, and a dog named Jack.

Jack was as sharp as a tack, testing off the doggy IQ charts. He was a house pet, not one of Dad's hunting dogs. He was regarded as an honorary family member, and judging from one story I heard about Jack, who I was too young to remember, he apparently thought of himself as human. Upon observing the other family members in their daily bathroom habits, which included making their way to that outhouse up the hill behind the house, Jack decided to forgo the normal dog protocol and do the same. He leaped up on the outhouse seat, but he lost his footing and fell into a cesspool of a thousand years of foul and disgusting human waste. The first thing Jack did after being freed was run like a streak of lightning past a line of cheering onlookers to baptize himself in Vallscreek.

Joe Trotter was an excellent barber, and although unlicensed, he made money cutting the hair of men and boys. He even cut the hair of white men when asked, although Jim Crow practices prohibited black men from getting their hair cut by white barbers. He trimmed hair in the house during weekends and the evenings following work in the mines or when he was laid off. When weather permitted, he cut hair on the front porch.

Barbering was not just about getting a haircut, it provided an opportunity for men to bond and joke and engage in animated conversations about a variety of topics—from sports and family matters to religion, politics, and civil rights, outside of work. My father had the gift of gab, and he was a trash talker, which was often expressed in its fullest form during those hair-cutting sessions. My cousin Pete Foster indicated that my father used to tease him about his generously sized head. He once said, "Pete, if your head was a hog's head, I'd work a whole month for it." Think of the amount of head cheese he could have made!

My father had both electric and hand-powered hair clippers. He used both with extraordinary skill, but the hand-powered ones required you to squeeze the handles as you would a hand exerciser, while positioning the blade on the head. When the handles are squeezed, the two blades work together to cut the hair. Since the manual clippers were mainly used as a backup in the case of the electric ones malfunctioning, the dull blades would often pull the subject's hair, resulting in some discomfort. It was my cousin Pete's opinion that my father seemed to reserve the manual method especially for his head.

My father's skills were not limited to the barbering trade or coal mining; he was also an able wood carver, although the family only became aware of this talent during one long session of unemployment. During this time, as my brother Joe relates, "He carved a gun stock for his hunting rifle in the back yard with a knife. He also carved his social security number into the baluster on the front porch." In these current days of identity theft, that would be unthinkable, but in those days the first social security checks were just starting to arrive.

The front porches as well as the back porches were traditionally very important in southern culture. Staying in the house where there was no air conditioning during the day was unbearable in the summer. Enjoyment of the porches was not just reserved for the social interaction of men. Women, children, and teenagers also enjoyed the porch as a space to socialize with their friends and associates. Many a courtship germinated from casual conversations with the opposite sex, perhaps while sitting side by side on a porch swing. My brother Joe recalls himself and his friends "checking out and greeting the local females as they strolled by our porches." The front porch was the place where women and teenage girls carried on the latest gossip about others in "hush hush" tones. Neighbors often engaged in friendly verbal exchanges while on their porches.

Following World War II, my father purchased a Dodge pickup truck. I am sure ownership of an automobile gave him a sense of pride and accomplishment—not very many people owned their vehicles at that time—and the freedom of greater mobility that the truck afforded was an additional benefit. The truck also became a source of extra income, necessary to support a growing family, as

Joe collected and sold scrap iron and moved people and materials for a fee.

For the children, however, the truck was mainly a source of recreation and family fun—Fourth of July picnics, drive-in movies, baseball games, carnivals, and pleasure trips to visit relatives and friends in the coalfields. I have vague memories about going on one family picnic in the truck, and to the drive-in. All I remember about the drive-in is a giant image of Popeye and Olive Oyl on the screen, and the taste of popcorn. I'm sure I fell asleep. Nevertheless, what I really remember about that time was the feeling of safety and security in the presence of my mother, father, and siblings on a family outing in my dad's truck. This vivid memory is more valuable than any photograph I could have of my father.

two

=====================================

TROUBLED WATERS OF VALLSCREEK

COMPLICATIONS SURROUNDING MY BIRTH hit my dad like a freight train as he awaited my arrival at the Clinch Valley Clinic Hospital in Richlands, Virginia, right across the border from West Virginia. In addition to navigating the regular winding roads of the hilly West Virginia and Virginia terrain, travelers from Vallscreek had to cross the exceedingly steep and treacherous Stoney Ridge Mountain leading into Tazwell, Virginia, on the road to Richlands. It was bone-chilling cold that early morning in January 1954 when I, the family's third son, was born.

After spending some time with my mother postdelivery, my father made his way back home, navigating the normally treacherous, hilly roads of McDowell County, West Virginia, made even worse with the fresh accumulation of snow. The chains used on car tires back then were invaluable in providing greater traction on snow- and ice-covered roads.

The rest of the family was waiting when Dad got home. My brother Joe has told me, "I remember very well when you were born because you, the twelfth out of fourteen children, were the first to be born in the hospital. Before then, the family got to see the baby right after it was born, but this time we had to wait, and we were concerned about our father's reports of your struggles. The family was happy, though, when Mom and the baby came home."

Though I was born on time, and weighed in at a hefty nine pounds, it was apparent at birth that there were some issues with my health. According to my mother, I was immediately taken by the medical staff and put in an oxygen tent due to my bluish color and the difficulty I was having in breathing. Fortunately for me, the technology for treating physiologic oxygen deprivation in neonates existed at this time.

The specific medical terminology describing my condition was patent ductus arteriosus. This is a condition that exists when the fetal circulation physiology fails to change to the postgestation condition. In other words, if the duct that connects the aorta to the pulmonary artery, which is supposed to start closing when the neonate takes its first breath after birth, does not close soon, an abnormal strain is put on the heart and lungs, due to much of the blood being rerouted back to the lungs instead of flowing to other parts of the body.

Some of the symptoms associated with this condition are bounding pulses in the neck, fast breathing, tiring easily, and slow growth. However, the heart muscle itself could be normal. While these symptoms may seem dramatic, their very existence reflects the beauty in how nature tries to compensate for a condition such as this to preserve life without compromising neural functioning. The brain is taken care of first while body growth is secondary.

Medical issues were not the only thing that concerned my family: the ever-present matters of race permeated the family consciousness. Although West Virginia offered substantial attractions for blacks from other parts of the South, it nonetheless maintained a separatist order; it was truly not a color-blind state. From the beginning, the West Virginia legislature had decreed that black and white children would not be educated in the same schools. The state also mandated the separation of the races in the state's social welfare institutions, including hospitals, homes for the aged, and schools for the deaf and blind, among others. Although recorded lynching were far fewer in West Virginia than elsewhere, racial violence and hostility still marked the experiences of blacks in the Mountain State. In 1919 a white mob lynched two black coal miners in Chapmanville, Logan County. Moreover, the potential for violent racial conflict simmered just below the surface of class and race relations through the interwar years. However, it was the declining demand for labor in the coal industry that soon led to a drastic reduction in the black population in the state.

Threats from Mother Nature in the form of flooding in the hollow of Vallscreek were an ever-present possibility, especially during the annual spring thaw after the heavy snows of winter. When I was five, Vallscreek rose above its banks, and the water advanced toward the row of houses running parallel to it about two hundred feet away. Our house was one of those. The creek had been slowly rising since the evening before with the steady rain. The community observed the rising creek nervously, contemplating what to do if the water overflowed the bank and surged toward their homes. About seventy-five feet behind the houses was a large hill, the base of which would contain the forward flow of water and cause it to rise vertically and flood the houses. Although I was very young, I can remember people discussing fleeing to the hills if the creek continued its advance.

The adults' tone of concern and recognition of the possibility of danger was clear, but I being a child found the situation exciting. Watching the steady parade of debris floating by in the raging waters—old tires, furniture, trees, children's toys, outhouses, and even an occasional mooing cow—was another exciting aspect of the flooding for me.

A major concern about the rising waters was the potential of the creek to flood out or destroy the bridge that spanned Vallscreek. The community was already relatively isolated from any town with considerable resources, so if the bridge was taken out, our side of Vallscreek would be totally cut off. In this particular instance, the bridge was spared and there was no significant damage to houses. But on one occasion prior to my birth, floodwaters did cause the bridge to collapse. When the waters receded, for months the residents on our side of the creek had to negotiate the perilous ruins to get back and forth across the creek. Loss of the bridge was especially hard on young people who had to catch a bus for school. One time my sister Bobbie, rushing to catch a bus, slipped and fell into the creek, then had to return home and miss a day of school, since the high school was eleven miles away and there was no alternative transportation.

Though troubled waters in a literal sense was a periodic concern, the metaphorical troubled waters of poverty, racism, medical issues, unemployment, and family tragedy were more constant problems. Until recently, it was common to think of floods as natural disasters completely beyond human control, but Hurricane Katrina has taught us otherwise. The predominantly poor and working-class Ninth Ward of New Orleans endured the brunt of the suffering and devastation from the storm. Fortunately, in Vallscreek there were no recorded deaths due to flooding in our area. Nonetheless, our lower camp, almost exclusively black, sustained the worst of the annual flooding. The upper camp, basically beyond the railroad trestle, a little more than a quarter of a mile from the Vallscreek bridge, was where the post office, the company store, our church, and our school were. The upper camp was predominantly white. Poverty and racism, compounded by natural disasters, could be like a two-hundred-pound weight around your neck, causing you to drown in a sea of despair.

During the 1950s, as unemployment among coal miners escalated, black men found themselves with increasing amounts of leisure time on their hands. In our area, just across Vallscreek, unemployed black men carved out a space on the side of the hill, where they gathered to talk, tell jokes, engage in male gossip, and drink moonshine. In addition to lots of laughter and joviality, heated debates, disputes, and insults regularly characterized the hillside gatherings. Following one heated exchange with another man, Ollie Crawford bounded off the hill for his house across the creek and seized his rifle, pledging to return and kill the man who had insulted him. Only the skillful intervention of Ike Barron, a neighbor, prevented him from returning and carrying out his threat.

An unemployed man unable to support his family is subject to feelings of anxiety, low self-esteem, doubts about his manhood, and even rage. A home chronically without a breadwinner is a home under stress and tension. Any medical situation would undoubtedly be aggravated directly by the stressful circumstances and indirectly by the inability to obtain the necessary treatment due to lack of insurance, resulting from the breadwinner being unemployed. Even southern West Virginians having the best insurance in the 1950s, and needing major surgical or trauma intervention, still faced poor odds of survival unless they could get to a major medical center. It's a miracle that my family and I survived and thrived in spite of the troubled waters of McDowell County, West Virginia.

With my father gone, my mother was faced with the responsibility of raising the remaining twelve children. Two siblings, Josie and Eva, had already graduated from high school, had married, and were living in Massillon, Ohio. Various relatives from Alabama had offered to help Mom raise some of the children, but she'd decided to keep us all together.

It's incredible that she raised the remaining twelve of her children without the assistance of a spouse for many of the years. All fourteen of us are still living, our ages ranging from fifty-six to seventy-eight. Mom credited her great Christian faith and lots of prayer with giving her the strength to endure the hardships associated with the challenges. She strongly believed in and lived those central tenets of Christianity emphasizing love and compassion for others, forgiveness, and trying to live a life that is pleasing to God.

My mother found other effective methods of venting the tensions from the daily grind of life. She coped with emotional stress through the writing of poetry, which she intensified later in life. She probably wrote at least a hundred poems. I'm sure that if she'd had the right connections, she could have gotten some of them published. Unfortunately, many of her poems were destroyed in a house fire in 1982, and some that had survived the fire were tragically lost in the process of moving her into a nursing home. Incidentally, my sister Bobbie shares that same aptitude for poetry.

My grandma, her mother, lived with us, providing another source of income for the family, as well as emotional support and adult company for my mother. My grandma was also a convenient live-in babysitter when my mother had to leave the house or when she was hospitalized for medical reasons or for the depressive episodes she suffered from time to time. Her brothers provided emotional support and financial benefits to the extent they were able. Her association with women in her church allowed her to communicate with and confide in peers who may have been going through difficulties of their own. Of course her older children, especially the girls, were able to help her perform household chores and tend to those of us who were younger.

My brother Joe was a source of financial support for the family as well. He operated two paper routes, selling *Grit,* a weekly newspaper, and the *Pittsburgh Courier,* a black newspaper. Joe recalls his experience selling those papers, saying, "I carried two bags, one for the *Pittsburgh Courier* and the other one for the *Grit* paper, and I would go door to door throughout the local area on foot, soliciting prospective customers. Usually the white people after a quick scan of the black newspaper would decline, but often follow it up with 'I will take one of them *Grits.*'" The black people, not surprisingly were the predominant customers for the black newspaper.

While most young males with paper routes expected to retain and enjoy the profits of their labor, Joe turned most of his earnings over to our mother. Nevertheless, he did not mind doing this, because he felt an obligation to help out the family.

Joe also collected old whiskey bottles to sell to the bootleggers. Their continuous demand for a steady supply of containers to bottle their brew kept Joe hopping and on the alert for discarded liquor bottles. Just as our father had been a hustler, Joe "got his hustle on" in response to that demand from the bootleggers. My mother, who was not a drinker and frowned upon the idea on religious grounds, did not refuse the money that Joe made from selling those whiskey bottles. I can imagine her saying, "Forgive me, Jesus, but we need this money."

In addition to Joe's enterprising activities, he had his assigned household chores. He chopped wood and gathered coal from the slate dump to use as fuel for the kitchen stove and the potbellied coal stove in the living room.

Though my mother could have benefited financially from marrying again, the probability of this happening is much less when you have twelve dependent children. Moreover, my mother was pretty leery about the idea of bringing another man into the household. She had eight daughters who were still under her care, and she couldn't forget the horror stories of sexual and physical abuse she had heard during her youth in Alabama.

One thing among many that she worried about was how she was going to get me the medical attention I needed for my heart problem. In a poor state like West Virginia, without the medical insurance that my dad's job had provided, alternative funding was virtually nonexistent. In addition, the procedures for treating congenital heart conditions were new and still in their early development, and access to major medical centers in southern West Virginia did not exist in the 1950s.

In the late 1950s and the early 1960s, the civil rights era was starting to heat up. The *Brown v. Board of Education* case overruled *Plessy v. Ferguson*, making racial segregation in public places illegal. The Montgomery Bus Boycott against racial segregation on city buses was implemented in 1955. Black people across the country as well as many whites were outraged over the brutal killing of Emmett Till in Mississippi. African Americans living in southern West Virginia were subjected to the Jim Crow laws of the South. Social services to assist poor people were limited. The struggle for civil rights and the social changes that sprang from the social philosophy associated with it led to the development of programs to help less economically advantaged families, especially in northern states. This factor influenced my mother's decision to move her family to Ohio a few years later.

Quite naturally, institutional inequalities and prejudices have impact on the limitation of one's potential, but to a young child, those things are abstract. Discomfort, suffering, pain, and sadness are usually comprehended through children's concrete experiences—such things as painful lacerations, bumps, bruises, foot punctures, and fractures from accidents associated with the environmental hazards of living in poverty, and in mountainous and forested surroundings.

I think the words from my sister Isalene best summarize the feelings of my siblings about our family's experience in West Virginia. She indicates that it was a "happy childhood with a lot of challenges that we didn't realize because everybody was going through the same thing." A large family such as ours encountered greater obstacles than some, but, as Isalene goes on to say, "All of the families did basically the same things. The fathers were coal miners, and the mothers were housewives. Most of the people were poor, though some were better off than others, having better clothing and other possessions. There was no one, however, who could be considered affluent."

Though the men brought in the money, the critical role that women played in promoting the welfare of the family should not be underestimated. Historically, the real economic worth of work done by women in their traditional roles as caretakers, housewives, and cooks in their own homes and the homes of others, has been grossly suppressed. Cleaning toilets, sinks, and bathtubs and scrubbing floors is not easy work. Being strategic in how one plans and prepares a meal that will both please and nourish those who eat it within the constraints of a defined or limited budget requires significant forethought and ingenuity.

How do you put a price on something as critical to the collective health of society as child rearing, teaching children right from wrong, and giving them the morals and values that will maximize their chances of having a successful life in this society? Surely it is worth a lot more than the monetary value traditionally associated with it.

These good basic morals and values usually embraced by the families tended to promote peace and harmony between the residents of Vallscreek. The families usually got along well, but when there was a conflict, as Isalene said, "All the children did was throw rocks at each other all day long, but they rarely hit each other." Another thing the young people would do when they were mad at each other was to engage in the silly act of making fun of each other's names. Isalene would become Gasoline and Trotter would be changed to Trot Trot Trot, or something to that effect. Conflicts were generally just limited to inconsequential children's arguments, and if parents got involved, it was most often from the standpoint of deescalating the situation rather than exacerbating it. The "soccer mom mentality" was nonexistent during this time.

Some of the games my older siblings and their friends played in Vallscreek were hopscotch, checkers, horseshoes, baseball, football, basketball, and shooting marbles. Though I was not old enough at the time to have the skills to acquire a vast collection of marbles, I have a vivid recollection of boys boastfully displaying the ample supply of beautiful marbles they had taken from some unfortunate, less-skilled victims. Boy, those "cat eyes" were magnificent!

Dee said, "Most of the time we didn't have real balls. We just balled up newspapers and put tape on it." When they played touch football, usually the girls would play against the boys. "The boys would always win," Dee said.

In Vallscreek, a paradox existed in regard to protecting children and teenagers from "sinful" activities such as drinking, premarital sex, and gambling but allowing them the freedom to explore the potentially dangerous natural environment surrounding them. Children would walk through the dense woods and across railroad trestles and go swimming in the local swimming holes, things that parents would be fearful of their children doing today. Back then, parents did not have the fear as they do now of child predators, or of being accused of neglect, so they felt more secure in letting their children explore nature. Now if a child ends up with broken limbs, noticeable bumps and bruises, or animal bites, an investigation may be done to determine whether some form of abuse or lack of supervision was involved.

We children then, in the summer, would venture off at the break of dawn into the woods and groves to pick blackberries and apples. We would not return until our pails were full. One of the concerns that we did have was the possibility of being bitten by a snake. To protect against this, Isalene recalls, "We put on old long pants, and big shoes to make sure our feet were covered very well, and sprinkled on liniment or turpentine to keep the snakes away." The blackberries and apples we picked would be made into cobblers, and some canned, by our mothers.

There was a frightening incident one time when Isalene and some of her friends went apple picking. They apparently had been picking apples from a grove that belonged to a white man. The man got his shotgun, and when he pointed it at them, they grabbed the pails of apples they had picked and started running. They came to a road. Another white man, driving by in his truck, and noticing that they seemed to be desperately trying to escape some danger, offered to help them. He put the apples in the truck and gave them a ride home, demonstrating that, even in Jim Crow southern West Virginia, some white people were willing to help others who were not of their race.

Whereas the incident Isalene recounted was frightening, my brother Joe recalled an experience that had had the potential to actually end in tragedy. "We were picking berries on the edge of a man's property when a white man ordered us off. James 'Hobby' Moss, one of our friends, brazenly challenged the man to meet us at the top of the hill. Instead of one man, we met a mob at the top of the hill, carrying a hanging noose. Hobby fought them off with rocks he had amassed, as long as he could, but we had to run as fast as we could with the mob in hot pursuit. As we escaped, we could see and hear them in the distance cussing and shouting racial epithets at us."

Activities for teenagers were pretty limited in Vallscreek and surrounding areas. One of the highlights of Sunday afternoon for teenagers, actually the whole family, was the promenade to Canebrake, about a mile from Vallscreek. The parents and young boys and girls, dressed in their Sunday best and looking like a million bucks, smiling and profiling, would enjoy a leisurely stroll into Canebrake to go to the place to be, Mack's Place, close to where we picked apples. The place sold sandwiches and things like pop, peanuts, and candy. Mack's Place also had a jukebox, and the teenagers' ultimate goal was to buy pop and peanuts, then dance a little while and go home. This would be their Sunday afternoon activity. In retrospect it seems like a lame outing, but that experience was as sweet as cotton candy for the youths at the time.

The store was owned by white people. Businesses owned by African Americans in the area were limited, consisting as they did of small family-owned businesses such as barbershops, home-based candy stores, or bootleg house bars.

The Do Drop In was a house joint that the young people would go to on their way home after choir practice or Bible study. A big incentive for them to be involved in church activities was the opportunity to get out of the house and maybe hang out with their friends a while at this place. The place sold beer, pop, and snacks, and it had a basement with a jukebox. As they did on Sundays at Mack's Place, the young people would just have a pop and a snack, dance to a couple of songs and then leave. They relished this golden opportunity to circumvent their parents' rules in order to be with their fellow teenagers without younger children or their parents around. They could not linger too long, for the parents knew the church activities only lasted so long. Isalene said, "One time we stayed too long, and Daddy came in there and caught us."

The formation of clubs was popular with the youth. Young people, bursting with energy, had to come up with activities they could do in an environment with paltry community entertainment facilities and few economic resources. Children had to become more creative in finding things to do. Clubs, societies, and circles were common entities in the churches, so children adapted the organizational structure and similar protocols used in church clubs to their own little informal clubs. They would take minutes and collect their ten-cent dues. Several times during the summer, they would have a wiener roast or fish fry. They would sell what food they could to raise money, and eat the rest.

Their biggest event would be at the end of summer. They would clear a field at the end of the road of brush that had grown over the summer and make a ball field to play softball. Isalene said, "We would enjoy the ice cream made from our ice-cream maker, and the wieners and fish from the wiener roast and fish fry we would have." All the children attending ate free that day, even if they were not in the club. I can recall munching on a hot dog and bun at one of those late summer events.

One exciting activity that Dee recalls is accompanying Dad into the woods to search for the family Christmas tree. She has fond memories of "thinking she was really something, following behind Dad as he would drag the beautiful tree home, anticipating indulging in the hot cocoa that Mom had prepared awaiting them when they got home."

Hunting was a great sport that engaged the attention and energy of many black and white men in West Virginia and throughout Appalachia. My father was one of those men. Dee said, "Dad would hunt for rabbits, squirrels, groundhogs, and possums."

My brother James said that he wanted to go on one of the hunting trips with my dad, but Dad would not take him. According to him, Dad would say, "Shorty [my father's nickname for my mother] said she don't want you to go, so I can't take you."

James would tell him, "You're the daddy, so if you say I can go, I should be able to go."

That was not how it worked. Dad, though the breadwinner, was bound by the wishes of my mother as far as the children's safety was concerned.

My cousin Pete Foster related his memories of accompanying my father and my brother Joe on hunting trips. Pete said, "They'd go way back in the woods. I would be sitting there all night on a log. Every little noise I heard, I would jump straight up. My head was on a swivel all night long." Constantly on the alert for any wild nocturnal creatures, he was barely able to get twenty winks in for the whole night. He said that my father and Joe could just lie there with their heads on a log and sleep like babies.

My dad had hunting dogs, which he spent considerable time and care in selecting. He looked up the dogs in the encyclopedia, trying to find the breeds that had the traits conducive to hunting. He would pay a hundred dollars for a dog. That was nothing to sneeze at in the 1950s.

Pete recalled, "Uncle Joe used to have a horn, sort of like a ram's horn, and when he blew it, no matter where the dogs were, when they heard the horn, they'd come right back." It took a certain skill to blow the horn. One could not usually just pick up the horn and blow it. It was something that had to be learned. Pete said, "Neither Joe nor I could blow the horn, but Uncle Joe could blow it beautifully."

I have only very hazy memories of my father preparing to go hunting. He and a couple of other shadowy figures would be loading crude packs of gear, his shotgun, and two dogs into his truck. I can recall the dogs shaking like leaves on a tree in the wind, and chomping at the bit in anticipation of a day of chasing down wild rabbits and other prey as they were led to the truck.

Pete related a sad and scary incident about one of Dad's dogs. "He had one dog that Levi Rogers, a neighbor, shot, leaving a big hole in its side. Everybody was afraid there was going to be a shootout when Uncle Joe got home from work."

When Dad got home, everybody stopped what they were doing. Boys cut their basketball game short, parents scooped up their little ones, shades on houses were drawn, dogs ducked into their houses, and chickens even stayed in their coops, but there was no shootout.

My brother Joe remembers our father saying to Mr. Rogers, "Levi, you shot my dog, so take him up in the woods and finish him off."

The wounded dog was under our house. Dad retrieved the dog and handed it off to Mr. Rogers. He took the dog to the woods and euthanized it. Nothing was said about it after that.

No violence involving humans occurred that day, but it could have. My dad, a dark-skinned man with wavy hair, had a reputation of being a tough guy, even though he was only about 5 feet 7 and 150 pounds. He was not a hateful or an antagonizing person, but he had little tolerance for anyone attempting to disrespect or abuse him.

My father often sported a small, neatly trimmed beard, accentuating his masculinity. He was conscientious about his overall appearance and hygiene; he took cleanliness seriously—daily baths, groomed hair, stocking cap, waves and all, and regular shaves, except of course during weekend hunting trips roughing it in the woods. On one of those weekend trips, he lost an eye in an accidental shooting, necessitating that it be replaced with a prosthetic eye. My mother mentioned on several occasions that he was just as meticulous in keeping that eye clean as he was about the rest of him, literally buffing it like a precious jewel.

Not only was my father of compact stature, he also had legs like baseball bats that his muscular torso could have sued for non-support. My mother said my father used to thrust his legs up on the balustrade of the front porch, enjoying his leisurely Sunday or Saturday afternoon after a long week of backbreaking work. He had earned the right to just chill out on his front porch, but my mother would playfully try to discourage him from displaying those meager specimens of human locomotion. He paid no attention to her teasing him about them, retorting, "These some pretty legs." I don't know about pretty, but that must have been a strong trait, because most of the Trotter clan has been cursed with it, including yours truly to the nth degree.

My mother shared some of my grandmother's features. My mother was a little darker, and her face was a little more angular, but it exhibited less distress. Though she was a bit overweight in her late thirties through her fifties, she was attractive. She slimmed down in her later years, which gave her an even more attractive appearance.

My mother and father had a good relationship: they respected each other and were mutually content with each other's performances of their respective roles of husband and wife and father and mother. They did not argue but communicated civilly. My sister

Dee related one incident when tempers did boil over, however, and my father slapped my mother.

Dee said, "Mom picked up a frying pan and hit him in the head with it. That was the last time he tried that." Dee also said that often, whenever Mom requested something of my father, he would salute her and say, "Yes, ma'am Shorty." The bump on the head from that skillet may have resulted in an even higher level of respect for her.

Though my older siblings enjoyed their life in the hills of West Virginia, their expectations of a bright economic future in that state were limited. In the 1950s, the coal industry was on the decline, and the prospects for employment were dismal, especially for African Americans. The situation for females with hopes of having a career other than being a homemaker was even more dreadful. Having some post–high school education would have given both females and males a greater chance to move up the economic ladder, especially in states other than West Virginia.

Some of my older brothers and sisters attended Excelsior High School in War, West Virginia. Extra encouragement was often reserved for certain students, those who had some special talent that the teachers recognized or for those children of the "elite." Isalene stated, "Never once did any of the teachers talk to the rest of us as though any of us had the potential to do whatever we wanted to do. They only talked to certain ones . . . and the same thing would be noted when we moved to Newcomerstown, Ohio. We got our encouragement and motivation to aspire to greater heights mostly from Mom."

My brother Joe, however, has a somewhat different perspective on this. He remembers that trade schools, emphasizing fields that included brick masonry, carpentry, and auto repair, were heavily promoted for boys. Even though a dearth of occupational prospects for young black males existed in southern West Virginia, evidence that some things were starting to change outside of West Virginia was becoming clear. The hopes were that more options would open up in West Virginia as well, and that students would be ready to take advantage of them.

While I knew my mother had a great interest in the educational advancement of her children, I found out later that my father, too, had been extremely interested in his sons, in particular, becoming well educated. He felt it was of critical importance to his sons' ability to take care of their families. My brother Joe stated, "Just knowing that my father had articulated his wishes for his sons to be well educated was a strong motivating force for me when I was in college."

While my older sisters and brothers were busy contemplating their adult futures, I was just preoccupied with being a child, trying to figure out what makes the world go round. We had one of those big floor-model radios. I remember lying on the floor listening to it when I was four years old. It was such a mystery to me about how people could fit into the radio. I had to live with this puzzle until I got older. In the meantime, I just accepted things as they were, and enjoyed listening to the "little people" in the radio.

When I was a child, I liked looking at my reflection in my parents' dresser mirror, when I got the chance. This was another mystery I could not comprehend. I just enjoyed exploiting that phenomenon in my private relationship with the boy in the mirror that looked just like me, down to the distended, prominently pulsating artery in my neck, due to the heart problem. The boy in the mirror had a smooth, unblemished, dark brown complexion like the surface of a Reese's peanut butter cup, with slightly chubby cheeks. He also sported a neat haircut that his dad or some other adult had given him. I thought that kid looked pretty good. Oh wait, that was me.

We enjoyed many duels with our identical cowboy holsters and guns, never failing to shoot each other at the same time, but never killing one another. We always remained standing, and smiling at each other.

When I was around seven or eight, I started noticing something about my teeth when I looked in the mirror. My four front teeth on the top and the four bottom front teeth started to take on an unsightly rust color and a rough texture. The teeth looked like they were rotten, and that was what people thought. My brother James used to call me "cornbread teeth." That did wonders for my self-image.

Years later I saw a dentist who said it was not decay but that I must have taken an antibiotic when I was young that was known to discolor and roughen the enamel. Another dentist thought it was due to some developmental problem with the teeth.

Regardless of the cause, I hated them. But there was nothing that could be done about them. We were a poor family without dental insurance. I had to endure them, along with the teasing and the resulting self-consciousness, throughout my teen years and young adulthood. Correction of the problem had to wait until I was able to save up enough money from my summer jobs while in college to at least get the front, more visible teeth addressed. I was then able to smile confidently, as I had when I was a little boy looking in the mirror.

Around 1958 we got a television set. We could only get three channels, and these, with the outside antenna we had, were unclear. Occasionally, the channels would get clear when a plane was passing overhead. The excess "snow" would disappear from the screen, allowing images so sharp that one could detect beads of sweat on the foreheads of people on the screen. We really appreciated those fleeting forty seconds of visual clarity. On rare occasions, a "colored" person would appear on television. Our family and other black families around there derived as much excitement from that as someone would observing Halley's Comet. Whenever someone spotted a black person on television, the excited pronouncement "There's a colored person on television!" would be shouted down the road.

Sometimes one of the Carringtons, who lived about three houses up the road, would come to our house and accuse us of taking their "siganal." This was ridiculous. How do you take someone's television signal? We could not control the electromagnetic waves. Even if we did interfere with their signal, we did not do it intentionally. They had a superior antenna setup, allowing them better reception, probably because their antenna was mounted on a distant hill. I remember being able to trace their antenna wire from their house to the antenna perched on top of the hill.

The Carringtons were the elite people on that road. Their family surname even sounds rich. They had nice hardwood floors in their house, and a modern bathroom. Mr. Carrington, due to more education, had a better job in the mines, and he also sold life insurance. Though they seemed to be quite well off compared to the other black people around there, in retrospect the Carringtons were probably not as prosperous as we thought. Wealth and affluence are relative.

When the end of summer rolled around in 1959, I can recall contemplating attending school for the first time. I remember it because my sister Isalene and all of the older kids were having their end-of-summer wiener roast. I was gorging on my hot dog and bun as the rest of the children were talking about the impending school year, and I remember feeling so proud that I was going to be starting first grade that fall. I had already mastered the prerequisites of being able to count to a hundred and recite my alphabet, and I was ready to go.

Managing sleeping arrangements and getting ready for school in the morning in our large family were challenging. We would get up from our crowded beds at the crack of dawn. The bedroom I slept in was shared with two brothers, my grandmother, and two sisters. My two brothers and I slept in a rollaway bed, my brother David and I at one end and my brother James at the other end. The one blanket we had to keep us warm during cold nights was reinforced by an assortment of coats laid on top. My grandmother, on the other side of the room, shared her bed with two of my sisters. Other siblings slept on two couches and another rollaway bed in the living room. Two of my youngest sisters slept with my mother, in her room. This situation would not seem mathematically possible by today's standards.

I can vividly recall my first day of school. One of the older siblings heated a big pot of water on our wood- and coal-burning stove. My brother Joe's responsibility was to get up early and fire up the stove in the kitchen as well as the pot-bellied stove in the living room. I washed up from the heated water added to cold water in a washtub in the kitchen. Several of us would use the same water before it was replaced.

I recall getting dressed, and sniffing the new smell of my Wrangler jeans and multicolored cotton plaid shirt. Over time, that fresh-from-the-store aroma would gradually fade as I simultaneously got used to the mundane routine of getting ready for school. Every day was mad chaos as we literally bumped into each other as we got ready for our day, but my mother was somehow able to bring some order to the confusion. By delegating certain responsibilities to older siblings as a CEO would do with lower-level managers, and monitoring them as closely as a prison guard, things got done.

After eating a breakfast usually consisting of salt pork, biscuits, oatmeal or grits, pancakes with Karo or Alaga syrup, and eggs, prepared by our mother, we would wash our teeth with soap or clean them with soda. We did not consistently have toothbrushes. Dressed and ready to go, we headed for school. The younger of us walked to the primary school about three-quarters of a mile away. The older siblings waited at the little parking area, across the creek, for their bus, and we would say good-bye to them as we continued on our way.

We walked to the one-room schoolhouse for black children. I did okay walking most of the way, but the last forty or fifty feet were up a hill, which seemed to cause me as much fatigue as swimming the English Channel. As a "macho man," I find little pleasure in admitting to this, but my sisters, Voncille and Effie, would alternate in helping me up the hill, especially in the wintertime.

We had just rounded the curve one day on our way to school when we encountered a woman, screaming hysterically in her yard. I only knew her as Miss Marie. Smoke and flames were pouring from her brick house. A man named Mr. Porter was running about indecisively. He finally picked up a water hose, jumped over a small brick partition between his house and the house on fire, and directed the feeble stream of water toward the flames, but to no effect. The fire was too far gone.

Slowly making our way to school but periodically looking back, everything appeared to get smaller as we increased our distance, except for the monstrous fire that continued to grow exponentially. We felt bad for the woman, but as children, we could do nothing. When we made our way back home after school, there was nothing left of her house but smoldering embers.

Thoroughly imbedded in my memory from school is telling my teacher, Miss Bessie, that it was my birthday and I had turned six. It was the custom back then to give boys swats equal to their age in years. I was happy that she was going to recognize me for my sixth birthday with six swats. Little did I know that I would receive real swats, administered with full force, not the little baby swats I had been expecting. I guess she was making up for the spankings my dad never gave me. Needless to say, I never told her of another birthday. My sister Effie, now called Mecca, recalls that spanking, saying, "I was really upset with her doing that."

Mecca's own recollections about school in West Virginia were pretty painful. Reflecting on those memories, she says, "I just always felt afraid. Afraid of the teachers and afraid of being whipped, and ridiculed, and if you didn't do well, they were going to punish you. It was very strict, and I was afraid that I was going to get paddled or hit with the strap. I had seen our sister Doris get strapped before. That school used to represent fear to me instead of being a learning environment." She therefore tried to do as well as she could. Mecca recalls that, when she was sent to the board to write or do arithmetic, "Mr. Hutchinson had me so nervous that my hands would be trembling when I wrote my letters or numbers on the board." According to Mecca, those experiences stayed with her throughout her school career.

Mecca suggests that Miss Bessie at the one-room school in Vallscreek had a preference for the lighter-skinned children, who tended to be her pets. She does, however, recall Miss Bessie bringing cornbread and beans and cold milk to feed the students in the school.

My older sister Isalene said this about Miss Bessie: "She was the best. She was the teacher, the mother, the principal, and the janitor." The school was equipped with a coal stove, which she had to get going before her pupils got there. She would often during the winter find it necessary to take off some children's shoes and socks and warm their feet before class could start. Reflecting back to that time, and putting myself in her situation as the teacher, I can only surmise that her heart ached when contemplating the futures of many of her bright students, whose potentials would be stymied by the sociopolitical realities of southern West Virginia and the nation as a whole at the time.

Miss Bessie taught the first through third grades by herself. Isalene said, "There would be a table for each grade, with seven or eight chairs. She would first teach the first grade something. While this was going on, the second and third grades would be working on something she had assigned them to do." This process would be repeated for each grade and for different subjects.

Every morning, though, before starting class, the children would sing, pray, and say the Pledge of Allegiance. At the end of the day they would sing a song, some of the favorites being "Home on the Range," "Yankee Doodle Dandy," "The Negro National Anthem," and "Old Black Joe."

My brother Joe said, "I use to hate this song because I thought she was talking about me." Of course the song had nothing to do with him, but in the 1940s and 1950s black consciousness had not evolved to the point where most blacks unabashedly embraced their darkness. In an atmosphere of white supremacy in the South, where blacks were relegated to an inferior position in society and caricatured in exaggerated, cartoonish pictures, it was no wonder that Joe had such an aversion to that song.

At recess, on nice days, the students would go outside and play. The playground was equipped with a maypole, sliding board, see-saw, merry-go-round, and swings. There was an outside toilet the children had to line up to use. The water pump adjacent to the outhouse was a center of activity on hot days, as children eagerly lined up and waited to quench their thirst after playing hard.

The first time I learned that embarrassment can sometime be the best teacher was in the first grade, when I was asked to spell a simple word and missed it. An informal spelling bee was being held in the class, and the word I had to spell was "is." I got confused when I was asked to spell it and I spelled it s-i. I felt stupid and embarrassed when informed that I was wrong. I never forgot the spelling after that.

Some of the other memories I recall as a child in West Virginia included hiking up the big hill behind our house. We would go as far as we could. I suppose the limiting factor was me, due to my heart problem. I remember jokingly, but seriously, getting myself a stick to use as some sort of leverage to scale the hill. I said, laughingly, "I am an old man." The older brother I was with, realizing my limitations, stopped where I stopped. From this distance up on the hill, we rolled small boulders down. It was fun to listen to the boulders as they gained momentum rolling down the hill, crackling as they made their way through the debris of dead brush and vegetation. Fortunately we never hurt anyone through this thoughtless activity. Some woman could have been in her backyard hanging clothes on a line to dry. Small children could have been out playing, or some poor soul could have been making his way to an outhouse up the hill from his house. We could have caused damage to property. Thankfully, as far as I can recollect, none of these things happened.

Like most little boys, I liked to play war when I was a child. Back then, we indulged in it more actively and creatively than boys do now, when war is often played electronically, via PlayStation. I have recollections of engaging in war games with other boys when I was five and six years old. We would be running and pretending to carry and fire guns, making the sounds of gunfire with our voices, as we portrayed American and German soldiers. I did okay playing with the other boys until they started running and I was not able to keep up. As I ran out of gas, I watched them surge ahead with more energy and excitement than a group of dogs chasing a car dragging a hundred-pound piece of fresh bacon.

I can't say I felt bad because I could not keep up. This was just the way it was. I think my mom felt worse than I did, because she could see clearly that I was not physically on par with my play-mates. By nightfall I was fatigued from playing all day, and was ready for bed.

One thing that I fancied doing as a child was fishing. A wooden swinging bridge spanned the small creek between the dirt road we lived on and the rural highway on the other side. I remember being on that bridge on warm days, and feeling the cool, pleasant breeze blowing down from the surrounding hills sweeping across my face. I remember being amazed at the little fish and minnows swimming under the water in the creek.

An older brother, a couple of other boys, and I would occasion-ally attempt to catch fish. Our crude equipment usually consisted of a pole made from a small tree branch with an old string tied to it, and a bent nail attached to the string. We would put a night crawler on the nail as bait. Despite our considerable efforts, we were never successful. Had we snagged an old shoe, a piece of wood, a can, or an old chicken bone from the creek, we would have been almost as thrilled as if we'd reeled in a nice fish.

The small dirt parking area on the other side of the bridge was adjacent to the highway. On two occasions I can recall traveling evangelists setting up there and preaching to the local people. They always came with the fiery message that hell and eternal damnation and fire and brimstone awaited you if you did not accept Jesus.

They would then collect whatever money they could and leave. They really scared the hell out of people. I remember going home feeling terrified about going to hell, thinking about all of the honey buns I'd stolen from my dad's lunch bucket before his death, the little fibs I told, and the not-so-nice things I did to other children. I did not want to burn forever.

Another frightening experience I had was caused by familiar members of the community. I awoke one morning to hear a commotion right outside the house. I looked out the window and saw my uncle Luther and several men from the neighborhood standing at the side of the house, laughing and talking in an animated manner. Among them I recognized Ike Barron, Joe Jackson, Ollie Crawford, and Fletcher Blackmon. Joe Jackson was holding a large knife.

As I watched, a hog came into sight, running as it tried to flee my uncle, who was frantically grabbing at the hog's leg. It was painfully obvious what the men were trying to do. The ear-piercing squealing of the hog was terrible. I saw Joe Jackson lunge at the hog with his big knife, and he managed to stab it in its side. The hog seemed to squeal even more as the blood gushed out. This initial stab was followed quickly by a stab to the hog's neck. Though felled by the lethal stab to the neck, the hog continued to squeal and thrash in agony for quite some time. I could only wish that the gruesome episode would end. Even to a young child, it seemed like a barbaric act.

After they killed the hog, the men spent the day boiling the animal in some kind of large container. At one point they took the hog out and strung it up by its feet on a horizontal pole whose ends were attached to vertical poles firmly secured in the ground. They next skinned and gutted the animal, after which it was cut into sections and divided up. Though it had been horrible to observe that really brutal scene, I derived great satisfaction from feasting on the final products of ham and bacon.

At the time of my father's death in 1957, black miners faced frequent and increasing periods of unemployment. Technological changes like the mechanical coal loader in post–World War II dramatically reduced the need for laborers in the coal industry. In his recollections of life in the coal mines of West Virginia, the veteran coal miner Robert Armstead described in *Black Days, Black Dust* how coal-loading machines were displacing increasing numbers of hand loaders: "With giant, crablike arms, the coal-loading machine, or loader, scooped the coal up onto its belt-type surface. The belt tumbled it back out of the way, usually onto the bottom or into empty cars. . . . Some timbermen, trackmen, and loaders kept their jobs, but the mining machines created massive layoffs. Every two or three months, three hundred or more men got laid off" (p. 64)—and just before his death, my father was one of them.

In West Virginia the number of black coal miners declined precipitously from nearly 35,000 in the 1940s to only about 3,000 as the civil rights movement got underway. The decline of the coal industry in the state spurred a mass exodus of blacks from the coalfields to the urban-industrial North—New York, New Jersey, Michigan, Illinois, Ohio, and the Washington, DC, area. Growing numbers of African Americans migrated to cities from the southern Appalachian coalfields of Virginia, Kentucky, Tennessee, and Alabama, as well.

In the summer of 1960, my mother made the decision to move her family to Ohio. I had often heard about Ohio. As a little boy, about six years of age, I remember the curtains hanging in the bedroom that I shared with my five or six siblings and my grandmother that had little pictures of the state of Ohio all over them. We used to say, "Look, there's Ohio." I had two older married sisters who lived there with their families. My concept of Ohio was of a place far away where everybody had a lot of money and lived in big houses. The excitement of anticipating the move to Ohio, where a comparably easier life awaited us, could not be contained.

I am sure some of my older siblings who were closer to graduation from school had mixed emotions about moving and not being able to finish school with the friends they'd grown up with.

The night before and the morning of the big move, my mother and the older siblings were busy packing everything up of any useful value for the big move. By late morning, the mood was one of anxiety, as we wondered when Ralph Harris and Marvin Jones, the husbands of my two older sisters, Josie and Eva, were going to arrive here from Ohio to move us. Finally, at noon everybody broke out in glee as the men announced their arrival, blowing their car horns as they rounded the last curve coming down the mountain into Vallscreek. Looking across the shallow creek, we could see two nice-looking cars, each towing a small trailer.

By about two o'clock that afternoon, everything that we could carry was loaded up. My brother James was disappointed because not enough room was available in either car to carry the family dog with us. He pleaded with one of our brothers-in-law to maybe somehow secure the dog on the trailer, but he would not allow it. I'm sure my brother thought this was pretty callous and cold, but we children had no say-so. It was decided that the dog would be left in the care of a neighbor. There would have been eight of us children, my mother, and my grandmother making the trip. At that time, Josie, Eva, and Bobbie lived in Massillon. Dee had moved to Alexandria, Virginia. Isalene and Joe were still in school, but they had spent the summer in Massillon, and were assisting Josie, Eva, and Bobbie in preparing the house for us in Newcomerstown, Ohio, where we were moving.

After saying our good-byes to friends and neighbors, we all got in the cars and headed up the hill and down the road toward a future in Ohio that we hoped would be brighter. A mixture of apprehension, sadness, and happiness came over us, as we witnessed the rows of company houses, and the personalities who had touched our lives, fade into the distance and from view as we moved further up the hill and around the bend, making our way toward that Promised Land we knew as Ohio. My sister Mecca indicated that she was petrified about leaving West Virginia. She did not want to leave her friends. Mecca now feels that the move from West Virginia was the best thing for us to have done. Had we not moved, she says, none of us would have progressed, and I would not have survived.

We were joining others from Vallscreek—the Carringtons, the Barrons, the Blackmons—who had decided to make that trek out of the coalfields of West Virginia that last year or two. This was in a way our Middle Passage, only this time we were not African inhabitants taken from our land by force to a place of certain bondage and suffering. We were moving under our own volition. We only hoped that the road we traveled on this middle passage would lead to a more positive mode of existence.

About an hour into the trip, an appropriate song came on the radio in our car—"Hit the Road Jack" by Ray Charles. Everybody burst out laughing. Even the younger of us children could understand the concept of hitting the road. That was what we were doing. We were hitting the road out of West Virginia to, hopefully, a better life in Ohio.

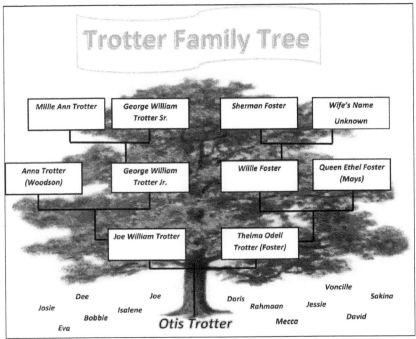

Trotter Family Tree

| Millie Ann Trotter | George William Trotter Sr. | | Sherman Foster | Wife's Name Unknown |

| Anna Trotter (Woodson) | George William Trotter Jr. | | Willie Foster | Queen Ethel Foster (Mays) |

| Joe William Trotter | | Thelma Odell Trotter (Foster) |

Dee   Joe   Doris   Voncille   Sakina
Josie   Isalene   Rahmaan   Jessie
Bobbie   David
Eva   Mecca

Otis Trotter

Trotter family tree.

Coal mine in southern West Virginia. Photo by James T. Laing, "The Negro Miner in West Virginia" (PhD diss., Ohio State University, 1933).

Coal camp home in southern West Virginia. Photo by James T. Laing, "The Negro Miner in West Virginia" (PhD diss., Ohio State University, 1933).

Miners eating their lunch, from the Pocahontas Operators Association collection, courtesy of Eastern Regional Coal Archives, Craft Memorial Library, 600 Commerce St., Bluefield, WV 24701

My mother, Thelma Odell Foster Trotter, and my maternal grandmother, Ethel Foster, with my sister Dee as a toddler.

Rock Elvy Missionary Baptist Church, my father's family church.

From left: My brother David, I, my brother Joe, and my brother Rahmaan, standing on the spot where our house once stood in Vallscreek, 2010.

From left: My brother David, my nephew Carson, my brother Rahmaan, and I standing next to Vallscreek, 2010.

My brothers and I in front of the old church in Vallscreek, 2010.

Rahmaan reminiscing about our childhood exploration of the railroad trestle, 2010.

three

========

THE NEWCOMERS

THOUGH THE DISTANCE BETWEEN Vallscreek and our destination, Newcomerstown, Ohio, was approximately three hundred miles, the trip seemed like a voyage to the moon. The usual question from children in this situation is "Are we there yet?" Well, we weren't.

In those days, many segments of the superhighway system were not completed yet, so most of the trip was via old state, county, and US routes that took us directly through the hearts of small cities and towns. I can still hear the loud clanging of steel and metal objects being moved about, the sound of giant blowers, the high-pitched hissing from pressure tools in the many factories and plants that we passed on our way. I remember the swarm of cars and trucks going to and fro as we slowly made our way through these towns.

I also remember that in the late afternoon, I would guess around four o'clock, my thoughts turned to those fried chicken sandwiches that my mother had prepared for the trip. They tasted so good—words could not express how much we appreciated them. To me no restaurant along the way could hold a candle to my mother's cooking. In those days, my mother could not have afforded to feed all of her children in restaurants even if she had wanted to. Furthermore, many diners in 1961 probably would not have served black people in West Virginia, at least not in a dignified manner.

The next thing I knew it was nearly dark. I had been sleeping like a log for a couple of hours. Someone said we were in Ohio, and

51

that we were almost there. My heart beat with excitement, expecting to arrive shortly, but after driving miles and miles we still were not there. As it turned out, that "almost" was about two hours.

After what seemed like a journey to eternity to children who'd never been more than ten or twenty miles from home in West Virginia, we arrived in Newcomerstown, a small village of approximately four thousand people nestled in the Ohio valley in eastern central Ohio. Major industries here included the W. M. Brode bridge and road construction company, the Heller Brothers tool manufacturing firm, the Goshen Brick Company, and James B. Clow and Sons Company, manufacturer of iron pipes and radiators.

Our family was to move into a house on Clow Avenue, the main street of the small African American community, most of whose inhabitants came from Alabama. In the early 1900s, James B. Clow sent representatives of his company down South to recruit potential black employees to work at his piping company. Many of those early blacks specifically came from Rock Run and Anniston, Alabama. The Clow Company was so successful in recruiting skilled blacks from a foundry in Rock Run that the company there filed a lawsuit—which ultimately failed—against the Clow Company for taking its workers. Clow relocated several dozens of black families from Alabama to Newcomerstown. A few others came from Kentucky, Georgia, North Carolina, and from other towns in Ohio over time. The Clow Company established a community center in 1924 to assist blacks who had recently moved from the South to work at the Clow Company to get acclimated to their new life in the North.

The Clow Company, not surprisingly, was the major economic engine that drove the development of the African American community and its institutions in Newcomerstown between 1900 and the 1950s. More so than for our larger urban counterparts, our lives revolved almost exclusively around our families, churches, and a few mainly home-based enterprises. Income earned from the company allowed blacks to establish churches, which were a vital part of life in Newcomerstown. Trinity Baptist Church was organized in 1908, under the leadership of Mr. Lowery. Destroyed by fire in 1925, Trinity Baptist's present building was constructed by the Clow Company in 1926 and was donated to the community when the company terminated its operations in 1956. St. Paul African

Methodist Episcopal Church was founded in 1920. Reverend Hairston, its first pastor, oversaw the construction of the building.

Candy stores in homes, and barbering establishments operating from homes, were some of the businesses that were created by blacks during that era, mirroring the business environment of our community in Vallscreek. Sanitation services and at least one bar were among other enterprises created by blacks. In the late 1960s, an African American resident, Paul Simpson, selling cleaning supplies, would make his mark as the most successful black business owner, eventually expanding his business to at least one other community, Uhrichsville, Ohio, fifteen miles away. Simpson broke another barrier in the town, becoming its first black police officer in 1969.

One of the local barbers was a man named Mr. White, about 5 feet 7, with a caramel-colored skin and black wavy hair. It was said that he was part Native American. Mr. White also ran a small candy store out of his home, and shortly after relocating to Newcomerstown, our family became patrons. My younger brother, David, and I would purchase candy from him whenever we were lucky enough to get a little change from our mother or perhaps from the relatives who occasionally visited us. Mr. White's neatly kept living room was always crowded with older boys intensely watching sports on his grainy black-and-white television, hardly noticing us, while apparently waiting to get their hair cut.

I remember that Mr. White's wife, a very light-skinned woman with long, graying hair that was often tied in a bun, slightly built and with a pleasant, welcoming smile, would retrieve our choices of candy from the glass case and accept our money. She died a couple of years after we came to Newcomerstown. Not long after her death, Mr. White's house started to deteriorate structurally as well as hygienically. And according to my brother James, without the watchful eye of his wife, the teenage guys were robbing him blind of candy from the case.

Mr. White continued to cut hair, however, and by this time my brother David and I were two of his few remaining customers. I conjectured that many of the older fellows had finished school and started their lives in other places, or perhaps they began cutting each other's hair while watching the television that was increasingly becoming a part of home life. Our mother would send us to get our hair cut when it was needed and when she had the money. Sometimes Mr. White would cut it on credit and she'd pay him later. It never failed that when he turned the light on before cutting our hair, roaches would scatter to hiding places like legions of soldiers fleeing to foxholes during an air assault. We hated this, but over time we became more tolerant. The roaches were par for the course, and I just made sure the barber chair was free of the critters.

When the Clow Company closed its plants in Newcomerstown in 1956, its workforce needed to find employment with other companies in town, such as the Heller Tool Company or Kurtz-Kash, or to start their own businesses. Some people, especially blacks, moved to other cities and towns in Ohio, resulting in a significant decrease in the number of African Americans in the town.

Newcomerstown was, in a way, a study in contradictions as far as race relations were concerned. From the turn of the century through the early 1940s, blacks in Newcomerstown were pretty integrated residentially with whites, while in most of the rest of the country races were greatly segregated geographically. Blacks in Newcomerstown lived all over the town during most of that period and attended school with whites. Most of the blacks did concentrate around Clow Avenue, South College Street, Center Street, and Cheery Street, which were considered the residential area of the black community.

Shirley Coker-Kerr recalls that "Newcomerstown became a melting pot, as people of varied nationalities made their homes on Clow Avenue. Along with the Yanais and Gumbars from Hungary, the Lenzos from Italy, and the Kings, who were Native Americans, we lived with a sense of community, enjoyed our differences, and developed friendships which have lasted through generations."

The broader geography of Newcomerstown consisted of several major thoroughfares and streets. These were Canal, State, and Church Streets running east and west and north of the northern end of Clow Avenue (now martin Luther King Drive). The principal streets traversing the village in a north and south direction were River Street, west of MLK Drive, and College and Chestnut Streets, east of the Drive. The main streets of the business district, which we referred to as Uptown, consisted of Main, Bridge, and a portion of Canal Street, and the businesses and institutions on these streets included the five-and-dime, a luncheonette, the library, the Eureka Hardware Store, the meat market, the post office, police and fire departments, and the Touraine Club, a bar and restaurant.

Schools in Newcomerstown have always been integrated. Shirley Coker and Cora Russell were black cheerleaders who were on the cheerleading squad as early as the 1950s. A black band director, Mr. Curtis, worked with the school system in the early 1960s. These things occurred even in the context of a predominantly white town.

But segregation was not unknown in Newcomerstown. The Clow Company, even though it had an integrated work force and was thought to pay its black employees equal to what it paid white employees for equal work, promoted segregation in its company outings, with blacks and whites having separate picnics. And by the late 1960s, it was predominantly blacks who lived on Clow Avenue. Many whites who had resided on the avenue had either died or moved away. A couple of black families lived on College Street, adjacent to Clow Avenue. No blacks were on the school staff except Mrs. Willy Dale Harris, who was part of the janitorial staff. I do recall, in the late 1960s, a very dark-skinned man from India who taught chemistry at the high school for a very short time. It seemed ironic that while Newcomerstown during the period from the late 1960s through the 1970s seemed to be more segregated, the country as a whole was becoming more integrated.

At my age of seven years, however, the name or history of the street, Clow Avenue, onto which we made a left turn upon our arrival in Newcomerstown, had no more significance for me than any other street, apart from being the one that my family and I would live on. At about eight p.m. we arrived at the house, rented to us by a man by the name of Odis Dansby Jr.

The house seemed huge to me. Our house in West Virginia had been about seven hundred square feet, and this house was more than double that. The first thing I and the younger siblings wanted to do was to rush into the house and go on an expedition. We found two large bedrooms and two smaller bedrooms, a living room, a family room, and a small back room that could be another sleeping room. There was a basement, which I remember few people having in Vallscreek, and there were plenty of places for children to play hide-and-seek. The other great feature of the house was that it had an inside bathroom with a bathtub, commode, and sink supplied with hot and cold water. We had officially entered the modern age.

I did not know it at the time, but my mother and some of my older siblings were not happy about being resettled in Newcomerstown. The initial plan had been for us to move to Massillon, Ohio, but for some reason the prospective house there had not panned out, so we ended up in Newcomerstown, where we really did not know anybody. In effect, we were like refugees in our own country. This was the town where my oldest sister's in-laws lived, so the thinking had been that this was a better alternative than to continue living under the difficult conditions in West Virginia. My mother, with her strong faith, I'm sure prayed for days before making the decision to move, and prayed even more that God would give her guidance to successfully raise her children here.

The smell of the house is still etched in my mind. It had a strong smell of ammonia, Pine-Sol, and other cleansers I cannot identify. These odors did not bother me: they signified a house that was fresh and clean. Five of my older siblings, three of whom were no longer living at home, had arrived days earlier to help clean and prepare the house for our arrival.

The only downside of the house, as far as I could see, was the appearance of the ceiling in the kitchen. It was bulging from an old leak in the bathroom above and was riddled with unsightly, ragged scraps of wallpaper.

After the initial inspection of the house, most of us children went onto the porch to meet and talk to the many young strangers in the town who had congregated in our yard and on our porch to meet this large family of black "hillbillies" from West Virginia. The story of our impending arrival had preceded us. Who were we? What were we like?

We were the "newcomers" of Newcomerstown. We had no relatives or former acquaintances or friends from West Virginia who were now resident here to help ease our transition. In the eyes of the people who did live here, we were just this huge, ragtag family suddenly inserting itself into the fabric of their lives.

Unquestionably, we did stick out—not only for the size of our family but for the way we talked as well as the way we dressed, even though at the time we were not aware of being so different. But the differences that were so often to make us a target of derision did not deter us from striving toward an education, in hopes of enhancing our future quality of life. Our efforts would pay off in that we did relatively better than others in our community, but this was another factor that was to undoubtedly invite scorn upon us.

My family was to feel not too long after our move that it had been a mistake to come to Newcomerstown, due to issues of harassment. My brother Rahmaan, then James, has voiced this strongly, saying even many years later that he resented the decision that was made to move us there. Decisions were made, the die was cast, the milk was spilled, and cards had been dealt, so there was nothing we could do but try to make the best of it.

Without a doubt, many of the young teenage boys in the community had heard stories of the imminent arrival of a black family from West Virginia that included numerous females in or approaching their teens, and were eagerly awaiting us. There seemed to be a couple dozen young people milling around outside, talking, laughing, and generally shooting the breeze.

One of the youths in the crowd approached my younger brother, David, and me. He said his name was Victor. He must have been about twelve. I was knee high to a grasshopper, so he towered over me. Of a medium brown complexion, he was gregarious and animated, with an air of mischievousness. He wanted to know how old we were. I was older than David by a year and a half, but we were about the same size. Because of my heart condition, I had not grown as fast, so I appeared younger than I was. Victor was not aware of this, of course. He probably thought we were twins, as other people had thought when we were younger.

Victor thought our similar size would make for a good boxing match. He enticed us to box by offering the winner a nickel. Though my physical endurance was limited in prolonged, high-demand cardiovascular activities such as running, I had no problems with lower-demand activities of short duration. In the boxing match, I was able to connect with a quick right to my brother's nose, and the fight was over. I was ready to collect my five-cent prize, but Victor reneged on his agreement. That made me angry, and I also felt bad for hitting my brother in the nose for nothing.

As the night wore on, the crowd gradually dissipated, and the sound of the crickets chirping in the dark could now be heard. Our young visitors had to go home and prepare for school the next day. We had to retire as well, because all of us had to get registered in our new schools the next morning. It was good we'd moved when we did, because the school year had only been in session for a few days.

I was reminded again of my heart limitations when I had to climb the stairs to go to bed that night. After a few steps, I was exhausted. It seemed as though I was trying to climb Mount Everest. I practically had to crawl up the steps. This young boy with the imperfect heart would have bigger mountains to climb in life.

I went to sleep quickly that night, but I woke up around three o'clock in the morning to the humming and hissing of the plant bordering the alley on the other side of the street. One might think that the noise from a two-block-long plant might interfere with sleep, but on the contrary, I found the regular rhythmic sound strangely soothing at night, and it tended to help me to sleep.

The next morning after David and I got ready for school, we went out to the backyard expecting to see a swimming pool. We had heard talk about people having swimming pools in their backyards in Ohio. To our distinct disappointment, no swimming pool could be seen, no matter how hard we squinted to see it. I learned later that a "swimming pool in your backyard" was not meant literally. It probably just meant there was one not far away, in the park.

Shortly everyone was ready for school, and we started on our way. Though we were poor, my mother had managed somehow to get us all new outfits for our first day of school. I can still remember the pleasant smell of my new jeans and plaid shirt. We found ourselves walking in single file, nine of us, including my older sister Bobbie, who had already graduated. She was leading, with the rest of us following her like newborn chicks, on our way to the school to get registered. Three of us were in high school. The rest of us would be attending the West Elementary School. My youngest sister, Denise, stayed home; she was not old enough for school at this time. There were no hills to negotiate, so I was able to manage the walking pretty well.

We got registered, and I was assigned to my class. I was in the second grade. I don't remember too much about the first day of second grade or too much of the whole year. I remember being awakened, on at least half the days I attended school, when it was time to go home. Clearly, my heart condition was sapping my energy.

One thing I can vividly recall from the foggy experience of my first year of school in Newcomerstown was the profound conflict I had when I went to the restroom at school that first day. The teacher directed me to the restroom, but when I went in, I was faced with the dilemma of what fixture to use for a bowel movement. The choice was between the urinal, which I had never seen before, or the commode, which initially I did not see, as it was concealed by a partition. (A commode hidden from view behind a partition was new to me, too.)

After I discovered the commode, I said, with relief, "Okay, we do have one of those at home"—which of course I had used. So I ultimately made the right choice, but for a minute I literally sweated, in a state of panic, over what the consequences would have been of me selecting the wrong fixture.

During my first year of school at West Elementary, I remember taking tests and not having a clue as to what I was doing. My grades were evidence of how abysmally I was doing academically—many Us (unsatisfactory) and VSs (very slow) on my grade card. These were basically failing grades. Obviously, I did not pass that year. Due to my being sick with colds and the flu, my days of school attendance were shockingly few in number—surely contributing to my cluelessness in school.

Children with a congenital heart problem such as patent ductus arteriosus are probably more prone to respiratory infections. Another recurring problem was nosebleeds, probably due to higher pressure in the upper body, among children with this condition.

One late evening my nose started bleeding and would not stop. It bled continuously for what seemed like hours. Someone summoned a woman from down the street who was thought to have some kind of nursing or medical experience. Her name was Edith Newby. She was a light-skinned black woman who could have been mistaken for a tanned white woman. In her early fifties at the time, she had the appearance of a much younger woman.

She said, "Run a tub of cold water and put him in it."

My mom did as she instructed, and shortly my nose stopped bleeding. We were all pleased that my nose had finally stopped hemorrhaging, and I was put to bed. Everything was fine, but then suddenly my stomach started feeling like I had downed ten hot dogs in three minutes. I threw up huge amounts of the blood that I had swallowed while my nose was bleeding.

I know it was gross. My siblings, who minutes earlier had been happy to see that my nose had stopped bleeding, vanished immediately from the room in horror. My mother did not, remaining there and stoically helping me get cleaned up. I felt much better after getting rid of that blood in my stomach.

We had been in Newcomerstown about a year, and for the most part everyone was adjusting well. My siblings were doing well in school, completely destroying the expectation that we would be completely "backwards" West Virginians, although some disadvantages of coming from an underprivileged school system in West Virginia did shine through in certain situations.

Isalene recalls one incident in a typing class at school when she was experiencing difficulty operating the typewriter, and the teacher, watching her struggling, said, snootily, "Oh, you're from West Virginia, and you've never been to an integrated school, have you?" She turned around and walked away without offering any assistance or encouragement.

Social life outside of school for teenagers was another point of adjustment from the life my elder siblings knew in West Virginia. The teenagers here seemed to be a lot more streetwise. They would hang out at a place across the street called the Flats. In West Virginia after nightfall, everybody went in the house and things got quiet. We had no streetlights in West Virginia, so this may have been a factor in things shutting down much earlier there. Nightlife was different in Newcomerstown.

My sister Isalene says, "At nightfall, that's when everything got started. People started to get loud, and run up and down the street, whooping and hollering."

Living in Newcomerstown only about a year before graduation, and being kind of shy in addition, did not allow Isalene enough time to cultivate any deep relationships. She says that the best two associations she can recall while in Newcomerstown were with two white classmates. She recalls being invited to their homes and being "treated very well." Ironically, her relationships with blacks in her age group were not that positive.

My sister Mecca, then Effie, reminisces about her impressions when we arrived in town. "When we got to Newcomerstown, everybody made fun of us, about how we dressed and how we talked." Mecca remembers getting into a fight the first night we got there. She said, "This neighbor girl kept making fun of the way I talked and proceeded to push and hit me." When Mecca decided to start defending herself, the girl left her alone.

In the fifth grade, Mecca complained repeatedly to her teacher, Mrs. Smith, about a girl harassing and threatening her. Mecca said the teacher told her sternly, "You've just got to stand up for yourself, you've got to stand up for yourself." Feeling that she couldn't even get the teacher to help her, she had no other option but to do what she'd been told, stand up for herself against the school bully.

But after a really bad year of being harassed in the eighth grade, Mecca went to stay with our sister, Dee, in Washington, DC, for the summer, making her one of the family members for whom Dee has been an anchor in that town. For Mecca, this was a totally different world. She had never seen that large a concentration of black people in her life. She was not just a lone stranger, as she had been in the school at Newcomerstown. Tens of thousands of teenagers resided in the city, and many of them did not know each other, so being new was not such a big deal.

She was also amazed by the number of blacks who owned businesses and had relatively powerful positions, something she had never seen before, and, as she recalls, "I remember how thrilling it was to see nationally recognized entertainers such as James Brown, the Temptations, and the Supremes perform at the Howard Theatre."

Mecca got a job that summer and was able to buy herself more nice clothes than she had ever had in her life. Having all of these experiences, and with her natural beauty being accentuated by the stylish new clothes she wore, her self-confidence was boosted. When she returned to Newcomerstown that fall, she felt much better about herself.

Mecca's aspiration was to become a model when she graduated from high school. She did attend a modeling school in DC, and obtained a few modeling jobs when she was younger. Befitting her desire to establish a more chic image that modeling would entail, it was then that Mecca relinquished the old, unglamorous southern name of Effie for her current name. Before long, however, her interest turned toward law enforcement. She studied criminal justice at the University of District of Columbia and has worked in the criminal justice field for many years in Washington. She has a daughter, named Sherita, who is in her late thirties. Mecca is married to Douglas Roeser, and they have two children, Shawn and Honey, who are now in their twenties. Mecca and her husband spend much of their spare time involved with an organization they created to expose underprivileged youth to auto mechanics and auto racing.

My sister Doris reminisced about the apprehension she'd experienced in moving to a new town. "When moving to Ohio at thirteen years of age, all I could think about was how scared I was, and how was I going to make new friends and whether they were going to like me. I also wondered if color would be a factor, since I was moving from a segregated school to an integrated school." She indicated that in the end everything turned out okay, and when she graduated from high school in 1967, she was awarded a scholarship of six hundred dollars from the Citizens Scholarship Foundation to help with expenses in attending school at the American Institute of Business Secretarial and Stenotype in Washington, DC, to be a keypunch operator.

As had Mecca, Doris stayed with our sister Dee when she first got there. Dee had been living in the DC area since finishing high school in West Virginia in 1959. She was married to Sam Pannell, who was also from Vallscreek. Together they raised three children. Sam was a skilled brick mason, and did not have trouble finding good jobs in the building trades in Washington during that time or anywhere for that matter. In fact, Dee and Sam lived in Newcomerstown for a year during the midsixties. Sam had the reputation of being one of the best brick masons in Tuscarawas County.

Another sibling, living in nearby Alexander, Virginia, at this time, was Bobbie. She was married to David Plenty, and they eventually had five children. Later on, in the early 1970s, Bobbie started her own beauty salon business, and it has served her very well. Additionally, in the mid-2000s, she started an online business called "My Towels Talk," selling personalized towels and washcloths embroidered with her own creative slogans.

As my older siblings were making progress with their own challenges of adjusting to a new school environment, I continued to struggle in school due to my illness and the high absenteeism from school associated with it. Fortunately, things were soon put in place, enabling me to get the medical attention I needed.

Between our family doctor, the school system, and my mother being aware that I had a serious medical problem that needed to be addressed, the process was initiated to connect me with agencies and specialists that could assist me with getting treatment for my condition. Our family doctor, Dr. Agricola, even came to the house to help my mother complete papers to get the ball rolling. I remember him saying, "Something can be done."

Fortunately, the basic medical research and procedures to address these congenital heart problems had begun in a serious way just fifteen years before my birth. Techniques were being perfected at Johns Hopkins University Hospital based on research largely done by an African American, Vivian Thomas, behind the scenes.

Thomas was an unemployed carpenter who had aspirations of going to college to work toward his goal of becoming a doctor. The Depression came, and without a job and income, he had to spend all of the money he had saved for college to care for his family. Thomas was hired by the man who was to become the main cardiologist at Johns Hopkins, Dr. Fred Blalock, who was at Vanderbilt University in Tennessee at the time. Although his job was to take care of the animals in the lab, it was soon discovered that Thomas had a sharp mind and a great aptitude for physiology. He and Dr. Blaylock were able to develop techniques for correcting blood flow in limbs compromised by crushing injuries, as well as treatments for hemorrhagic and traumatic shock. They had done experiments on dogs where connections were made between the subclavian and pulmonary arteries. These were done to test theoretical treatments for other conditions. The unexpected effect was that blood flow to the lungs was increased.

Vivian Thomas also had a knack for creating different surgical gadgets and instruments, and Dr. Blalock, highly valuing Thomas's abilities, was successful in getting him to accompany him to Johns Hopkins Hospital in Baltimore, where Dr. Blalock had accepted a position as a lead cardiovascular researcher and surgeon. There he and Thomas continued the research that led to the first successful surgery to treat the congenital heart condition called "tetralogy of Fallot." This complex condition involved four different defects, the net effects of which were to decrease the oxygen level in the blood and to greatly increase stress on the heart. Though this was not my specific diagnosis, it would be noted later that I had features of it.

The procedure to address this problem brought Dr. Blalock and Dr. Helen Taussig worldwide acclaim in 1944. Vivian Thomas was virtually ignored, even though at the request of Dr. Blalock he had accompanied the surgeon to the operating room to help guide him through the surgery. A black person being present in operating rooms was prohibited at Johns Hopkins at the time.

Though Vivian Thomas is now credited with training a host of young surgeons and many laboratory technicians, he would not be given fair credit for his work until the 1970s. At that time he was given an honorary MD degree for his contribution to the advancement of the understanding and treatment of congenital heart disease. One of the more nationally renowned surgeons who trained under him was Dr. Denton Cooley, who remarked in the *Washington Magazine* in 1989, "There wasn't a false move, not a wasted motion when he operated." To be clear, Thomas did surgical procedures on animal models as a researcher and leading lab technician at Johns Hopkins, but he did not operate on humans. There was no way I or any of my family could have known that one day I might benefit from surgery and medical knowledge that an African American medical researcher had contributed so much to advance.

Doctors and researchers were making contributions to the understanding of the physiology and the development of cardiovascular surgical techniques at numerous other institutions around the country. There was Dr. John Gibbon at Pennsylvania Hospital in Philadelphia and Dr. John Kirklin at the Mayo Clinic. Both of these doctors were instrumental in perfecting the heart-lung machine. That technological development made it possible for the heart to be stopped so that more complicated intra-cardiac procedures could be performed—and thereby defining the term "open heart surgery." Other surgeries on structures associated with the heart prior to the advent of the heart-lung machine and after have been characterized as open heart surgery, but in fact they were not, hence the confusion surrounding the term.

Dedicated researchers at the University of Minnesota, University Centers in Texas, Harvard University, and other institutions contributed to the advancement of cardiovascular surgery. At Harvard University Medical School's Children's Hospital in 1938, when he was the chief resident in surgery, Dr. Robert Gross was planning his technique of correcting patent ductus arteriosus by practicing in the postmortem room and the animal laboratory at Children's. He normally worked under the surgeon in chief, Dr. William Ladd, but he conducted these practice sessions when Dr. Ladd was on summer vacation. Dr. Ladd never forgave him for doing this without his permission. Dr. Gross was certain that if he had informed him about his intentions, Dr. Ladd would not have allowed it. Not infrequently, some of the most revolutionary advances in science and medicine occur when one strikes out on a "lone wolf" mission, violating the usual protocols and guidelines.

After perfecting his technique with the cadaver and animal models, Dr. Gross was ready to try his procedures on a human patient. The patient was a seven-year-old girl. When he did his thoracotomy (an incision starting from under the left nipple and curving back and up toward the left scapula) to expose the patent's ductus arteriosus— a fetal connection between the aorta artery and the pulmonary artery and one that usually obliterates shortly after birth—her defect could clearly be seen. Before he proceeded to close this connection, he wanted to see what effect the ligation would have on the patient's symptoms and general condition, so he first just closed it with a clamp. When he put the stethoscope on the patient's pulmonary artery, the loud murmur had disappeared. He left the clamp there for three minutes, occluding or blocking the flow of blood, and noted that there was no bluish color of any degree, suggesting that the defect was not compensating for some other more complicated condition.

A series of blood pressure readings taken showed some rise in her pressure during the relaxation phase of her heart. The blood flowing out of the aorta into the lungs in the setting of patent ductus arteriosus does not allow the main pumping chamber to fill sufficiently while it is relaxing, resulting in lower pressure. Simultaneously, the amount of blood pumped out to the body is decreased. Dr. Gross also noted that the pulse rate decreased somewhat during the occlusion, suggesting that the heart did not have to work as hard.

In view of these positive findings, and satisfied that he could ligate the shunt permanently, he proceeded to close it with sutures. After the ligation, an amazing calm prevailed in the patient's chest: the constant buzz and thrill conducted through vibrations to his fingers were gone.

Dr. Gross's success with this patient ushered in the initial wave of modern surgical correction of congenital heart defects. The patient, Lorraine Sweeney, is still alive today, and in her eighties.

Several years later, Dr. Helen Taussig at Harvard Children's Hospital noticed children who were afflicted with heart conditions that caused the "blue baby syndrome" did better when there was an accompanying defect, patent ductus arteriosus. She approached Dr. Gross about the possibility of developing a surgery to relieve the symptoms until a more permanent treatment was available.

Dr. Gross refused to do it. Perhaps he was concerned about the ethical implications of creating a second heart defect to address another issue. This may have seemed to violate the Hippocratic Oath—including the directive "First do no harm"—that all doctors take.

Learning of the groundbreaking cardiovascular research that was being conducted at Johns Hopkins, she contacted Dr. Fred Blalock. She suggested the concept to him, and to her delight, he indicated that he had been working on a similar technique to address a different problem. That is when he and his very able lab technician, Vivian Thomas, went to work to develop that technique called the "Blalock-Taussig shunt" to treat that "blue baby" condition.

Four hundred miles away and a decade later in Columbus, Ohio, a protégé of Blalock and Taussig, a young cardiologist by the name of Dr. Donald Hosier, was busy in the early 1950s setting up a heart laboratory at Columbus Children's Hospital.

It is amazing, almost supernatural, how all of these seemingly disparate events—in civil rights, medical developments, and changes in a family's situation—would result in dramatic and positive shifts in the course of my life. When we moved to Ohio in 1961, my mother had high hopes that we would experience a better way of life and that—with God's grace—I would obtain the medical care I needed for my heart.

An appointment was made for me to see Dr. Hosier in Columbus, and several months later I had the surgery.

four

NEW LEASE ON LIFE

ARMED WITH CUTTING-EDGE MEDICAL KNOWLEDGE, particularly in the specialty of pediatric cardiology, gleaned from his fellowship at Johns Hopkins University Hospital, Dr. Hosier started building the first heart catheterization laboratory at Children's Hospital of Columbus, to be completed in the mid-1950s. When Dr. Hosier passed away, in 2003, Dr. Grant Morrow, a former medical director at Children's Hospital, said at his memorial service, "He was the engine for starting pediatric cardiology in central Ohio." Dr. Hosier's mission was to provide a regional center for children with heart disease in central and southeastern Ohio and West Virginia, so parents would not have to travel as far to seek help for their children. I was born around the time the center was completed. No one could have known that I would one day be a beneficiary of his efforts.

The cardiology department of Children's Hospital is now well known around the world. Dr. Hosier and his wife, Marcia, were successful in their great efforts to solicit donations from foundations all over the state to help fund his project. One foundation, the Kettering Foundation, pledged $5,000. Dr. Hosier returned the check. As Mrs. Hosier recalls, "Bud [his nickname] wrote back, 'Thank you, but we need $100,000.'" A month later, the foundation sent them $50,000.

Then the Kinder Key, a Christmas caroling group, learning of their efforts, decided to adopt the heart lab as its mission. It has since collected well over $1,000,000, as of 2003. The hospital now has at least thirty cardiologists, three surgeons, and state-of-the-art diagnostic equipment. Later on, Dr. Hosier also worked with the Crippled Children's Fund.

The first open heart surgery at Children's Hospital was done in 1957. Dr. Howard Sirak, trained at the prestigious Columbia Presbyterian Hospital, was the surgeon, and Dr. Hosier assisted. "The equipment used in the first surgery was developed here," said Dr. Sirak, recalling how a team in the cardiovascular laboratory that included George Funakoshi, the chief perfusionist at the time, assembled the device with its pump and a rotating disk and trained to operate it. That first patient, James Elliott, to Dr. Sirak's great satisfaction, was to help relay the Olympic Torch to the 1984 games in Los Angeles.

Under Dr. Hosier's leadership, Children's Hospital, which served central and southeastern Ohio, made great strides in the diagnosis and treatment of children with congenital heart disease. He was instrumental in the startling growth in numbers of various diagnostic procedures, electrocardiograms, phonocardiograms (graphical sound recordings), cineangiocardiograms (motion picture recordings of a portion of the cardiovascular system), increasing from 456 to 1,147, 0 to 38, 19 to 67, and 0 to 101 respectively, between 1952 and 1960 at Children's Hospital. Another measure of the hospital's progress in addressing the needs of children with congenital and acquired heart disease—that is, rheumatic fever–related conditions—is the drastic increase in the number of clinic visits to the hospital. There were 479 in 1957 and 731 in 1960, which is about a 53 percent increase in just three years.

By the time I became a patient at Children's Hospital, great leaps had been made in addressing a variety of congenital heart defects, and I was just in time to benefit from its services. About a month or so after my mom and I had the consultation with our family doctor, the Reverend George Gilmore from our church offered to take us to Columbus so I could see that cardiologist Dr. Agricola had recommended.

I remember when we got to the city, making our way through the maze of streets and traffic and finally finding our way to the area where the doctor's office was located. The city was amazing to me—it seemed huge. I had only seen a town with more than three or four thousand people when we'd passed through them quickly on our exodus from West Virginia. But it was nothing like this. This was a world that I had no reference to even imagine. I gazed in astonishment as I observed the mass of humanity—especially the throngs of black people—walking the streets, the many hundreds of cars, and the transit buses. Another thing I noticed were the many temporary makeshift sidewalks made from plywood. Roads and sidewalks looked like they were being rerouted. Buildings were being torn down. At the time I had no concept of what was going on. Looking back, I now understand that this undoubtedly represented the early phases of urban renewal in Columbus, and many of the people I saw walking the streets were probably displaced victims of this development. The whole scene is filed away in my mind as a neural snapshot on the frame of life moving through time and space.

We finally arrived at the doctor's office, a large, majestic-looking house, old but very well maintained. It appeared to be a late 1800s building, one that radiated historical charm and possessed strong "bones." I was called by the nurse to the examination room after only a brief wait. Following a short but thorough examination, Dr. Hosier said to my mother, "Your son definitely needs to have surgery to fix his problem, and if it is not done, he may not live to be twenty-five." He added that even if I did survive that long, I would probably be bedridden and suggested that the heart problem was interfering with my growth and development. I was really short for my age of eight years, and I weighed only about thirty-eight pounds. Dr. Hosier said, "He will start growing normally after the surgery, although he may not catch up with boys his age." The choice my mother had to make was a no-brainer, given the alternatives. Although the doctor had a good idea what the problem was, he said that I would need to go to the Children's Hospital in Columbus to have more definitive tests.

A couple of months later, my mother and I, with the assistance of another neighborhood friend, Raymond Dansby, made our way to Columbus again. Raymond said to my mother, "I have a good friend in Columbus that I talked to about you, and she said it would be okay for you to stay at their house while your son is in the hospital if necessary." The woman, who lived near the hospital, did allow my mother to stay with her while I was in the hospital for a couple of days. I am sure my mother appreciated this. She would not have been able to afford to stay in a hotel.

Besides x-rays and blood work, the main test I had done that really nailed down the diagnosis was a heart catheterization. This test involved threading a catheter into a vein or artery in the groin, or in my case, through vessels at the bend of my arm. The catheter was maneuvered up through the brachial vessels into the chambers of the heart, then dye was injected up through the catheter. Using an x-ray machine taking serial pictures, the doctors could track the flow of the dye and detect where the abnormal flows were. At the same time they could assess the pumping capacity of the heart and the structural integrity of the heart muscle and valves and even make some assessment of the electrical function of the heart. This was in 1962; now, of course, much improvement has been made in heart catheterization.

When a heart catheterization procedure is done, you are not completely knocked out but only heavily sedated. You may go to sleep, but much of the time you can be pretty conscious, and know what is going on. In my case I did fall asleep, but I woke up in the middle of the procedure. I remember my forehead really itching, and I tried to scratch it, but my arms were tied down. I remember asking an assistant in the room to scratch my forehead, and she did. That was such a relief.

I can still visualize the room. Painted in light colors, it had a sterile quality, and it was packed with complex-looking equipment and apparatus. There were doctors and assistants in white coats intensely focused on trying to analyze the problem with my heart. This must have been pretty exciting for Dr. Hosier and the others.

The heart studies did confirm what they had suspected. I had patent ductus arteriosus. It would take open heart surgery to correct it. I was released to recover from the studies as the next course of action was being contemplated.

The hospital notified my mother in a few weeks that I had been scheduled for the surgery in two months. They sent various books and pamphlets to prepare children for what to expect when going to the hospital for heart surgery. I don't think I was afraid. In fact, the prospect of getting my heart problem fixed made me feel kind of excited.

When the time came to go, and again with the help of Raymond Dansby, we traveled to Columbus. My heart beat harder than it usually did in anticipation of the nighttime ice cream and cookies that one of the books the hospital sent me had mentioned. The thought of being able to keep up in playing with the other boys my age after the surgery made my heart beat faster, too.

After I was checked into the hospital at the admittance desk, my mother and I were ushered to an area a short distance away, where I was given a bag of toiletries, coloring books, and crayons. I guess these were donated by some agency or other to make a child's stay in the hospital a more pleasant experience. Shortly after this, my vitals were taken, my finger was pricked to draw blood, and an identification tag with my name and my doctor's name was put around my wrist.

One of the nurses I saw down there was a brown-skinned, pleasant-looking woman who was slightly overweight. She seemed to be really nice. I would see this nurse, or one who looked exactly like her, later on during my stay at the hospital—when my opinion about her will have changed.

When I got to my room, I was changed into hospital clothes, and my street clothes were put in a bag and given to my mother. Soon a multitude of doctors and medical students started coming in to examine me and ask my mother all kinds of questions about my medical history and my family medical history. There were questions about whether or not I had had all of the common childhood diseases—mumps, chickenpox, measles, whooping cough. My mom was asked about any known history of rheumatic fever, strep throat, pneumonia, as well as questions about diseases she may have had before and while she was carrying me. They were concerned, too, with my developmental milestones—when I started walking and talking, and whether or not I was born on time. I remember my mother saying with emphasis that I had talked and walked rather early.

The leading physicians involved with my care at that time were, besides Dr. Hosier, Dr. Josepha Craenen, and the surgeon, Dr.

Howard Sirak. I would have a series of different x-rays taken, and the hated finger pricks for blood draws would be done repeatedly. One x-ray they did was not bad. They gave me a chocolate-flavored paste to swallow as a contrast material, and I actually thought it tasted pretty good.

The surgery was scheduled to be done two days from my date of admission. I remember that the night before the surgery I had a terrible nosebleed. Dr. Hosier came and helped get it stopped.

I went to sleep and was awakened early that next morning, hours before daybreak. I was bathed and prepared to be taken down for surgery. I remember feeling the pleasant wooziness from the sedative I was given before the surgery. The next thing I remember in that dazed state was my mother, my grandmother—wearing light-brown sheer stockings tied below the knees—and Reverend Gilmore from the church walking in what seemed like slow motion toward the bed transporting me to the presurgery area. I don't remember them saying anything. In the operating room, I remember seeing the big bright light above the operating table and being told to count to ten. I faded out before I got to three or four.

I remember vague flashes of semiconsciousness after the surgery, when I could see blurred images of people—probably medical personnel, my mom, and Reverend Gilmore again. I became fully aware after about two or three days, and about the third day after the surgery, they got me out of bed and tried to walk me around the intensive care room. My body seemed contracted; I was bent over like a little old man. The pain from the large incision was excruciating. As I walked, everybody seemed to want to reinforce me with positive statements like "You did good" and "Great job." I did not walk too long, but I was happy when they put me back in bed.

Every day things got better, and my appetite started to come back. About the fifth day after surgery, I was able to start eating solid food again. Many people complain about hospital food, but I personally had no complaints. I was glad to get that food. There was no problem with my appetite. And I looked forward to the ice cream and cookies at night.

After about a week, I was removed from intensive care to a regular room. I was happier than a kid riding his first bike about that. I was starting to feel stronger and stronger. It was nice to be in a regular room. Quieter than the intensive care unit, it had a television, and a lady came around every day with a cart with books on it that you could choose from. I was also able to color pictures in the coloring books I was given when I was first admitted.

One thing I didn't look forward to at night was the nurse I mentioned earlier, the one I was pretty sure I'd met during the admissions process. What she would do is go from room to room and stick a rubber tube down the noses or throats of young patients who were recovering from chest surgery and suction out their lungs to clear them of excess mucus and old blood. I now know it's important to do this to help prevent pneumonia and other problems, but to a child it just seems like torture.

I could hear children scream in agony as she made her way from room to room transporting her hellish apparatus, an aspirator mounted on a cart with wheels, with rubber tubing and a large collection bottle and its nasty-looking contents sitting on a shelf of the cart below the aspirator. I would hear her coming and wish I could somehow escape this angel of child torture, but unfortunately I could not. I resisted her with every fiber of my being, but with her being bigger and stronger, I would always lose the battle. I would have to endure the horrible gagging feeling and the nauseating smell of rubber as the tubing traveled down my nose or mouth.

On one of the nights she paid me a visit I guess I had been in a deep sleep, because I woke up to find she had tied my arms to the bed. She stuck the tube down my throat and suctioned away. After that experience, until I was old enough to realize the necessity of what she did, I was convinced that this woman was truly working for the devil.

After I was taken to a regular room, many doctors and medical students visited my room to check on how I had responded to the surgery. They all seemed pleased, my main doctors especially so. I felt like I was their badge of great surgical and medical success. And while I'm sure they were justifiably proud of what they'd accomplished, I believe they had a genuine sense of altruism. They would pick me up and carry me around, and let me sit at the nurses' station and color or write.

One day a doctor asked me to push another patient in a wheelchair around the floor of the wing. After I did this for a while, he listened to my heart, and I realized he just wanted to see how my heart responded to the stress of pushing the girl around in the chair.

Now that I was feeling better, I started to relax and enjoy myself. I certainly enjoyed the attention I got after my surgery. I received get-well cards from school and neighbors and a fruit basket and a few dollars from church. One thing I particularly liked doing was looking out the window and marveling at the sights of the city. I could see a multitude of cars and trucks traveling in all directions on the streets below, and people of various races and colors walking to and fro. The leaves on the trees were at their peak of transition to the colors of fall, and I could see in the distance the skyline of downtown Columbus, dominated by what I learned later was the LeVeque Tower.

After about two and a half weeks, the doctor said I was ready to go home. It was now just a matter of my mom coming to pick me up. She came to get me the next day. So excited about the prospect of going home, I no longer wanted the lunch I had been ready to chow down on before she got there—a hamburger, French fries, and some kind of vegetable. My oldest brother, Joe, had accompanied my mother. I asked him if he wanted my hamburger. His eyes widened with excitement as he asked me, "You sure you don't want it?" I said I didn't, and he downed it eagerly.

The doctor came in shortly with some last-minute instructions for my mom. I can't remember everything he said, but the one thing he said that stuck with me was "Don't hold him back—let him go." I guess he was saying that my mother should not be too protective, that she should let me enjoy running and playing like boys my age. Otherwise, and unnecessarily, I could end up being a cardiac cripple. My mother, Joe, Reverend Gilmore, and I headed to the car to make our way home to Newcomerstown.

I walked with much more energy now, and I felt more aware, as if I'd come out of the fog of my illness into a state of clarity. With great excitement I looked forward to getting home to see the rest of my family—and to being able to run and jump with my playmates like the doctor said I could.

When we got home, they were all glad to see me. One thing I remember being asked was "What happened to your voice?" This surprised me. Because you don't hear yourself talk the way others hear you, I had not even thought there was anything the matter with my voice. I did learn later that sometimes during this surgery the laryngeal nerve, coming off the spinal column going to the larynx, could be injured, or the respirator could directly traumatize the vocal cords. The problem with my voice, it turned out, was that the volume was low and people had trouble hearing me.

But this gradually got better. One day I was lying in bed, being pestered by flies. I guess I got frustrated and said, "You darn flies!" My mother and several of my siblings downstairs reacted in amazement, exclaiming, "Otis got his voice back!" From that day my voice went slowly back to normal.

The main signal to me that the surgery had been a success was when I was able to walk up the stairs without getting out of breath. Before this I had literally had to crawl up. This had to have been a miraculous thing for my mother to behold.

The doctor had instructed my mother to not be so protective of me, but instead of letting me go back to school when I felt I was ready, she kept me out for what seemed like three months. I didn't really complain about this at first because I enjoyed playing in the house and even outside.

Finally, however, I did return to school. I was treated like a celebrity. Open heart surgery is still a major operation, but back then it was a really "big freaking deal." One of the first things my classmates asked me was, of course, "What happened to your voice?" I would just say I didn't know. "They just put me to sleep for my operation, and when I woke up, I was talking like this."

My performance in school after I got back was better, and so was my alertness, but I had missed so much that it was difficult to catch up, and I was ultimately retained in the second grade. I did, however, derive greater joy from playing outside during recess, my energy level having increased so much. And by then I'd had a significant growth spurt.

The next year in the second grade, I did pretty well. I got many S+s (satisfactory plus) and a few Os (outstanding). Now my foundation for advancing to the next grades was solidified.

I can recall while I was home recovering spending some relatively rare moments with my grandmother. I'd always asked her questions about her past and the grandfather I had heard about but never met, but she seemed reluctant to talk about them. Her relationship with my grandfather seemed to be one of those mysterious pieces of family history that would always be hidden to me. I later learned about the physical and emotional abuse she'd suffered at my grandfather's hands—which is maybe why I can't recall many times when she laughed out loud or even smiled. Grandmother never seemed to be overly affectionate, either. I remember trying to hug and kiss her when I was little, but she always seemed to recoil, shyly.

Though Grandmother lived with us, she spent much of her time to herself. She cooked her own food, food she would occasionally share with me. This was a special treat for me. My mother's cooking rivaled the top chefs', at least in my estimation, but on rare occasions to indulge in my grandmother's was an experience that really perked up my taste buds and made them cry out for more.

There were two unpleasant things I associated with my grandmother. One was her habit of "dipping" snuff. This meant that there were cans strategically placed around the house into which she would spit the resultant revolting liquid.

My grandmother was also in cahoots with my mother in dosing us children with dreaded castor oil. There must be others out there today who remember vividly their traumatic encounters with that disgusting substance. Those were the days when the belief was firm that for a medicine to be good for you, it had to taste horrible. My mother and grandmother swore by this stuff, having almost as much faith in it as they did in prayer.

My first encounter with castor oil occurred back in West Virginia when I was four years old and had a cold. Believing that it was good for relieving congestion but knowing how it tasted, my mother decided to give it to me in my orange pop. After drinking about a quarter of the pop, I realized it didn't taste right. I can still remember my exact words. I just said, "This pop don't taste good." As I looked around at the rest of the family, they all seemed to look guilty, as though they were players in a grand conspiracy that had gone awry.

At times, I tried to enlist my grandmother as an ally in disputes with my mother. One time when I didn't get my way, I threatened to "go up the chain of command" and report my mother to my grandmother so she could straighten it all out. Of course my grandmother did not interfere. She told me, "You better do what your mother said."

My grandmother had her own part of the large bedroom, which she shared with three of my sisters. One of my sisters slept with her until the others graduated. Eventually this freed up enough space so that she could have a bed to herself.

Sometimes going to my bedroom, which I shared with my brothers, I would catch a glimpse of her sitting in a chair with her back to me as she looked in the mirror and combed her hair. I always thought she looked like an elderly Indian woman with that long, gray, wavy hair. Undoubtedly, as was evident in both her hair and her face, flowing through her veins was blood representing hundreds of years of genetic blending of African, European, and Indian ancestry.

One night while my mother, brother, and I were on our way back from a doctor's appointment in Columbus on a Greyhound bus, I kept thinking that things were not going well at home, an apprehension that would not go away. After we arrived in Newcomerstown, my mother called a cab to pick us up. When we turned onto the street and approached the house, we noticed that a light on the porch was on and that a couple of cars belonging to church people were parked outside, an ominous sign. Why would they be there at night when my mother was not home? It was clear from my mother's reaction that she knew something was wrong. She seemed reluctant to go into the house.

We learned that my grandmother had died, apparently from a massive stroke. She had been found collapsed in the closet. Nothing could have been done to save her; in those days, high-tech trauma centers were nonexistent.

Though the thought of my grandmother dying, due to advancing age and certain of her ailments, was always in the back of my mind, I was nevertheless not prepared for it. I was stunned and grief stricken. It was as if my whole world had changed in an instant. She had been a significant fixture in the household, one that helped define the rhythm of my own daily routine as well as that of the family. I would no longer be awakened by her frying bacon and baking biscuits in the predawn mornings or have brief chats with her before leaving for school or coming home. No longer would I see her working in her little vegetable garden in the back or observe her as she struggled home with a bag of her own personal groceries from the local IGA.

In my state of shock and sorrow, I cried at first, briefly, then stopped. In a desperate attempt for comfort, I asked the woman from the church who was at the house, Mrs. Belcher, "Will she go to heaven?" Mrs. Belcher said, "Sure she will." This gave me comfort, convincing me that she was in a better place, with all the troubles of this life behind her, and I felt it was at this point that my healing started.

Over time I gradually adjusted to a life that did not include my grandmother's physical presence, but my mother slipped into a deep depression after my grandmother's death. This was not the first time she had suffered severe clinical depression; she'd had bouts before I was born and when I was too young to remember. My father dying only seven years before, and now her mother and confidante, along with the perpetual stress of caring for numerous children, were all too much to bear.

As a child, I did not know what was wrong, but I sensed an overwhelming sadness enveloping her like a massive dark cloud. She would often just sit motionless, almost speechless, in total contrast to the way she usually behaved—talking animatedly, joking around, and enjoying the interaction with her children. My older sisters, realizing she needed help, arranged for her to be admitted to Massillon State Hospital. At that time the techniques and medications used to treat severe depression were not as effective as they are today. Patients such as my mother often got better independently over time, rather than as a result of the treatments. Sometimes the treatments made things worse.

I remember traveling with some of my siblings to Massillon to see her, an experience that in some respects was just as depressing as her illness. The visit was so impersonal and devoid of intimacy. We had to wave and yell to her as she stood at a window, with bars, on the third floor. There was no way we could reach out and embrace her. All of us were sad, but it was clear to me that our moroseness paled in comparison to the utter despondency we could see in her face, a sadness that even a bright sunny day did nothing to lessen. The realization that she was unable to physically reach out and touch her children pushed her spirits, I am sure, to greater depths.

Mental illness is something that has been traditionally taboo in society. While now there is more understanding for and acceptance of people suffering with mental illness, nevertheless it's still an issue that many people are uncomfortable with. Consequently, far too many people affected with the condition not only fail to get treatment but are at risk of social isolation. I found out many years later that in the early 1950s my mother was subjected to electroshock treatment for her depression. My lack of awareness of this, I think, reflected the veil of secrecy surrounding mental illness that permeated even my own family's attitude about it.

My mother took me back to see the doctor in Columbus periodically for a couple of years, but then she stopped. I don't know if the doctor said I did not have to come anymore or if it just became too much of a hardship for her to take me while dealing with her depression. Luckily I was doing well, and I continued to do well symptomatically for the next four or five years.

When our mother was hospitalized, my sister Dee came from Washington, DC, to stay with us at my mother's request. Dee was and is a very loving sister. Never once did I hear her complain about taking care of us, even though she already had two children of her own, five-year-old Geneva and two-year-old Thelma. At times we children—especially my brother David and I—were as rotten as Mister's kids, the kids Celie took care of in *The Color Purple*.

One day my brother David and I didn't want to go to school because of a little half-frozen ice and a smattering of snow. We were hoping school would be canceled, but it was not. We kept stalling around, hiding around the garage and the house instead of walking to school. Dee spied us from the kitchen window and yelled, "Go to school!"

We headed to school, intentionally slipping and falling, hoping someone would have mercy on us and chastise my sister for sending us to school in such terrible weather. That did not happen, however, even though we pulled our little stunt of slipping and falling all the way to school.

Later that evening after school, my brother James said, "I saw you fools keep falling on the ground, looking stupid." He would have had a clear view of us from his classroom window at the high school, which we had to pass on the way to West Elementary.

While Dee cared for us, her husband, Sam, remained in DC to work. Sam was only about 5 feet 6 and 145 pounds, but he had a big personality. He talked and laughed loudly, and he liked to brag. No, he was not a big man, but he was not a pushover. I can see him now with that wad of tobacco in his jaw, talking about what he'd do to someone if he caught them trying to cheat him in gambling, always ending with "B'lieve that!" When he eventually joined his family in Newcomerstown, he got a job with a construction company as a bricklayer, proving his proficiency in that trade. He was also taken seriously in the streets of Newcomerstown. With his reputation for carrying a pistol and knife, and with his street-hardened persona, he was nobody to play with.

Dee was pregnant at the time she was staying with us. I was not aware of it at the time. I thought she was just getting fat. One day, out of the blue, I looked at her and said, "Your belly look like a beach ball." That was probably not the most considerate thing to say to my sister, and it may have knocked her hormone-challenged emotions for a loop. I regretted what I said when I was older, but children tend to say whatever is on their minds and not be too concerned about people's feelings.

The baby was finally born, and it was unquestionably one of the most beautiful babies ever. It had the face of an angel. But when the child was about three months old, tragedy struck about eight o'clock one morning. Everyone was alerted by Dee's piercing screams. She ran down the stairs with the baby and paced the floor while desperately blowing in the baby's mouth, trying to get her to breathe, but she didn't. She just flopped limply in Dee's arms. Everyone was hysterical, but in the pandemonium someone managed to get a neighbor to take Dee and the baby to Coshocton Memorial Hospital, fourteen miles away. Needless to say, the situation seemed hopeless.

Nevertheless, I remember going behind a door in the back room, crying and praying to God for a miracle. Why I chose to retreat behind a door in that darkened back room was most likely my feeling that solitude and quiet allowed me to establish a personal and direct connection to the Almighty so he could hear my pleas.

It was devastating when my sister returned shortly from the hospital, dazed and consumed with grief. I instantly knew what the outcome was without her speaking a word. It had only been about three months, but we all had become strongly attached to the child, and we all suffered the loss. This was the first experience I had had with the death of a family member who was not an adult, and it gave me a sense that death may be a less distant threat than I had previously thought.

In these years I enjoyed all the normal activities that young boys love. Participating in physical education class in elementary school was a real treat. I was a fast runner, and everyone wanted me on their team. I was good in calisthenics and acrobatic-type activities, and I liked swimming. Though I was never a great swimmer, it was thrilling to just frolic in the water. I enjoyed tag, dodge ball, basketball, baseball, and football.

Although we enjoyed the usual boyhood fun, my brother David and I had certain chores to do, such as keeping our bedroom clean, taking out the trash, and helping my older brother James periodically clean up the basement. Back then, people who were low income qualified for food commodities from the government. We appreciated much of this food, especially the beef, cheese, and oatmeal. The problem was that we got far more powdered milk, cornmeal, and oatmeal than we could consume. Consequently, these commodities ended up being stockpiled in our basement, and they started to attract rats in droves. Our basement was like a land of milk and honey to these rodents, who feasted well on that food supply, grew fat, and multiplied prodigiously. Occasionally, those obese, waddling rats and their offspring would make their way to the upper levels, throwing the whole family into a panic. We had to do something about it.

So one day my brother James shot a couple of rats in the basement, scaring the crap out of everybody. My mother was not home at the time, and I don't think he would have done what he did if she had been. The family finally decided that the best thing to do was to get rid of the stockpiled commodities, and that is what we did. My brothers and I hauled dozens of bags of commodities out of the basement and burned them outside in the metal trash can. We also implemented the use of d-CON rat poison. Before long, the rodent population started to decline. We would collect the dead rat carcasses in the basement and those occasional ones upstairs, and dispose of them. Sometimes we would see one struggling in its last throes. That was a horrible sight. We would just put it out of its misery.

After that experience with the rats, we stopped storing so many commodities in bags. The food that we could not consume within a reasonable amount of time was just thrown away. By taking these measures, and maintaining our normal cleanliness, the problem with the rats was eliminated.

Even though we benefited from the commodities, my mother supplemented our diet by gardening during the spring and summer. As she had in Alabama and West Virginia, she grew various vegetables—tomatoes, cabbage, greens, potatoes, green beans. My brother Joe would help prepare the ground, forking it up and turning the soil, when we lived in Vallscreek as well as in Newcomerstown until he graduated. My mother would do the planting and cultivation of the garden along with Joe's help as well.

When my brother David and I were older, we would eagerly help out, too. After a couple of seasons, however, we grew tired of what we felt was tedious and grueling work. My mother, sensing our lack of attentiveness and accuracy, became weary of redirecting us and just decided to do the cultivation herself. We did, however, continue to do the initial preparation of the soil. After several years, my mother abandoned the larger garden and just put in three or four rows of her favorite plants.

Our family was large, which meant that on laundry day my mother had her work cut out for her. Even though we may each have had only three or four outfits, when this is multiplied by nine or ten, you are talking about a lot of clothes. We did have a washing machine, but it was one of those older models that did not automatically rinse and wring out the clothes. It had a wringer with two rollers on it that looked like rolling pins, with one situated horizontally on top of the other. When you want to wring out the clothing, you just pushed a lever, and the two rolling pins came together and rolled in the same direction. Clothes inserted between them were pulled through and wrung out. The lever on the washing machine could be activated to separate the rolling pins from each other. This was important because if anybody accidentally got a finger or a hand caught in there, a way was available to extract it. A parent's nightmare was children playing around with one of these machines and getting their hand caught.

Using this kind of machine, my mother would wash loads and loads of clothes on washday. And not having a dryer, she would go up and down the walkout basement steps, carrying baskets of wet clothes to put on the line with wooden clothespins to dry. It sounds archaic, but that was the way it used to be done.

Seeing our mother struggle with these clothes, my brother David and I, when we were a little older, were eager to flex our little muscles by pitching in to help carry those baskets of clothes up the steps so she could hang them on the line.

Around 1970, people who did not have the convenience of both a modern washer and dryer at home started going to the local Laundromat to do their washing. We started doing this as well. First David and I would accompany our mother there, helping her carry the clothes. Eventually, it became our responsibility to take the clothes to the Laundromat and do the laundry. We didn't mind doing it. It gave us a chance to just hang out. If we had enough change, we'd get a snack or soda from the machines. Sometimes you'd be able to rig the machines and get free stuff.

While going about her household tasks, whether it was washing clothes, cleaning up the house, cooking, ironing, or even gardening, my mother would sing Christian songs. Some of the songs she sang that still reverberate in the recesses of my mind are "There Will Be Peace in the Valley," "Precious Lord," "Swing Low Sweet Chariot," and "The Sweet By and By." I am sure the act of singing these songs lifted her spirits and sustained her against the stresses and strains of caring for a large family as a single mother.

My oldest brother, Joe, told me about something involving spiritual singing that he'd experienced when he was eleven years old. He had just joined the church, and he felt good thinking that Mom was so proud about his giving his life to the Lord. He said, "I kept singing that song 'Jesus, My Rock,' repeating that same refrain over and over." He got on our mother's nerves so badly that she had to ask him, gently, to stop singing that song. I guess too much of a "good" thing can sometimes be bad.

It is not an unusual attribute of traditional southern women, especially black women, to be good cooks. My mother was not an exception. I would say, and I don't think I am being biased, that my mother ranked high among those women in her cooking skills. She possessed the ability to make a scrumptious meal out of scratch. I can still savor her cornbread, black-eyed peas, pinto beans, greens, cabbage, and potato salad. For dessert I remember devouring her delicious rice pudding, sweet potato pie, bread pudding, and any number of cakes. I have not tasted bread pudding or rice pudding that comes close to equaling hers in my lifetime, although my sister Isalene does make a banana pudding that rivals my mother's.

Consuming my mother's good food provided me as a growing boy with an abundance of energy for play and exploration. I had much more energy than I used to have. A child with that amount of energy today might be diagnosed with hyperactivity disorder. I was literally bouncing off the walls. All I needed was some way to focus that drive into constructive or productive activity. This was achieved through playing baseball with friends, running and jumping, touch football, and yard work. My surgery was behind me, and I was ready to take on the world.

Sometimes when a child has an illness, parents have a tendency to acquiesce to the child's wishes. The unintended consequence of this is the child becoming spoiled, tending to want his or her way. When I was nine years old, I needed some twine for my kite. James was supposed to go to the IGA store, two blocks away, to get it for me, but he refused to get it as promised because he and his friends had other plans.

I asked my mother if I could go get it, and she said no. She wanted me to wait until my brother was able to get it for me. Well, I could not accept this. Against my mother's wishes, I snuck off to the IGA and bought the twine myself. I did not think it was such a big deal, given that the store was not far away.

I tried to slip stealthily back into the house with my new roll of twine, but David saw me with it and said, "Oooh . . . I am going to tell Mama!" He snitched on me, and my mother was livid. Expecting the wrath of Moses to be unleashed upon me, I ran to the back room and locked the door. She got her "loyal son," Joe, my oldest brother, to bust through the door. I really looked up to my brother, but I now felt betrayed.

After surviving that old-fashioned southern beatdown, my brother Joe took the opportunity to exploit my humble state by imparting his wisdom on the importance of obedience. He said that no matter how much you want to do something, you should never disobey your parents. After listening to my brother, I realized that I had been wrong.

A couple of days later, I was able to fly my kite. It was a warm and breezy early spring day, perfect weather for flying a kite. I was beaming with anticipation and excitement, nearly tripping over my feet as I rushed into the backyard to launch my hastily constructed kite into the clear sky. I had been looking forward to this moment all day at school, and now the time had arrived. I attached the twine to the kite, and the wind immediately and briskly lifted it into the sky. I could feel the tension exerted on the twine as the wind propelled the craft to greater heights. I decided to anchor the twine to the ground with a makeshift stake, but in the process, the pressure of the accelerating kite pulled the spool out of my hand, and the kite, with the spool of twine, went flying. I started chasing it like a dog chasing a rabbit.

The spool of twine unwound rapidly as it bounced wildly from side to side, with me in hot pursuit, across the alleyway at the back of our property line, through a field between the alley and College Street. Keeping within five to eight feet of the spool, I kept chasing it across College Street through people's yards. As I crossed the next street, Mulvane (fortunately not a major thoroughfare), barely looking out for cars, the momentum of the kite suddenly increased, resulting in a greater distance between me and the spool of twine. Continuing through residential properties on the other side of Mulvane and onto Chestnut Street, and brashly disregarding any trespassing laws, I was overcome by a sense of resignation to the awful reality that my beloved kite was being lost. Though it was fruitless, I pursued that kite as far I could—to the bank of the Tuscarawas River, about a block and a half beyond the backyards on the other side of Chestnut Street. There, breathing hard and recovering from my pursuit, I watched as my prized possession, its tail dancing in the sky, soared across the river with increasing velocity and greater height.

I wondered where it would end up. Would it finally come down in Uhrichsville or Dennison? Or would it turn north and travel to Dover or New Philadelphia or maybe even make it as far away as Canton or Massillon, forty-five miles away? Physically recovered from the chase, I headed home. I had given it a run for its money. Maybe if I had been a little bigger, with a greater stride, I might have been able to catch it.

My mother seemed concerned with David's and my growth. She would measure our heights periodically, making a mark on a doorframe to compare it to the next time she measured us, several months later. I suspect that she was more concerned about me, since one of the symptoms of the heart problem I had was slow growth. The doctors had assured her that I would grow after the surgery was done, but we knew I might not ever catch up with boys my age. I guess she felt compelled to check out my height herself.

She seemed to be happy when she could see that we were growing. Later on, she confessed that she was afraid that we were going to be midgets. I guess when we surpassed the magical height of 4 feet 10 or 11, she was relieved that we would escape the midget label.

I had the feeling growing up, and I'm sure my siblings would concur, that our mother loved all of her children. My assessment of her is that she viewed her children as beautiful flowers in a garden that she loved and nurtured. I may have had a special kind of relationship with her because of my medical situation. I do remember as a young boy recognizing how traumatic it would be for me if my mother were to pass away—my world would have ended. As a matter of fact, the death of any member of my family would have been horrific. Even though out of anger I might have momentarily had bad thoughts about a sibling, his or her death even then would have been heart wrenching.

One time, in an attempt to provide more for her family and herself, my mother tried her hand at selling Avon products. Though we did have the benefit of my dad's Social Security survivor's benefits, this was not enough for us to live on beyond a bare subsistence level. Mom's business venture was short lived, however. She frequently could not get enough orders, and often the people who did order stuff did not have the money when it was time to pay for the order, so she quit.

Eventually, though, as more and more of my older brothers and sisters finished school and obtained jobs, they tried to help out the family the best they could. They would send Mom money from time to time, and on a number of occasions they helped out greatly at Christmas time in making a better Christmas for the younger ones.

Often, the things that we wanted the most for Christmas we did not get. So we had to be more creative or turn to alternative activities to amuse ourselves. One of the things that David and I enjoyed was building tree houses. James, who had a knack for constructing things from wood, would help us. We would get up early on a Saturday morning if it was during the school year, and the weather was nice, to get started on our project. Scrap materials or whatever we could use would be scavenged from the dump, which was about a quarter of a mile away. It gave us a good feeling to construct what we considered to be a marvelous architectural feat out of discarded materials.

James's skills and creativity went beyond just building tree houses. Being a member of a family with minimal financial means forced him to tap into his creativity to create from scratch a toy or something else that appealed to him. For instance, he would make skateboards out of roller skate wheels and wooden boards. James recalls his friend Brad asking him, "What is that you made?" James said, "Well, it's a skateboard," giving it a name. This may well have been the original skateboard.

He could also make things that he saw someone playing with. I can't remember what one of these was called, but it looked like a judge's gavel, and it had a hole drilled in the top of the head.

Caps were inserted in the hole, and then a thing like a rocket was jammed down onto the caps. When you hit the thing on the sidewalk or curb or another hard surface, the vibration caused the caps to explode, and the pressure created from the exploding caps caused the rocket to fly into the sky. You get the picture? Anyway, he would make stuff like this all the time. I remember him saying once, "Shoot, I can make that."

He would also take the spokes from an old umbrella and use a slingshot to shoot the spokes at a target. Though this was potentially dangerous, it showed his ingenuity. He was such a tinkerer that our next-door neighbor, Terrell Russell, would at least on one occasion say, "What are you inventing today, Critter?"—Critter being James's nickname at one time.

With his creative ability, the excellent grades he got in mechanical drawing in school, and his basic facility with math, James probably had the potential to be an engineer of some sort. Given different family circumstances where this potential could have been nurtured and pushed, I am confident that he would have. He did attend school to study carpentry, and he's been working the last thirty years in construction. James, now Rahmaan Rasheed, having converted to Islam in 1974, currently lives in Washington, DC, with his wife, Winona. They have raised six children, five daughters and one son, all of them self-sufficient and contributing members of society.

Building little go-carts and vigorously competing against each other in go-cart races was another activity that we enjoyed. My brother David and a friend of ours, Tyrone Simpson, and I were one team. We were considered the underdogs. We competed against the more elite team of Mike Dansby, Brent Dansby, Vincent Belcher, and Kevin Brown, boys who belonged to what we thought were more affluent families.

We would spend one day in our garage building a go-cart from the most decent wooden boards, wheels, and axles that we could find around the house or the dump. After we and our competitors had completed the vehicles, we met at the area where we would race. About three-quarters of the time we, the underdogs, would win. The winners would receive a trophy, which was usually an old football or basketball trophy we had come across somewhere.

One incident that gave me pause during this period of my life occurred at the swimming pool. We were done swimming and were putting our clothes back on, preparing to go home, when my heart suddenly started beating really fast and hard. I said to my friend Mike, "My heart is beating real fast," and asked him whether his ever did that, and I think he said, "Yeah." Maybe he didn't really understand that this came on more suddenly and much faster than normal. It stopped as suddenly as it began. I did not feel dizzy, as if I was going to pass out, or short of breath. It was just weird. I would not have another experience like that again for several years.

Though apparently not life threatening, the episode made me fearful, made me feel that death was constantly lurking around the corner. I thought about my heart daily, wondering whether this would be the day that my number was up. During this time, I often wondered whether I'd live to be thirty, and if I did what kind of life I would have. In spite of my fear, I did not let it paralyze my desire to lead a normal life as a young boy—a normalcy that included getting involved in the occasional act of boyish misbehavior.

One of these acts, which I committed with David and our friend David Belcher, was a conspiracy to soap the school windows when we were in the fifth grade. This was around Halloween, and we planned it the night before. Our friend Tyrone was supposed to participate, but for whatever reason, he didn't. We went to the school after dark and soaped the windows good, the first grade through the sixth on one side of the one-story school building.

I don't know if Tyrone ratted on us or not. All I know is that the principal came up to me the next day and asked me if I'd soaped the windows. I thought, How could he possibly know to suspect me? Then, not wanting to get into more trouble being caught in a lie, I confessed.

Mr. Smith, the principal, rounded all of us up who were responsible for soaping the school windows—Vincent Belcher, my brother David, and I. There was another student, a white boy by the name of Richard Tiddrick, who was also being punished, but he was not with us. Apparently, he had acted independently. The principal supplied us with buckets of water, and we had to go the whole length of the one-story school building, washing the soap from the windows. As we washed the windows, starting with the windows of the classes for the sixth grade, the students inside the classrooms were laughing at us. I can imagine how thrilling it was for all of those white students looking at these black boys, except for the one white boy, being forced to wash all of those windows in payment for our transgressions. By the time we got to the first- and second-grade classrooms, the children looking out at us, being younger, were not as aware of what was going on, and tended to react as though we were big fifth- or sixth-graders doing something exciting.

We did get to eat lunch after we were done, although it was later than our usual time. I thought our punishment was over, but after we finished our lunch, Mr. Smith calmly told us to go with him to his office. I thought, This does not sound good. He informed us that he had contacted our parents and got permission to give us a paddling.

He had obviously devised a system. He had all four of us take a seat in one of the four chairs he had lined up. He allowed us the freedom of choosing what order we were going to go, so I decided to go first, wanting to get it over with. He reached way back and gave me three searing swats. At first my rear end was numb, and then what seemed like a wave of scorching fire spread out from my buttocks to my lower back and to my thighs. It felt like somebody had turned my butt toward the fire on a rotisserie and left it there. I felt as though if I sat in a bucket of water, I'd give off steam. After the paddling, I was directed into a little adjacent room—the recovery room, I supposed.

The next person in line was the white student, Richard Tiddrick. He got his swats and galloped into the recovery room like a wild horse. Even in the midst of my post-paddling agony, I could not help snickering. My brother David was next. After getting his licks, he ran in, stuttering—David was a stutterer—in excruciating pain.

Vincent Belcher was the last one to experience the principal's wrath. He ran into the recovery room squealing like a pig at slaughtering time, sliding on the floor on his knees while holding his posterior. By this time my pain was easing up, and I nearly cracked up at the sight.

Another mischievous but really dangerous thing we did around this time was drain some gas from an old car in our garage. The car belonged to our friend Vincent's uncle Frankie, who was in Vietnam at the time. My mom was allowing him to store the car in our garage until his return.

After we drained the gas, I decided, in a flash of vanity, that it would be a good idea to make a big flaming O for Otis on the floor of the garage with the gas. After I poured the gasoline for the O, I moved the pail with the rest of the gasoline to what I thought was a safe distance away. I lit the gas, and it went *whoosh*—and spread to the pail I had placed over to the side. The tires of the car caught on fire, too, and before we knew it, the flames were licking at the rafters. In a panic, I ran to get the garden hose to try to put out the fire, which seemed to make it worse—so much for my firefighting skills.

By this time, my mother and my sisters were on the back porch, yelling and screaming for me to get away from the garage. It was one of those carefree Saturday afternoons, and it looked like they had all been in the middle of doing their hair. With their hair sticking up all over their heads, and in their state of panic, they looked like trolls jumping around.

By this time, I could hear the fire trucks coming down the street. Before they could get to the garage to put out the fire, I ran into the house and hid in the closet in a desperate attempt to escape what I was sure was going to be my mother's wrath. I thought about trying to get up into the attic, but then I remembered that there were no stairs.

My mother found me pretty quickly, but, surprisingly, she did not give me a whipping. If the trembling in her voice and her shortness of breath meant anything, I think she had been too terrified. She was just thankful that I was not hurt. She already had to be concerned about a child with a congenital heart problem. To have to care for a "crispy critter" child would, I think, have been too much. She did not have to tell me to not do it again. It took only one time for me to learn that gasoline is nothing to play with. Fortunately, only minimal damage was done to the garage, but as for Vincent's uncle Frankie's car, it was ruined.

Sometimes my brother David and I and a few of our friends would buy boxes of the caps that are used for cowboy guns. Then, under cover of darkness, we would go down to the bar, Lenzo's, at the end of the street. When the coast was clear, we'd go to the back door, which would usually be open. We'd wait until the lady work-ing behind the bar got ready to put something on the grill or pour a drink, then we'd bust a couple of rolls of caps on the concrete steps with a brick, nearly giving her a heart attack. Then we'd take off running. She'd be really pissed, yelling, "You damn kids!"

That bar, Lenzo's, had an interesting history. Up until about the mid-1960s, though blacks could go to the bar, it was segre-gated inside. There was a black side of the bar and a white side, and blacks and whites stayed on their respective sides. Eventually whites stopped going to the bar, and it was sold to a black man by the name of Booker Russell around 1969. The bar ended up clos-ing, however, by 1970.

Booker Russell was our next-door neighbor, and he was defi-nitely one of Newcomerstown's interesting characters. Originally from Alabama, he was part of that migratory wave of African Amer-icans who relocated to Newcomerstown between the 1920s and the 1940s. Booker was an eccentric man who had an affinity for the processed hair style, and he sported his 1950s-style sharkskin pants and loud shirts into the late 1960s and early 1970s. We'd see him walk briskly by the house with the confidence of a male model on the runways of Paris, all decked out, gripping his cane in his right hand and barely acknowledging us as he passed by. His slight limp did not seem to slow his stride.

Other times he would stop and chat, usually to brag about how he was the "mayor of this town" and how he ran it. Throughout this monologue, he would jab the air with his cane for emphasis. Although it was obvious that he had no real social or economic power in the town, he was, surprisingly, somehow able on occasion to get people out of jail without them having to post bail. I could only guess that he had a certain gift of diplomacy to go along with his eccentricity.

I was in the fifth grade when I could sense the buzz of excite-ment in the air about an upcoming local talent show to be held at the high school. Two members of the black community were going to participate—my sister Jessie Trotter and Victoria Harris—so of course we were excited, too. I remember my family and me en-tering the old three-story building, constructed at the turn of the century, through large heavy doors held open to allow the hordes of people to make their way in. After walking up to the second floor and making a left turn, we found ourselves directly facing the doors to the top of the auditorium.

We entered the auditorium and quickly found seats. The place was starting to fill up fast. I noticed several of my classmates from West Elementary School sitting in the auditorium with their parents. Various people from the neighborhood—the Dansbys, Russells, Harrises, and Collinses—were sprinkled throughout the audience as well.

Soon the program began. To be honest, I only remember a few performances, especially the one by Ron Hooker, who, with his round face and rotund physique, did a very funny impersonation of King Louis of France in an act entitled, "Dear Ol' King Louie." He danced energetically and confidently during his routine, and his antics set off a chorus of laughter in the audience and loud applause at its conclusion. (Ron did become a ruler of sorts in real life. He made history in 1970, becoming the youngest mayor in the country when he was elected mayor of Newcomerstown. This became a national story on the *ABC Evening News*.)

The other contestants I recall are Vicky Harris and, naturally, my sister Jessie. I thought Vicky sang very well, but of course I wanted my sister to win. Finally it was her turn, and her performance of the two songs she sang—"The Soul of a Man" and "A Juvenile Delinquent"—was staggering. The crowd's response was thunderous.

It was clear to the masses of people there that Jessie's performance had been the best by far, and when it came time for the judges to make their decision, the vote went overwhelmingly her way. The whole family and many in the neighborhood were so proud of her. The local newspaper described her performance as "similar in style to that of Aretha Franklin, who is one of the foremost vocalists in the country."

Jessie also demonstrated considerable talent in acting. She played numerous prominent roles in high school productions, and later on, after high school, she got acting parts in the Little Theatre, an outdoor theater in New Philadelphia.

In 1971 Jessie sang with a group in Washington, DC, called the Soul Review. The group disbanded after about a year, but some members joined another DC group called the Black Heat, which in 1973 produced a successful album that had a hit song, "Your Fool Still Loves You."

Though my sister Jessie did not realize her dreams of becoming a professional singer, she did have a successful business career, having been employed by the Warner and Swasey Company for many years, until she resigned for health reasons. She was also able to raise her son, Carson Trotter, who has been a shining witness to the excellent nurturing and socialization provided by his mother as well as his grandmother.

Christmas time in the Trotter household was as bright and cheerful as Booker Russell's personality and attire was colorful, even though, materially, we did not have much. Even giving the living room or the kitchen a fresh coat of paint in anticipation of family members coming home for the holidays was exciting. It was such a joy to have the older siblings home from college or just visiting from the faraway cities and towns they lived in now. It was always interesting to listen to my brother Joe talk about his experiences in Chicago and Evanston, Illinois, and Kenosha, Wisconsin. I can still hear Lou Rawls singing "Tobacco Road," playing in the background on our little record player. That was one of Joe's favorite songs back then in the midsixties.

My sister Isalene would tell interesting stories of her life in Norwalk and Hartford, Connecticut, as a college student, and about her employment at a bank in Hartford. Her husband, Isaiah Jackson, whom she met while working at the bank, years later related to me a funny story about how he ended up dating her. Isaiah at the time was a young college student from Nigeria. Isaiah recalls, "I would come to the bank often, and would just always get in her line." Before he could summon up the nerve to introduce himself, someone at the bank, realizing that he was trying to meet her, suggested that he accompany Isalene and some of the other employees to lunch. Their relationship progressed from there.

Tragically, after nearly forty years of a marriage that produced two sons, Isaiah Jr. and Usen, my brother-in-law Isaiah passed away in May 2010.

My sisters Josie and Eva would come down from Massillon. They had moved to Massillon from West Virginia in the mid-1950s in search of better job possibilities, but as Josie put it, "For black women in Ohio, things were not much better." In company with many other women at the time, her main objective, she said, was to find a husband and have children. Josie and Eva did eventually find employment, with the Perry Rubber Company and the Central States Canning Company in Massillon, and both did get married, having five and three children respectively.

Their children are doing well, some earning advanced degrees and running their own businesses. Some of Josie's children moved to Atlanta in the early 1980s to try their luck in the entertainment business. All three of her sons, Donnie, Bruce, and Greg, as well as three of their friends, performed in a group called the Z-Band. After little success in such a competitive field, and finding themselves resorting to living in their van, they had to figure out other alternatives for survival.

One night they stumbled upon a storefront church engaged in loud worship. This church ended up being their savior spiritually as well as materially. They all joined the church, and before long their musical skills were discovered, and exploited to enhance the church's music ministry. Through this mutually supportive relationship with the church, they all eventually found work.

These young men were part of that new wave of reverse migration to the South in the mid-1970s and 1980s. The sharp edge of overt racism had dulled somewhat in the South, especially in Atlanta, allowing blacks greater access to economic opportunities. But for those couples who were involved in interracial dating or marriage, as were my nephew Greg Harris and his wife, Missy, strong taboos still persisted. This, Greg said, was the main reason they'd moved back to Massillon, where there was greater tolerance for such relationships.

A big topic of conversation among my family during their visits in Newcomerstown was always the well-known football rivalry between the Massillon Tigers and the Canton McKinley Bulldogs. Our cousin Will Foster, an outstanding football player for Massillon in the late 1960s, ended up playing for the New England Patriots for a while in the early 1970s. He was a source of great pride to his father, Thamon Foster, my uncle. I can still hear my uncle bragging in his deep baritone voice about his son during these holiday visits, and his laughing along with the rest of the family at his own jokes.

One big event in getting ready for Christmas was going to get a tree and decorating it, and another was putting up a few strings of lights on the porch. Though the lights were paltry in number, the colorful, blinking bulbs did ignite a mood of excitement and festivity. They also signaled to us younger ones that Santa Claus would be coming in a few days, and that made our hearts beat with anticipation.

In our house, Christmas Eve marked the season's greatest point of excitement. Everybody was home, gifts were piling up under the tree, and Santa Claus was on his way. We always said we would wait and open the gifts Christmas Day morning, but we always broke down and opened them Christmas Eve. Opening gifts on Christmas day somehow did not seem to be the way we wanted to spend the day.

The best Christmas I remember was in 1966. David and I got a Johnny Seven, a big toy army gun with a grenade launcher and machine-gun sound effects. It also had the capability of shooting out little round, soft projectiles. We played for hours with our new toy, killing each other hundreds of times but immediately coming back to life to fight an imaginary enemy in some faraway foreign land. Soon our grumbling bellies would reel us back to reality, and we'd suspend our war games temporarily, to eat, and then, after filling our guts, we continued to play until we succumbed to exhaustion and our emotional crash from the pre-Christmas high and fell asleep.

That Christmas, we had one of those artificial trees that changed colors as it revolved. I knew that a lot of people hated these, but I came to love it. I liked the way the colors were reflected on the exciting toys under the tree on that early Christmas morning. We all liked the fact that the tree did not leave a mess with pine needles. The firebug in me saw the tree's downside: I would not be able to enjoy the flames that exploded when we took a real tree out after New Years to burn.

I can recall the Christmas in 1969 when we put up a big Santa and sleigh display outside. In this period of rising black consciousness, my brother and I decided to make the Santa African American by painting his face brown. After we finished, I looked at the wooden snowman we had in the yard, and had a fleeting thought of making him African American as well, but then I said, "Nah, that won't work." Snowmen by nature are white, and that would be taking Afrocentrism to ridiculous extremes!

A power failure affected much of the town one Christmas, and we literally did have a black Christmas. We sang "I'm Dreaming of a Black Christmas" and the other traditional Christmas songs. This is was one of the sweet memories of life on the Avenue.

From left: My sister Eva, Ralph Harris, my sister Josie Harris, and a friend of theirs, 1956.

Josie's and Eva's children with my sister Sakina (in swing) and me (standing next to her) at Cy Young Park in Newcomerstown.

My sister Bobbie and my brother Rahmaan, dancing in the road on the opposite side of Vallscreek from where we once lived, when they were in town to attend the 1991 Excelsior High School Reunion in War, West Virginia.

My sister Jessie and her son Carson around 1974

TALENT SHOW IS

Jessie sings, "I'm No Juvenile Delinquent."

The Annual Talent Show sponsored by the Senior Class, scored a remarkable success in February. Bill Snader and Robin Rice acted as the Masters of Ceremonies for this event.

Jessie Trotter was presented with an award for first place with her songs, "Juvenile Delinquent" and "The Soul of a Man."

Second place was won by "The Unestablished," composed of a group of Juniors. They sang "Love Is Blue," "If I Had a Hammer," "The Rev. Mr. Black," Steve Guy was narrator.

Ron Hooker won an honorable mention with a pantomime. His impersonation of King Louis of France was well received.

Students from the seventh through twelfth grades presented the eleven acts which made up the 1968 Annual Talent Show.

Dear Ol' King Louie

"The Unestablished"

Jessie and other students in yearbook pictures of the talent show.

My sisters Jessie and Mecca (*top row, second and third from left*) in yearbook pictures as high school juniors in 1968.

My sisters Sakina (*left*) and Mecca in Washington, DC, around 1976.

five

LIFE ON THE AVENUE /
BITTER AND SWEET

LIKE MOST BOYS, upon entering junior high school, I had high hopes of participating in sports. Even though I felt good and was energetic, I knew I probably wouldn't pass the physical, due to my history of heart surgery. But many of my classmates, recognizing my speed and agility, were encouraging me to sign up.

My brother David, a couple of friends, and I went to sign up. We were issued our football uniforms. We took them home with us, walking proudly and carrying the jerseys, pants, shoulder pads, kneepads, and helmets on hangers. After getting home, we put on our uniforms. While posing in front of the mirror with the equipment on, I felt strong and powerful, like Superman. I had visions of running on the field, catching a pass, and dashing toward the goalpost, while hearing the thunderous cheering of the crowd.

I soon found that this was not to be. My short-lived fantasies were dashed when we went to take the physicals required before we could start practicing. We went to Dr. McCauley, who examined us one by one. First John Little came out smiling; it was obvious that he had passed. He was followed by Mike Dansby and Michael Belt. They all passed. I went in next. He checked my eyes, arms, legs, and body, saying, "Un huh," in approval as he went along. But then he checked my heart, and his facial expression changed as he moved the stethoscope methodically over my chest. Then he said those words I did not want to hear, but was expecting: "I'm afraid to let you play." The words stung for just a minute—I guess I had already prepared myself for them. I went back out to the waiting room. The other boys were waiting to see if I'd passed.

My brother David went in next. He passed with no problem.

Though disappointed, I had to accept it. Sports were not going to be the foundation upon which my adolescent self-image was going to be constructed. It was clear to me that I had to find another way to enhance my sense of self-worth during those insecure teen years.

Besides, I told myself, sports are not the most important thing in life. What if the doctor had allowed me to play and I had gone into some kind of lethal arrhythmia during the physical stress of a game? This would have been devastating. John Little, the first boy to pass the physical that day, was to be killed in a tragic motorcycle accident the summer after graduating from high school. He was a good athlete, smart and popular. This goes to show that there are no guarantees in life.

I swallowed my disappointment and went on with my life.

When my friends and I were around eleven and twelve, we liked to go to the movies and roller skating, activities that ranked near the top with kids in the 1960s and early 1970s. Because our parents often did not have the money, we would hustle pop bottles, rejecting none, not even the filthy ones. We just washed them out and added them to our cart. We were real troopers. We also shoveled snow or did whatever we could to get the money to go.

I also used to sell the newspaper *Grit*, and later on I sold all-occasion cards. One time I had gotten about twenty-five orders and was just about to mail them in along with the money, minus my profits. I had already made plans for going skating, saving some of the money to buy a BB gun and go to the dairy store on State Street and enjoy a delicious hamburger, fries, and strawberry milkshake. But then something happened. My mother, who was facing an especially difficult time financially, needed to borrow the money. I was reluctant, but I gave it to her.

I was horribly disappointed, but the thing that bothered me the most was the thought of missing that juicy hamburger and the strawberry milkshake. I actually dreamed about them one night, and I woke up slobbering on my pillow. I wanted to go back to sleep to finish my meal, but no matter how hard I tried, I could not. This was more frustrating than an interrupted sneeze or a good yawn cut off in the middle, or some other good thing interrupted while approaching its zenith. Use your imagination.

My mother fully intended to get the money back to me before too long, but it was several months before she did. At this point it was too late to order the cards, so I returned everyone's money. By that time, of course, I had misplaced the list, but I had in my head the customers who'd ordered and the amount I owed them. They all seemed to understand my situation, and were grateful that I'd given them back their money.

A few years later, between the ages of fourteen and fifteen, I would get a job through a government agency designed to employ disadvantaged teenagers. I worked in the schools doing janitorial work. I did this work during the summer, and during the school year I worked evenings a couple of times a week. The janitor was my boss. I liked the job—it gave me good spending money and it enabled me to buy school clothes.

One thing I did not like about the job was cleaning chewing gum from underneath the chairs and desks. I'd haul a bucket of water and cleanser into each classroom, and then, supplied with a scraper, I'd go from one desk and chair to the next, cleaning the gum from underneath them with the scraper. I would also clean the tops of the desks and chairs, and the blackboards. I didn't mind that.

When I wasn't trying to make money, I spent most of my free time engaging in socially acceptable activities and avoiding drama, but there were times that I did get into fights. I was not hesitant about standing up for myself. I didn't like starting fights, but I would finish them. Timidity was not part of my character, and I would fight if I found it necessary. An individual's size did not concern me. I did not care.

When I was in the fifth grade, a new boy came into my class. One would think that a new person would try to get along with others, but this dude seemed to be one of those tough farm boys who thought he could kick everybody's butt. He was like a preadolescent version of a villain in Western movies on television. I can't remember how we got into the fight—it just seemed like he wanted to fight me. Maybe, being white, he just did not like black people.

Anyway, we started fighting in the classroom during recess time. I think the weather was bad, or some of us did not want to go outside and play. During the tussle, I flipped him on the floor—a beautiful move, by the way. That startled him, and abruptly ended the fight.

One of the girls in the class commented in amazement about how I had flipped him.

He didn't like that at all, and he said, in a cocky cowboy manner, "Wait until we go outside. I need more space."

I said we could go outside and continue the fight another day, all the while thinking, This fellow is bigger and actually stronger than me, and I really don't want to fight him again.

A couple of days later during recess, though, he approached me and wanted to continue the fight. I didn't want to be a "punk," so I said okay. A big crowd gathered and we started trading punches. I would throw a couple of body blows—he was a bit taller than me—and he would go for my head, but I'd block the shot. Then he'd grab me and throw me to the ground. I would wiggle away, then get up and hit him a couple of times. I was fast and wiry. To paraphrase Muhammad Ali, I was so fast I could turn off the light in the bedroom and be in bed asleep before the room was dark. He would throw me down and try to grab me again, but I wouldn't let him hold me down. I'd get to my feet fast, because I knew he was bigger and stronger. I didn't want him to get me in a situation where he could pin me and then pummel the heck out of me.

We were both still on our feet, and I could feel myself getting fatigued. I was punching, but I was running out of steam and losing my effectiveness. My arms started feeling like lead weights, and I was huffing and puffing like a man who had smoked three packs of cigarettes for a hundred years. He was able to catch me with a couple of good ones to the head, my right eye in particular. When my eye was hit, it began to sting and water like I was in the shower, and I couldn't see out of it. I was happy that a teacher intervened at this point to stop the fight.

The guy won that round, and was soundly congratulated by his friends. But though I'd lost, he never disrespected me again.

This was just one of numerous fights I had in elementary school, most of which I won. The ones that I lost I still won because I defended myself and maintained my dignity.

It was a warm spring day in 1966, and Muhammad Ali had just soundly defeated Henry Cooper in a boxing match the night before. My brother James had been taunting classmates who were supporters of Henry Cooper all morning at school, imitating Ali's famous boxing moves. One of his classmates, Ernie Tripplet, said, "Oh, you think you can box like Cassius Clay?" My brother said, "Yeah." Ernie challenged him to a fight after school behind the Shell gas station on State Street, three blocks from the school. My brother agreed, thinking that by the end of the day Ernie would have forgotten about it. James was really not too eager to fight him because Ernie had a reputation for being really tough.

The back of the Shell station was notorious for being the place where high school boys settled the score. It was the Madison Square Garden of Newcomerstown, where I recall a small scrapper known as Beatle Bailey beating up a guy twice his size. James remembers preparing to go home after school that day and feeling thirsty. As he told it, "My mouth was really dry, and I needed to get a drink of water. I decided that I would just stop at the Shell station and get a drink"—meaning, of course, that he wanted to see if the fight was on. Upon arriving, he noticed that many spectators were already there, eagerly anticipating the big fight.

James said, "As I was about to take a sip of water, Ernie suddenly came up on me, pulled my blue Ban-Lon shirt up over my head, and hit me about three times in the head." My brother said that he just slipped the shirt off and started defending himself.

The fight, a combination of boxing and wrestling, went on for fifteen or twenty minutes. James said, "The fight seemed to last forever, until we were both exhausted."

Eventually Ernie said, "You ready to give it up?"

Then James, "You ready to give it up?"

This went back and forth until one of them finally said yeah, and the fight ended.

James said he thought the fight was about even. This fight went down in the annals of Newcomerstown as one of the most memorable high school fights in history. These were the days when young people could settle a score with a physical fight and it would be over. The next day, they could continue to be friends or at least get along. Rarely did things escalate to the level of violence that is prominent today.

Though her children would fight on occasion when provoked, my mother, consistent with her Christian values, was spiritual and peaceful. She often referred to "turning the other cheek," when it came to the possibility of physical confrontation, and she taught us to try to avoid fighting with others. My mother was human, however, and she had her breaking points, one of which occurred when I was eleven.

About seven of us children were in the kitchen playing Monopoly and cards. We kept arguing over the games, and she repeatedly warned us to stop. We would stop for a while, then start up again. She finally had had enough, rushed in, and started whipping butts with a belt. In the commotion, chairs, tables, cards, and game boards and all their little parts were knocked to the floor. Pop bottles that had been accumulating in the corner were rolling about. Screams of pain filled the air as we tried, futilely, to escape my mother's vengeance. When her reign of terror was over, a still, pervasive calm enveloped the room. Everyone seemed stunned, like, "What just happened?"

Needless to say, that was the end of games for the day. I guess my mother was simply channeling Jesus's righteous indignation when those people turned the Temple into a den of iniquity.

When my mother was not visiting the wrath of God upon us, which was a less frequent occurrence than we probably deserved, she was affectionate, which led to a problem for me, and I think for David as well. It strikes me now that as boys approach the dawn of puberty, they start rejecting their mothers' attempts at affection. In my own case, I may also have been growing tired of feeling like the overly protected one. I even said to my mother, "I'm getting too old for that."

At this my mother replied, with a sad little chuckle, "Well, I guess you boys are growing up."

I was relieved by her reaction at the time. I had been afraid that I may have hurt her feelings—which I now realize I probably did.

Often children are not mature enough to realize that what they say or how they act may have an effect on someone else or come back to haunt them later in life. Sometimes you are forced to reflect back on how else you could have handled a situation. Many years later, I have often thought about how I resisted Mom's attempts at affection, how I'd I failed to realize that I could have helped fill that void she felt because my father had died. I did get to the point when I was an adult of being able to show her affection, but of course it was impossible to reverse past actions. I was finally able to give her a spontaneous hug, tell her I loved her and how grateful I was for the care and guidance she'd given me while I was growing up.

My mother did all she could to protect me and keep me from thinking about my heart, but my anxiety about it giving out and causing me to suddenly drop dead was always in the back of my mind, intensifying when I was twelve or thirteen years of age. Premature heartbeats had become more frequent, and this was terrifying to me. Despite the assurances from doctors that these occurrences were benign, I was still fearful.

One day David and I were playing catch with a baseball, firing it back and forth to each other. I missed once, and the ball hit me in the chest. Terrified by the thought of the horrible damage that had been done to my heart, I ran into the house. My heart seemed to be jumping out of my mouth.

I told my sister Dee, "I got hit in the chest with the ball!"

She noticed the pulse beating in my neck and became petrified with fear, a reaction that made my own fear even worse.

When my mom found out, she was so alarmed that she called someone to take us to the doctor. When the man arrived in his car, I ran to it and jumped in the backseat, motioning to my mother to hurry up—I thought I was surely dying. Halfway to the doctor's office, though, it felt as though my heart rate had eased up, and when Dr. Agricola checked me out, he said, "It's nothing to be too concerned about, just a little cardiovascular."

On the way home, I remember my mother saying something to the effect of "*He* ain't never concerned about nothing!"

When I was not worrying about my heart, I managed to act like a normal adolescent and get into scrapes. One day, several of us boys were swimming in the pool at the park, and a cop came and kicked us out because we were harassing girls in the water. We were around twelve and thirteen at the time. We left the pool and walked up this big hill behind the park. When we got to the top, we walked about another hundred feet or so and came to the edge of a cliff. When you looked over the edge, you could see the new section of highway that had recently been completed. Little traffic was on the road at this time. I don't know what inspired us to do it, but we started chucking rocks over the cliff. I guess we were bored.

All of a sudden, we saw a police car down there. A policeman got out of it and blew his whistle at us, and we ran, confident that he would not be able to get up there before we got away.

I don't understand how, but shortly he appeared upon the hill, like Jesus, telling us to come out. I tried to hide behind a small bush, but when he came into view, I could see him clearly, so evidently he could see me. Besides, I was breathing so hard with fear I could be heard a mile away. I decided it was no use, so I came out, and the others followed suit.

I realized that this was the same cop that the people at the pool had called on us earlier. He didn't try to make a big deal of the pool situation. In fact, he said that our parents paid taxes and that we had a right to use the pool as much as anyone else. Since it was the pool employees who'd complained, he'd been compelled to ask us to leave.

I was sure he was going to arrest us when he said we had hit the windshield of a truck and the driver was livid, but he didn't. He advised us to leave the area by walking north about three-quarters of a mile, then turning left and keeping on walking until we got to Route 21. At this point, we could go south heading back to town. This way, he said, we could avoid the irate truck driver. I used to wonder if he was telling the truth or if this was his way of punishing us, by making us go on that long walk. I can't remember one of us connecting with a vehicle in our rock throwing, although it is possible.

Finally the four of us—William Mallone, Vincent Belcher, my brother David, and I—made it to Route 21. We had been walking south for a few minutes when suddenly William started going "Ah, ah, ah," and bending over in pain. He acted like he was going to die.

Something intuitively told me that he was going to be okay. I was thinking that if anybody was not going to survive this ordeal, it would be me, for I was the one with the cardiac history, and I was feeling okay. I was a little thirsty, though, so I suggested that we get some water as soon as we could. When we did this, ole William snapped back to life like a desiccated plant after a good rain.

When I was in the seventh grade, an event occurred that rocked the nation and marked the historical timeline of this country and even that of the world. It was April 4, 1968, the day that Martin Luther King was assassinated. I remember watching the news with my mother when the bulletin came on, and Walter Cronkite announced that King had been shot in Memphis, Tennessee. I remember saying to my mother, "Riots are going to break out all over the country." This turned out to be the case. Some degree of violence took place in virtually every major American city, as well as in many smaller cities and towns.

Even tiny Newcomerstown, Ohio, with approximately 4,000 people and about 150 or so blacks at the time, had its share of racial tension. There were a few isolated racial fights. Local African Americans formed little organizations in the town, and started advocating for more equal rights and better living conditions. In late 1968, after King's death, the Black Citizens Council, under the leadership of Rudy Russell, successfully petitioned to change the name of the main black street in town from Clow Avenue to Martin Luther King Drive. My boss on a job I had while in school, a white man, said to me at the time, "I don't blame the blacks for changing the name of that street to Martin Luther King Drive, because that Clow man suddenly shut down the company and went to Chicago, leaving those people without jobs."

On the first anniversary of King's death, a few of us blacks in school commemorated the event by walking out of class at a predetermined time. The principal of our junior high school seemed to understand why we were doing this and allowed us to go. He just had us sign out.

In the late 1990s, years after we had moved, history was made in Newcomerstown, when Shirley Coker-Kerr became the first African American council member. Ironically, the racism she was not as cognizant of in her youth revealed itself when a white man who wanted her position was caught on tape referring to her as a nigger. She said that this caused a "near riot." Shirley Coker-Kerr became a trailblazer again when she was selected to be president of the New-comerstown Chamber of Commerce. She also ran for mayor, but while she conducted a respectable campaign, she was not elected.

One of the issues she brought to the fore during her tenure as a council member was concern about the possibility of carcinogens from industrial wastes dumped at the landfill in proximity to the black community. A park at the south end of Martin Luther King Drive, which blacks in the town had campaigned for in 1969 so their children could have a safe place to play in the neighborhood, became a focus of concern about possible contamination. Coker-Kerr felt the park/playground should be closed because of the probability of contamination posing a health hazard. Blacks resisted because they felt a sense of pride about the park. This was something that they had worked to get, and they were not willing to let it go. As far as I have been able to determine, no official scientific connection has been made between ground contamination in that area and increased cancer rates, but many in that area seem to agree that cancer appears to be much more prevalent there than in other communities.

ADOLESCENCE comes with embarrassing moments, and mine was no exception. One experience I had causes twinges of embarrassment to this day when I think about it.

I was in the ninth grade. I had to do a mock campaign speech for a government class. I composed a nice speech and practiced reciting it at home until I got it down pat. The time came for us chosen ones to give our campaign speeches in the school auditorium. When I was called up to do my speech, I approached the stage confidently, but when I got to the lectern and faced the sea of faces in the audience, my throat and jaw tightened up and I felt as though all of the saliva in my mouth had suddenly dried up. I started to read the speech, but almost nothing came out. My lips were quivering, and my voice wouldn't project even with the assistance of the microphone.

Gripped with fear, my body became totally rigid, and my head and neck were frozen in place. All I could do was stare in horror at the audience. I had become a victim of a bad case of stage fright, and I must have been a spectacle to behold. In retrospect, my extreme stage fright may have been the result of a cardiovascular system already revved up from underlying cardiac problems.

The empathetic teacher, in an attempt to get me out of the humiliating situation, called upon another student to read the speech. The one she chose, Jeff Shivers, walked right up there with the confidence of a future president and read the speech flawlessly. Everyone clapped, including me. I was very grateful for the grade of C I got for the assignment. I guess my teacher gave me credit for writing a good speech and making the effort to deliver it.

A humiliating experience, but what could I do about it besides taking speech classes in school, which I did, and getting more experience speaking in front of people? I look back at it now and laugh at it as an embarrassing, but funny, paragraph in a chapter of my life.

The experience also made me more sensitive to, and able to identify with, people who have real difficulties in communicating with others. Imagine having a thought that you want to express and not being able to do it with ease. It is frustrating.

Take my brother David, for instance. He has struggled with stuttering all of his life, and as he could tell you, stuttering can have effects beyond just the ability to express thoughts. It can affect the stutterer's social and economic life. And while insensitive or uninformed people often seized upon my brother's stuttering as a vehicle for belittling him, he long ago learned to accept his problem, and in doing so, lessened much of the tension surrounding it. The result has been that he stutters significantly less now than he used to. David currently lives in Cleveland, where he works with elderly male patients at the VA hospital in the city. David enjoys drawing and painting, at which he displays considerable artistic ability, and he is proud that his seventeen-year-old daughter, Katie, shares his aptitudes.

One teacher who stands out during my junior high school years was Mr. Linwood Loomis. I did well in his class. I remember him because, besides being a good teacher, he exhibited plenty of enthusiasm in his lectures. Because his legs were slightly uneven in length, he would teeter from one foot to the other, at the same time gesturing with his arms, moving them in circles to emphasize the points he wanted to make. With his dynamic body language, Mr.

Loomis had the ability to make even the history of ants an exciting topic to the most uninterested student.

I didn't realize it then, but many years later I found out that Mr. Loomis and I shared parallel experiences in our lives. When my brother Joe attended his high school reunion in Newcomerstown in 2008, I accompanied him as a guest. Mr. Loomis was there with his wife, who was a member of my brother's class. I would have recognized him anywhere—he looked much the same as he had when I was in his class.

Mr. Loomis mentioned a book he was writing and promised to send Joe a copy when it was completed. Joe received the book, *One Man's Journey*, in 2011. After he was done reading it, he let me read it. It was then that I learned that Mr. Loomis, too, had experienced some significant medical issues at birth, and had not been expected to live. Due to his frailty, he was often bullied in school, as I had been as well, for a period of time in college. I had no idea that forty-three years later I would be making comparisons between my life and that of my former junior high school teacher.

While the official objective of school was to prepare you to take care of your material existence when your parents kicked you out of the house, church was to show you how to avoid the pits of Hell on Judgment Day.

My family belonged to the Trinity Baptist Church in New-comerstown. My mother insisted that her children attend Sunday school every Sunday morning. In my early teens, I participated in plays put on by the youth of the church on Christmas Eve. These Christmas Eve programs were well attended, as former residents often came back to town for the Christmas holiday. I remember being in *A Christmas Carol,* directed by my sister Jessie. I played Bob Cratchit, the terrified employee of Ebenezer Scrooge. I learned my lines quickly for this, and felt I did well—no stage fright for me here! In fact, many people—including my relatives, home for Christmas—complimented me on my performance.

Though I was effectively a member of the church and had been since childhood, I was not baptized until late 1969. My brother David and I were baptized on December 9 of that year at the church. I remember the day we committed ourselves to Christ. The preacher, Reverend Sherrell, had just reached the peak of his spiritual fervor and was now in the decrescendo phase. He said, "This might be your last chance. Tomorrow is not promised to you. I can feel the Lord tugging at your heart. Come, come, come to Jesus, right now!"

As the music played softly, he kept repeating this refrain, and I felt as though some inexplicable force was lifting me up out of my seat. Under the influence of that power, I walked toward the altar, followed shortly by my brother. Strong applause and repeated praises to God rang throughout the sanctuary as we made our way up.

I felt pure that day. My sins and guilt over my transgressions had been swept away. I pledged not to cuss, which I didn't do too much of anyway. Fornication was not a problem, because at the time I had not been sexually intimate with anyone, not that I didn't think about it. I guess I lusted in my heart. Attending park dances and the local hangout for teenagers was off limits too, as was R&B and rock 'n' roll music.

It took less than a week after our baptism for my brother and me to backslide to the depths of sin. We could not give up the fun of dancing with girls at the Chatterbox and at the dances in the park, and at least making an attempt to "cop a feel." We still went to church, but I knew now that I was not going to live like a Puritan.

I found out later that neither my mother nor the church people had ever expected us to live like Puritans, but that it was we who had been subjecting ourselves to that unrealistic standard. We failed to understand that Jesus took on the sins of the world and died on the cross for our sins, and by accepting him as our savior we are saved. No one is perfect but the Father. We are mere mortal creatures, and the flesh is weak. We can never be pure.

We lived on Clow Avenue, known simply to us as the Avenue and years later as the Drive, after the name was changed to Martin Luther King Drive. This was the main street, practically the only street in town dominated by blacks. This was the street where much of the character and identity of the youth who resided on it was formed. Our experiences of growing up in Trinity Baptist Church, partying at the Chatterbox Club, playing street football, or congregating and interacting at a one-story building that use to be a rooming house for single men years before. The walls separating the rooms were eliminated, creating one long open room. It was across the street from where we lived, and was called the Flats. This all contributed to fostering that unique Newcomerstown flavor in our character that remained with us like a brand, that makes us stand out no matter where we go, causing people to say, "You are not from here, are you?"

The Chatterbox was founded by a man by the name of Odis Dansby Sr. around 1964. The Chatterbox was a bar when he bought it, but he fixed it up and made it a place for teens. People of all ages socialized there, however. Older people would gather around the bar and drink pop, have snacks, and talk while watching all the young people dancing. Though the place did not sell alcohol, I would not now be surprised if some of those older folks hadn't been secretly spiking the pop in their innocuous-looking drinking cups with a little bit of alcohol. Undoubtedly, they had fun "tripping out" on some of the young people overconfidently "breaking a move" on the dance floor.

During the earlier parts of the day, preteens dominated the club. We loved dancing to the songs of James Brown, trying to imitate him. My friends and I frequently tried some of the really physical dance moves, like splits and flips. (If I were to do them today, not only would I be breaking a move, I would literally be breaking bones.) Some of the other performers we liked were the Temptations, Wilson Pickett, the Supremes, the Four Tops, Martha and the Vandellas, Smokey Robinson and the Miracles, Otis Redding, Chubby Checker, and Aretha Franklin.

It cost a nickel to play a record on the jukebox back then, a paltry sum in terms of today's economy, but to play four or five songs and buy a bag of potato chips and a soda pop was not an insignificant amount of money for a boy from a poor family. It took a day of hustling for pop bottles to cash in or hunting for scrap metal to take to Mr. White, the scrap man on the Avenue, to redeem for a little cash. My optimistic hopes of realizing a nice return on my efforts would always be dashed by Mr. White's minimizing the value of my supply of scrap.

Sometimes I would hit it big when I dug down under the couch and chair cushions at home, in hopes of retrieving coins that had fallen out of people's pockets. My heart would leap with excitement whenever I was able to pull out a shiny nickel, dime, or quarter. Visions of potato chips, popcorn, Chick-O–Sticks, and pretzels, chased by a delicious Coca-Cola or followed by a tasty Moon Pie, danced in my head. My conscience told me that the right thing to do was to turn this money over to my mother, but these ethical considerations were far outweighed by my desire for fun time at the Chatterbox.

At night the club was primarily frequented by teenagers. The club was popular, attracting teens from nearby towns such as New Philadelphia, Dover, Coshocton, Cambridge, Uhrichsville, and Dennison and as far away as Zanesville, Massillon, and even Canton. I am sure Odis Dansby made quite a bit of money running the place. He pretty much had a monopoly on providing entertainment for blacks at that time, facing no competition from any other establishment catering to young blacks in town. Incidentally, he had another monopoly of sorts—he owned a sanitation business in a town that did not, as far as I know, provide a sanitation service at the time.

From the perspective of our economically challenged family, Odis made plenty of loot, but he worked hard, and he deserved every penny. The Chatterbox was a nice place for teenagers to have fun, though by the time I became a teenager the place no longer existed. In Vallscreek, where we lived before, local black youth did have Mack's Place, which was white owned, and the Do Drop In, a black primarily bootleg joint for adults, but not a decent place of their own. On the contrary, the Chatterbox was black owned and geared toward teenagers. Older and younger African American adults in Tuscarawas County frequented Chicken's, the nickname of the black owner of the club in nearby Midvale.

It was in 1966 that a tragedy struck the Chatterbox. It was burned down by an arsonist, who I don't think was ever identified. In 1970 or so, a group of people got together to try to rebuild the club, and a structure had been built about three-quarters of the way to completion, when the funding ran out. Although it was never completed, the place did have walls, a roof, a cement floor, an unfinished door, and, of all things, a jukebox. Some young people did hang out there to listen to music and dance, but obviously it was sorely lacking the ambiance and management a real establishment would have provided.

After the demise of the Chatterbox, we had to come up with other things to do to compensate for the loss of the place. The older teens and young adults, however, still had Chicken's as an alternative. One thing we did in the mid- through the late sixties was to organize an informal gang. We adopted nicknames for ourselves. David was called Tough Cat because he was the strongest and more athletic one. Vincent Belcher was Sharp Cat, owing to his charming way with the ladies. Though he was short, girls thought he was kind of cute, proving that he had the luck of a leprechaun. I was Cool Cat because I had a cool and smooth aura, and because in the late sixties I sprouted an envy-inspiring Afro. That was my crowning glory, and I thought I defined cool. Our friend, Tyrone Simpson, was late joining the posse. He was called T-Bone because it rhymed with Tyrone, and he was lean and mean. Last, but not least, Mike was Top Cat because he was a natural organizer. He seemed to know how things were supposed to be, and was able to convince others that he knew the ins and outs of things, and the protocols of life in general.

We all even had our own cool pimp walk, which we really flaunted while showing off our Christmas, Easter, or back-to-school clothes. The girls' giggling, as we strutted down the street, was interpreted by us as admiration because we just knew we were five sharp cats.

The Avenue was the center of our community, the black area of Newcomerstown. Even within the confines of that small area, we always seemed to find something to do, from playing baseball or softball, dodge ball or touch football or tag, to go-cart racing or tree-house building. At the risk of getting into trouble with the law, we even occasionally broke into abandoned houses, just out of curiosity to see what was in there.

One time we broke into one of Booker Russell's old places. He had all kinds of stuff in there. There was a menacing, foreign-looking pistol, but we barely touched that. I still had an aversion to any kind of weapon, I suppose because of what happened to my father. The only things we took among the many enchanting things we found there were a couple of girlie magazines that looked to be from the 1940s—which, as one would expect, sparked the most interest in us budding adolescent boys—and a bunch of turn-of-the-century postcards. (My brother took those to school to show his teacher, apparently to get some idea of their potential value. Well, he never saw them again after she got hold of them. I think she took them.)

The next time we ventured into the house, Booker Russell's son, Terrell, caught us going in there and chased us away, saying, "I'm going to tell my daddy y'all breaking into his old house!"

I don't think he ever told, he just wanted to scare us. If he had, my excuse was going to be that I was just going along with Booker's grandson, Vincent, who conceived the idea of breaking into the place. But now, not wanting to run into the feared Mr. Book, which is what we called him for short, we scurried down the back alley behind the building, making a right turn toward State Street, which ran perpendicular to the north side of Clow Avenue. In this tiny community, it was not easy to hide, and consumed by fear, we lingered in the alley for a while, because you did not mess with Mr. Book!

This was an alley we played in a lot. Here we use to pitch pennies, nickels, and dimes toward a line drawn in the dirt. Whoever would get the closest without going over would win. Often my brother David and I would play against Paul Simpson Jr., who was known as Fuzzy, and William Mallone or Paul and Vincent or, alternatively, William and Vincent.

Had we known then what we know now, we would have limited our time playing in that alley. That alley was found to be saturated with years of finely granulated plastic fibers, belched out by a venting system all along the alley side of the plant, possibly exposing us to carcinogens.

In the summertime, when not engaged in our other activities, our inflated perceptions of our abilities led us to dare entertain the idea that we could be musicians and singers. We formed a little band. Mike was on guitar, a simple nonamplified, nonelectric guitar. Vincent played garbage can tops as cymbals, and my brother David played drums, which were the actual garbage cans. Finally, I of all people was on vocals. I had a tune in my head, but I couldn't carry it for anything. We all know now that our sound was so horrible that it could have awakened the dead and killed them all over again. But for that moment, we thought we were ready for *American Bandstand*.

Back then, *American Bandstand* was the dance show that all the young people watched, whether you were black or white. It featured music and acts that appealed to a wide variety of American youth. Until *Soul Train* came about, *American Bandstand* was the dance show that the kids from my community watched.

Local black radio was nonexistent in Newcomerstown in the 1960s, but starting in the early 1970s, a radio station from Canton, WHBC, had a block of time during which black music was played, from eleven p.m. to two a.m. Monday through Friday and about three or four hours in the afternoon on the weekends. It featured a deejay known as Butter Ball. Before that time, the black community had to rely on a distant AM station from Nashville with the call letters WLAC. The reception usually was only fair, but at times it came in booming. That is how we kept up with the latest black music.

Two of the deejays I can recall at WLAC were Gene Nobles and one called Hossman. Many people assumed that these deejays were black, an idea reinforced by their use of slang or colloquialisms, but they were white. Their use of slang may have been intentional because they were targeting a black market throughout the South and the southern Midwest, areas that often did not have local black radio stations. On the other hand, the speech patterns may have been absorbed through osmosis in their business relationships with nationally recognized R&B entertainers.

Many young white youths secretly listened to this forbidden "jungle music" in the privacy of their bedrooms, with earphones, late at night. I recall talking to some white schoolmates who were very familiar with the station and were "hip" to the latest black music.

The station always advertised records from different artists that you could order and have sent to you. Some of the deejays owned the record shops. I even ordered records a couple of times from record shops that were sponsors of the radio station.

Those were the days when it was common for blacks in small towns to order all kinds of things through the mail because local stores often did not carry merchandise, such as music or clothes, that we liked. One mail-order clothing company that catered to blacks, especially black males, was called Eleganza. I once ordered a silk shirt patterned in gray and red and a large "apple cap." I had seen that cap and shirt combination in the Eleganza magazine, and I thought it was sharp.

After a few weeks, my order arrived. The cap, which came in a box the size of a large pizza, was flat and elliptical in shape, and had a large prominent brim. I tried on my shirt and cap while looking in the mirror, picking out my 'fro as it sprang from the edges of the cap. I was pleased with the way the cap framed my face and matched perfectly with my shirt. I thought I was the shit, and couldn't wait for the dance coming up on the weekend.

On the weekend, I got all decked out in my dress pants and new shirt, with my apple cap to top it all off. It was nearly dark when I went outside, and Shorty Scott, our neighbor across the street, looked at me and did a double take.

He motioned me over and asked, "Where did you get that hat?"

He called his wife, Rose, to the door to take a look. She smiled, shook her head, and went back in the house.

Shorty was a connoisseur of style and fashion, known for dressing sharply. Any positive endorsement from him would have been impressive. The problem was that I couldn't tell whether or not I had passed his fashion inspection. His facial expression, reflecting a conscious effort to stifle laughter, and his statement, "It's cool, though," sent me into a state of cognitive dissonance. I chose to take what he'd said as a vote of confidence, however, and continued on my way.

Half the people I encountered said they liked my hat. Half the people laughed or didn't know what to think. My sister Jessie's boyfriend, Lloyd Dansby, said, "When I saw Otis coming up the street, I thought it was a flying saucer!"

It was not long before I retired that hat and deposited the whole experience in my memory bank of life's embarrassing moments.

I recall another memory, a painful one this time, of something that happened at one of the park dances when I was fourteen years old. The dances were held on the tennis court at the park. About thirty feet up the side of a small hill on one side of the tennis court was the restroom. A group of us had gone to the restroom, and we were on our way back down the hill toward the tennis court when the song "I Can't Get No Satisfaction" began to play. The song got me so pumped up I ran down the hill, and like a real genius, tried to jump the last five or six feet onto the flat ground at the bottom. I did not make it but tumbled down the hill.

When I got up I felt dazed and shaken, and I could not flex my wrist. To me, my lower left arm was obviously broken. I wobbled over to the tennis court where the dance was being held to show my arm to my sister. She freaked out when she saw it, but her boy-friend, Lloyd, kind of brushed it off, saying, "That arm ain't broke."

I knew it was broken because it was just hanging there, use-lessly. In retrospect, I think Lloyd did not want to have his date with my sister interrupted. Too bad for Lloyd—my arm injury meant that any member of my family at the dance had to skedaddle, too, so it could get taken care of.

A trip to the doctor's office confirmed the break, and my arm was put in a cast. This was the second time my arm had been frac-tured within two years, and it worried me to the point of thinking that it might have to be amputated.

Incidents of injuries like this with my arm and others in-curred by my brother David, such as the severe laceration of his leg from falling on a piece of glass while playing baseball, requir-ing stitches, earned us the title the Headache Brothers, bestowed upon us by Lloyd.

I asked Lloyd one day, "Why do you call us that?"

He said, "Because y'all always give your mother headaches."

Though I went about life normally in my adolescence, aware-ness of my cardiac history and uneasy thoughts about the possi-bility of further problems lurked in the back of my mind. By the eighth or ninth grade I was starting to notice heartbeat irregularity more and more, and a number of times I thought I was surely going to die. Each time, however, Dr. Agricola didn't seem too concerned, saying it was nothing to worry about. But when I asked if I should be participating in physical education class, he said I shouldn't be, which of course was worrisome. And this was around the time that the other doctor had disqualified me for the football team.

So, although I had done well for years after my first surgery at the age of eight, now I could hear the distant drumrolls of trouble ahead. Heart issues would continue to reappear, like evil demons, in some form throughout my life.

six

=======================

NAVIGATING HEART DISEASE
AS A TEENAGER

THE TEENAGE YEARS usually represent the time of life when people are at their peak of health and energy. For me, much of this period was dominated by concerns about my heart. I had begun to notice a distinct increase in fatigue at the end of the day after strenuous physical activity. When I felt my chest, I could detect a palpable thrill, and I could hear a harsh sound when I lay down on the bed with my ear against the mattress, a pronounced murmur I had not discerned earlier.

Though it was unfortunate that I had to deal with heart problems and the resulting surgeries right smack in the middle of my teen years, in a couple of ways they may have been a blessing in disguise. The unpopular Vietnam War was going on, and many older teenage boys were concerned over the possibility that they might have to go, so I felt a certain relief that I would not have to deal with this because of my medical history. But at the same time I still wished I hadn't had the heart issues and the surgeries that they entailed.

The fact that heart problems threatened my very long-term survival meant that any teenage issues I had took a lower priority on my list of concerns. The medical issues relevant to my immediate heath were paramount. I had to make a conscious decision to pursue a course that would most likely lead to a more socially productive outcome, rather than one that would increase the chances of my ending up in the criminal justice system. That would have further complicated a life that was already becoming more complex medically.

To address my medical issues, I was once again referred to Dr. Don Hosier in Columbus. I had not seen him in six or seven years. He was amazed by my development since he'd last seen me. He checked me out and concluded that it was time to do another heart catheterization to more accurately evaluate my situation.

The evaluation was done a few months later, again at the Columbus Children's Hospital. When I was taken to my room, doctors and medical students, led by Dr. Hosier, started to arrive, obviously eager to get their hands on this amazing medical specimen. They listened to my heart with their stethoscopes, thumped my chest and back, probed and prodded my arms and groin to feel for pulses. Electrocardiograms and blood pressures were taken. Technicians would come in to take blood.

Though it was not apparent to me at the time, racism existed in medicine as well as in American society at large. Doctors and interns do not infrequently bring into their practices preconceived notions about people of other races. It was rather shocking to me to discover, in old medical records I obtained while in the process of writing this book, unflattering comments about me. The following is a direct quote from one of the residents who examined me prior to my surgery in 1970: "This is a well-developed, somewhat dull appearing Negro male." Another intern made a similar comment about me. How can a doctor make an assessment about someone's intellectual ability during a preliminary physical evaluation? The fact that the descriptions "well-developed," "dull," and "Negro" occurred together clearly reflected, in my view, at least unconscious racist attitudes. Negative nonmedical comments or opinions should be excluded from medical evaluation reports, especially if they are not expected to have any bearing on the diagnosis or treatment. Fortunately, my main physician at the hospital did not, as far as I could tell, harbor any of those attitudes.

Later, after the doctors left, I was taken down for x-rays and other tests. It was kind of exciting to get out of the room and tour other parts of the hospital. The hospital seemed bigger than I remembered it years ago. It was apparent that new additions had been made, even if you didn't notice the lines of demarcation between the newer, updated parts and the older parts. .

In a couple of days, I was transported to the heart catheterization lab. The procedure was similar to the one I had had before, but the technology seemed more advanced. The tests revealed that I had two defects that had not been evident when I had been tested eight years before. These defects—severe pulmonary stenosis and coarctation of the aorta—needed to be corrected with surgery.

Pulmonary valve stenosis is a congenital heart defect in which the pulmonary outflow tract is constricted, and the blood cannot flow freely out of the right side of the heart when the right ventricle contracts. The valve leaflets may not move freely or there could be greatly enlarged muscle tissue in the outflow tract. One distinctive symptom is a machine-like murmur over the center of the chest. The risk posed by a condition such as pulmonary stenosis is right-sided heart failure, which could eventually lead to total heart failure if not corrected.

Aorta coarctation occurs when the flow of blood into the aorta is impeded due to narrowing of the aorta artery. The consequence of this is abnormally high blood pressure. Heart enlargement as evidence of cardiac stress is usually visible on the chest x-ray. The danger with this condition is that heart failure can develop over time, due to the heart muscle working too hard to overcome the impediment to blood flow. Also, the patient is at a greater risk of stroke due to hyperpressure in the head.

After the tests, the doctor released me from the hospital to recover. In about two months, we received a letter indicating that the surgery had been set for late March of 1971.

I was in the ninth grade at the time, and was older than my classmates because I had been held back because of my earlier surgery. I didn't want to be held back again because of extended absence from school. I did not want to be like Jethro from the *Beverly Hillbillies*, still going to high school at age twenty-two. As for worrying about the surgery, I think my mother and the rest of the family had more anxiety than I did. I just wanted to get it over and return to a normal life.

The day came to go to the hospital in Columbus. Deacon Belcher from our church agreed to take my mom and me to the hospital. I confronted these procedures with confidence because I had been assured that after they were done, I would eventually be able to do just about anything I wanted to do.

The usual preliminary tests and examinations at my admittance were conducted by a slew of medical professionals and medical students, and early in the morning of the third day, surgery was performed by Dr. Sirak, the same doctor who'd operated on me when I was eight years old.

He first addressed the aortic coarctation, the defect that posed the greatest and most immediate risk to me. To correct it, the surgical team removed part of two ribs from the left side of my chest, a procedure necessary because of dense adhesions from the surgery I'd had when I was eight years old. During the thoracotomy, a surgical approach that exposes the chest cavity, my aorta was narrowed in a section right before it loops downward toward the lower parts of my body.

In some cases, doctors perform an anastomosis, in which they simply excise the narrowed segment of the aorta, pull the two ends together, and stitch them. In my case, they used the left subclavian artery coming off the ascending aorta, disconnecting it from where it fed the shoulder area, and used that end to widen the aorta at the narrowed aortic arch. This allowed less obstructed blood flow through the aortic arch to the descending aorta to supply the lower part of my body. By doing this, the blood pressure did not need to be as high.

These techniques and procedures had side effects, however. When ribs are removed, there's quite a bit more postoperative pain. There is also more risk of developing a pneumothorax or collapsed lung, which actually happened postoperatively. The other significant side effect is curvature of the spine due to removal of parts of ribs. Until the ribs grow back, it is necessary to do exercises to counteract that tendency.

The rerouting of the subclavian artery, in addition to its therapeutic benefits, had the undesired effect of causing my left arm and shoulder to get smaller than my right arm and shoulder. The pulse in my left wrist was weak as well. Over time, collateral circulation in the chest region can, amazingly enough, develop to compensate for surgical alterations, injuries, or obstructions. I reinforced this tendency by doing exercises to strengthen my upper body, putting more stress on the left side. Building up the amount of activity gradually, I did a lot of arm circles, pushups, pull-ups, and light weights.

It was a while, though, before I actually got to do extensive postoperative rehabilitation. I remained in the intensive care unit for about a week. I remember my mother and my older brother Joe coming to see me when I started to wake up—I was in and out for a couple of days, I guess. On my third day in the ICU, they got me up to walk around. Consumed with nearly unbearable pain, I just wanted to get back in bed.

A few days later, a nurse told me that there were some people there to see me. They couldn't come in, but they could see me through the ICU window. The nurses sat me in a chair, and I waved at the people—three of my sisters and one of my brothers. They waved back, but it was not the same as being face to face. I was glad they'd visited, but it was pretty depressing for me to be seen in such bad shape, and I am sure it was for them as well.

About three days after this, I was transferred from the ICU to a regular room. One thing I kept complaining about was that it was so difficult for me to breathe. Finally one night the doctor came in and said an x-ray showed that I had a collapsed lung. He had to do a painful procedure of cutting a little hole under my left armpit and sticking in a tube that ended in my chest cavity. This was left in place for a couple of days to get the air out of the cavity so the lung could inflate. The site was only numbed a little with some mild spray anesthesia, so I was pretty uncomfortable. The doctor said, "It has to be done, or you will have all kinds of problems."

In a day or so, I started to feel much better. My breathing started to return to normal, and I had more energy. The doctors wanted to keep me there to correct the other heart defect, pulmonary stenosis, but I guess my mother was emotionally drained, and she pressed for them to allow both of us to recover from the current ordeal. They agreed to let me go home, but one of the doctors said that when they called for me to return in a month or so, I'd better come if I didn't want to have heart failure.

When they did notify us to come back, my mother understandably was a little reluctant. She knew these were major surgeries, and I had already survived two. I think she was just afraid that my system could not tolerate another serious invasive procedure. I not only wanted to live, but I did not want to be seriously disabled, so I told her what the doctor had said about facing heart failure if I waited too long. At my urging, she agreed to take me back at the scheduled time.

The pulmonary stenosis surgery was done, by Dr. Sirak, in May 1971. I remember when he came in to check on me while I was still fuzzy from the anesthesia. The ability of my eyes to focus was impaired. All the objects in the room seemed to be distorted, even the doctor's face, as he said, "Well, we got those vessels straightened out." This was nice to hear. I felt like I was finally done with all of that surgery.

Right after the surgery, though my visual field was foggy, my auditory system seemed to be functioning slightly better. I could hear the constant chatter of nurses and doctors, though I didn't understand what they were saying. Speaking as they did in their medical vernacular, they might as well have been speaking Greek. The moaning and groaning of patients, and the various heart monitors chirping on their own frequencies, surrounded me like a cacophony in an echo chamber. Amazingly, this did not disturb me, and I went back to sleep.

It was discovered that I had the complication of bacterial endocarditis, a bacterial infection of the heart, meaning that my temperature had to be monitored especially closely. I will never forget the time a doctor came into the ICU to check on me and picked up a thermometer that was lying on the stand next to my bed. She put it in my mouth. I immediately told her, speaking in a garbled manner because of the thermometer in my mouth, "That's a rectal thermometer." She promptly took it out, and said, "Oh," with a look of embarrassment on her face. I was quickly given some water and a toothbrush so I could clean my mouth out.

I was moved to a regular room in about a week. The doctors frequently came in to change the bandages and assess the incision. They were amazed at how good the incision looked and said I was healing well. The incision from this surgery was straight down the middle of my chest. It didn't hurt nearly as badly as the aorta surgery. The incision for the aorta surgery, being more curved and being situated along more movable body parts, caused more pain

My progress had been pretty good, but one day I felt kind of bloated and lethargic. One of the doctors came in with his wife. It was a Friday, and they were getting ready to enjoy their weekend, I supposed. The doctor looked at me quizzically, asking me, "How are you feeling?" I told him, "I feel kind of tight and heavy." He had my weight checked, then told me that I was gaining weight due to fluid retention. He had me put on some diuretics, and I felt much better the next day.

My main doctor, Dr. Hosier, told me that I had had a little heart failure. He indicated that with the two big surgeries back to back, and the bacterial endocarditis causing heart inflammation, failure was not surprising, and my heart would recover after the underlying issues were resolved.

The diagnosis of heart failure depressed me, but I was more disappointed with what it meant as far as my prospects for a quicker recovery were concerned, about being able to be active, about going back to school. My doctor kept telling me to be optimistic, saying that in time I'd be able to do just about anything I wanted. Because of that, I remained hopeful that I'd be able to lead a normal life.

After about a week of being in a regular room, I was released. I was glad to get home to see the rest of the family. The weather was nice and warm. Spring was in full bloom. All of the neighbors were waving to me and welcoming me home. All I could do was wave back, because the vocal problems I had faced when I had my surgery as a small child had reappeared. The trauma from the ventilator or laryngeal nerve injury had affected me again.

I spent the next few weeks catching up on assignments from school. I was able to complete enough work to pass to the eleventh grade.

I went back to Children's Hospital in Columbus for my follow-up in about two weeks. My mother and I made our way toward the cardiology section of the large outpatient area, an area sectioned off into different divisions designated by large signs—Urology, Pulmonary, Neurology, Cranial-Facial, Physical Medicine. Many children of different ages and races were sitting with their parents in the various sections, with chairs and walls so brightly colored that the spirits of the most ill children would have been lifted.

We finally made it in to see the doctor, who was not too pleased with my progress. I was not getting worse, but my heart was still too big. I had to go back in a month.

When I went back, things had improved a little. I was cautioned again not to be too active, and to take it easy, and I was told I had to come back in three months. The doctor said I would have to get a tutor to come to the house until I was able to go to school. The school did arrange for me to have a tutor when the new school year started. I still did not like the idea of not being able to go to school. It reinforced my perception of being different, sickly, and weak, but I felt hopeful that a brighter day would come.

When I went back in three months, the doctor indicated that things were looking much better. He told me again that in time I would be able to do just about anything I desired. In the meantime, however, I still was not permitted to return to school, and I was to come back in three months for another checkup. After this more positive report, even though I had not been cleared for more activity, I started doing little exercises like arm circles and pushups to help develop my left arm and shoulder, which had atrophied after the surgery. The shrinkage on the left side caused my shoulder to droop on the right.

My tutor's name was Eric Parks. He was blind, but amazingly he was able to go anywhere around town using his cane. He would assign me textbook sections to read, and we would discuss them the next session. He also gave me math assignments, and had me write little essays, which I read to him as he listened intensely, seeming to be impressed with my writing skills. He also tested me frequently.

Eric let me borrow a kinesiology book he had, possibly because I told him I wanted to exercise to help in my rehabilitation from surgery. The point is that I never gave the book back to him. When I had my next doctor's appointment and was told I could go back to school, Eric's services were no longer needed, and for whatever reason I never returned the book before he left. It might sound silly, but for many years I still had the book in my possession, and still felt guilty about it. Finally, when I moved five years ago, I donated the book to Goodwill, hoping that the book would be as valuable to the next owner as it had been to me in enhancing my knowledge of the body.

Having a brother who had gone to college, and was now a teacher, had inspired me to start doing more reading a couple of years before my latest surgeries, and that continued during my convalescence. During my recovery, I spent much of my time reading books, accumulating knowledge, and developing my vocabulary—which I enjoyed testing using the *Reader's Digest* vocabulary tests, on which I always scored well. This, another unintended way I was able to capitalize on my medical situation, may have kept me from going astray of the law with the restlessness that had plagued me in my earlier teens.

Luckily, too, I had a mother and older siblings who were good role models and who tried to steer the younger ones straight. Ironically, my mother, having had only an eighth-grade education—which was actually good for an African American raised in the South—was herself inspired by her children who were getting a higher education to make efforts to improve her own proficiency with grammar and vocabulary. I would observe her on a number of occasions going through some of the old English grammar books, once used by her children who had moved on, that had never been returned to the school but ended up in the house. (I can imagine certain school officials turning up their noses over "some of those Trotters not returning their school books.") She would also spend time looking up words she did not know in the dictionary. She said often that she'd done well in school, and that her teachers had encouraged her to go further. The likelihood of black females in the South continuing their education back in those times was nil unless your family had money and you were going into teaching.

When I went back for my next appointment, in December, the doctor, after examining me and looking at my latest x-rays, said things were looking better and better. He gave me the okay to return to school as long as I used transportation to get there and back. Since we did not have a car, arrangements were made for the bus to pick me up. It felt good to get back to school, but I did not like feeling different from the other students who walked or rode in cars.

In three months, when I had my next appointment, the doctor examined me and then studied the x-rays and electrocardiogram. The next words he uttered were the most beautiful I had ever heard. He asked me, "How far do you have to walk to school?" I said about a half mile. He gave me permission to walk to school. I was ecstatic, and the next day I walked there without any problems.

In the midst of my recovery from all of my surgeries, something happened that had the potential to literally shatter the heart emotionally and physically—not just mine, but that of every member of my family.

Early one morning in the middle of April 1973, my brother David, my sister Denise, and I were getting ready to head to school when two people—Vicky Harris, the same girl who'd been in that talent show at the high school with Jessie, and her brother David—rode up to our house on a motor bike. My older sister Jessie was on the porch when they rode up. Vicky walked onto our property and started arguing with Jessie. A fight started, and Vicky pulled out a razor blade and started slicing my sister's face. My brother and I, seeing this, grabbed her to pull her off. David Harris started fighting my brother. Since he was older and bigger, he was able to overpower my brother, bloodying his nose.

My brother, seething with fury, went into the house, got the shotgun, and returned, his face contorted with rage, to shoot the man who'd attacked him. At that moment I was witnessing death ready to strike, and had I not been able to talk my brother down, I have no doubt that David Harris would have been dead. But the murderous fury in my brother's eyes caused the two Harrises to get on their motor bike and roar off.

My mother had called the police, and when the aggressors' brother, Richard Harris, saw the police car arrive, he came up the street, armed with a pistol, and—exhibiting behavior that was beyond irrational—challenged the policeman on the scene, intimidating the small-town cop so much that he got in his car and left. Harris fired a shot at the police car as it retreated.

Later that day, when we returned home from school and my mother and sister came home from an excursion to New Philadelphia, we saw that the window in our door had been broken and learned that physical threats had been made against us.

Neither my brother nor my sister was seriously hurt in the fight, but this disturbing incident, resulting from an ongoing disagreement between Jessie and Vicky Harris, could have led to a great tragedy. The thing that made the situation even more regrettable and unfortunate was the fact that our sister Josie and their brother Ralph were married to each other. One would not have expected something like this to occur between the two families.

My mother was fed up with her family being the target of people's aggression in that town. In spite of encouragement from some family friends to stand our ground and fight back by any means necessary, my mother, averse to violent confrontations, stuck with the decision she had made, to move.

I think people tended to target our family more because my mother was religious and "turned the other cheek" more than most people. This would not have been the case if my father had been living. Though not a large man, he had been strong physically and mentally. He did not let people harass him, and he would not have put up with anything like this. My mother being a widow with many daughters, and for much of the time with no older sons around, made us attractive targets for harassment.

Though we suffered the brunt of the harassment, different families fought frequently among each other in general. One month it might be the Collinses against the Trotters, the next month the Harrises against the Collinses. Then it might be the Harrises against the Russells or the Jordans against the Collinses. Alliances were formed and broken quickly.

I can recall an occasion about six years prior to the incident that prompted our moving, when there was a big family feud in the street one night, one did not involve us. All of us were in the house. My mother always got us in the house when trouble was brewing. We had the lights off and were looking out the window at the angry crowd in the street. My sister's boyfriend, Lloyd Dansby, who was with us, said, with a big smile on his face, "This is better than *Saturday Night at the Movies*!" I must admit that I, and no doubt others in the family, did derive a perverse sense of excitement from disturbances such as these, especially when they did not involve us.

The phenomenon of interfamily disturbances, in Newcomerstown at least, seemed to occur mostly among the black population, at least back then. I've heard that families don't fight each other like they used to. It's well documented in social psychology that individuals or groups that are abused or oppressed, or have the perception of being so, have a tendency to direct that frustration and anger inwardly, in the form of self-hatred. This is especially true when they can't confront the perceived perpetrators of injustices against them.

While blacks in the town had their degree of disharmony, I must say that I had a profound sense that intraracial animus within the white population also existed, in the form, I believe, of classism. I can recall numerous episodes when poorer whites were excluded from certain circles and ridiculed by more affluent whites. The terms "upper crust" and "lower crust" were used to refer to different classes of whites in town. One could make the argument that poorer whites may have suffered greater psychological effects from intraracial classism than blacks suffered from racial discrimination in Newcomerstown.

General social separation between the races was a given at that time, so the emotional trauma of not being accepted into a certain social or economic class was not intense. Based on my experience, no clear evidence of classism within the African American community existed at that time. I would suspect that had there been, it would have destroyed the only buffer we had against racial prejudice in Newcomerstown. Our unity, though fragile, did serve in a strange way to provide morale support in general. Nevertheless, for my heart's sake and the safety of the rest of the family, we felt we had to get out of Newcomerstown.

My mother called my uncle in Massillon, Ohio, about forty-five miles away, and told him our situation. He said we could live with him until we got a place. By this time, it was only my mother and the three remaining children—Denise, David, and me. We left town that day with an escort by the county sheriff. It felt like that scene from Alfred Hitchcock's movie *The Birds,* when the family drove slowly out of town in that car. My brother, sister, and I would have preferred to finish out the school year in Newcomerstown, but our mother was insistent that we move immediately.

My Uncle Thamon, standing about six feet tall and weighing around 230 pounds, along with his stern expression, projected an air of authority and elicited respect from those around him. He and his family had moved to Massillon in 1950 from West Virginia. Though a compassionate man, he was strict and had particular ways of doing things. During the times I spent at his house, whether during the summers in the 1960s or when we stayed with him after leaving Newcomerstown, I experienced firsthand his sternness. Even something as simple as washing dishes was a science to him. To satisfy him, certain defined sequences of steps had to be followed.

He could also be rigid in his thinking. Once, at a time when I was nearing the end of my senior year in high school and planning to attend college, he was reading the paper, and he asked me to look at a part of the article that cited a monetary amount. The amount was $4.5 million.

He asked me to state the monetary amount. I said, "It's four and a half million dollars."

When I said that, he frowned and said, "No, it is four million dollars and five points."

In response, I said, "The correct way to say it is four and a half million dollars."

He became really irritated with me, wrinkling his brow and flaring his nostrils. He looked not unlike a black Bob Hope, and he seemed really disappointed that his supposedly intelligent nephew was not able to say the amount correctly.

After going back and forth, I just conceded to him, thinking perhaps he was going by some old math. Then, a couple of days later, I went back to his house and found him with a couple of old math books, books that had probably belonged to his children when they were in school. Apparently, he had been engaged in research. He continued debating me about the $4.5 million, but nothing he said changed my position. I just let him win the debate because he was so entrenched in his position, and nothing I said would have mattered.

Though my uncle had his math facts wrong, he was an intelligent man. This was evident by his demonstration of common sense, his penchant for reading the newspapers, and his flair for keeping track of and making logical analyses of world events. With little formal education or training, my uncle had built his own house, from the ground up, basing his design on a picture of a house his wife, Aunt Innie, got from the lumber company she cleaned for in downtown Massillon. It took him several years, working on it in his spare time, and he completed it around 1967. He did have help, of course, with the electrical and plumbing work.

We loved our uncle's house—it seemed like a mansion compared to what we were accustomed to. It was modern, immaculate, and had that new house smell. I felt a certain amount of pride living in my uncle's house, and I would sometimes brag to others about how great it was. I'm sure his pride far exceeded mine because his own creativity and sweat had gone into constructing it, whereas mine was purely vicarious.

After living with our uncle Thamon Foster and aunt Innie for a month or so, we were able to rent a house a block away from them. We three children enrolled in Washington High School in Massillon a couple of days after moving, our school records from Newcomerstown arriving soon after. We were not total strangers here because we had relatives who attended the school, and we had met people while visiting Massillon in the summer.

The sudden disruption of our life in Newcomerstown had a profound and lasting effect on my youngest sister, Denise, who now goes by the name Sakina. Sakina states, "Well, it was apparently something we had to do. I didn't have time to really think about how I felt, and really this is the first time that someone has asked me about it. It was scary, and I was somewhat shy, but in some ways very opinionated and feisty. However, when we moved that kind of shut that part of my personality down a little bit, I think. It seemed that I became really shy, and lost all of my confidence." She says that she lost her concentration and interest in school, and her grades dropped. She adds, "I knew there was going to be some collateral damage with a move like that. For me the collateral damage was that I lost my interest, focus, and confidence, and never regrouped."

Sakina felt no allegiance or emotional connection to her new school in Massillon. She recalls the following: "The day I graduated, there was no party, and I didn't get a graduation ring. There was no one really there celebrating that time of life for me. No one was really at my graduation, I don't think anyone came. It was kind of sad." Sakina suggest that in some ways the lack of connection she had with schoolmates in Massillon was coming from her. She relates, "I was very guarded and very private. I didn't want to tell people anything about my life. I did not want to talk about why we moved here, because it was embarrassing."

Sakina reflects on her outlook when we lived in Newcomerstown: "I had the feeling that after high school I was going to college and do great things because I felt and knew that I was smart. I felt that if I did not go to college, it would have been an embarrassment. That positive feeling just kind of dwindled when we moved from Newcomerstown."

Sakina did go to college in Wisconsin for about a year after high school. She did very well, but she had to drop out due to lack of funding. She admits that part of the problem was that she was by nature a private person, and that she did not network with people to find out about different financing options.

Sakina valued her privacy and anonymity, which is why she chose to attend the virtually all-white Mount Senario College in Ladysmith, Wisconsin. The other blacks attending that college were almost all male, almost all athletes, and mostly from Chicago. My sister, being very attractive, caught their attention, and they wanted to date her. Wanting to "get lost in her studies," she was not too receptive to their advances. She says, "They had a difficult time understanding me. They thought I was ignoring and disrespecting them. They were extremely hurt and angry about my obvious aloofness." This perception of being "dissed" led to her being bullied. "They would walk behind me and call me vile names. They would pound on my dorm windows, bang on my door while calling me names, just taunting me over and over again. They had white girlfriends, but they would go crazy if they saw me just talking to a white boy."

I guess those guys must have felt guilty about how they treated my sister. Sakina says, "At the very end of my semester there, all the big bullying black jocks got together and told me they needed to talk to me. They said they were wrong for bullying and taunting me, and they were truly sorry. I could see the tears in their eyes, and even when I think of that experience to this day, I can feel the hurt, and the tears come to my eyes."

I would experience some bullying when I attended college, but not to this degree. And I was not aware of the problems she'd had with bullies until she told me in 2012.

Sakina currently lives in Bethesda, Maryland. She enjoys work as a patient coordinator in the radiology department at a hospital in the DC area. A very outgoing social butterfly who has traveled the world, a real "globe-trotter" no one would ever suspect was once a shy and aloof girl.

Massillon and Newcomerstown had many differences. Whereas Newcomerstown was a small town, Massillon was a small city of approximately 32,000 people. At the time we moved there, Massillon was a steel city in the early stages of decline, but the industry was still fairly strong. Many young people were still able to graduate and look forward to a good-paying job working in the mills.

The other stark difference between the two was that Massillon's black population was about seventeen times greater, having around 3,500 black residents. Many of the older blacks, including my uncle, had migrated there from the South looking for jobs in the steel mills. They came mostly from Alabama and Mississippi. Even with Massillon's greater black population, the interfamily tensions we'd experienced in Newcomerstown did not seem to occur there, at least to anywhere near the same degree.

Our new school, Washington High School, had a student body about three times larger than our old school, approximately 1,200 students, about 200 of those being African Americans. There had been only about 15 blacks in the high school in Newcomerstown. When the three of us left Newcomerstown, the black student body of the high school decreased twenty percent.

I thought I'd had a nice-size afro in Newcomerstown, but when we moved to Massillon, the size of mine was dwarfed by the many gigantic 'fros that were being sported at the school. The black students here, especially the males wearing those plush 'fros, seemed to exude an attitude of "coolness," and to walk with a certain swagger. Many of them displayed quite a few more street smarts than I'd been accustomed to in Newcomerstown. I was just this skinny, green young man, from a country town, in the later stages of recovery from recent heart surgeries.

This was around 1973, the peak of the black awareness and Black Power era. Though blacks had control of a smidgen of economic power, and not much political power at the time, we had a psychological sense of power, a power that emanated from our unified stance in boldly advocating for our civil rights and seeking redress for generations of injustices. Our growing perception of racial identity and pride was manifested by our mass adoption of afro hairstyles, while repudiating the processing and straightening of hair, and our public flaunting of intricate "soul shake" rituals.

Even though I was a little "snowed" by the slick dudes in my new school, I quickly got wise to the game, and quietly adapted. My health was continuing to progress as well, and before long, I got an after-school job. Also, by the time my next appointment came up, I was old enough and my heart had recovered enough that I was able to make the trip to Columbus on my own, which I did on a Greyhound bus. It was now only required that I make the trip every six months. My checkups at this time were always good, and I was no longer in any immediate danger.

The summer before my senior year, I got a job supervising young children in an inner-city day camp, which luckily made the time fly by, because I could not wait to begin my last year of high school.

The lineup of courses for my senior year was impressive: college prep English, geometry, chemistry, Latin, psychology, and social studies. My maintaining about a B– average earned me the reputation of being a decent student. It was important for me to do well in school so I could get into college. Opportunities for a young man with a history of congenital heart problems were limited if he wanted to be hired at a mill. With a good education, I would have the chance of getting a good-paying job that would not be as physically demanding.

After talking with my guidance counselor in the first half of my senior year, I decided that I would attend Central State University, a historically black university. My plan was to major in medical technology. Being involved in the medical community as a patient for so many years, I had developed an interest in science in general and medical science in particular.

In spring of 1974, I received good news from Central State University. I had been accepted into the class of 1978.

From left: Me, my brother David, and David Harris.

Our Clow Avenue house in Newcomerstown.

My sister Voncille on the steps of Trinity Baptist Church, September 2014.

Candy
Shingler

Jeff
Shivers

Bobby
Smart

Phyllis
Smith

Phyllis
Smyth

Brenda
Starkey

Vicky
Starkey

Dona
Stevens

Beverly
Stokes

Patricia
Sweitzer

Marty
Tabor

Harlan
Tharp

Carla
Tish

David
Trotter

Otis
Trotter

Jaynaise
Welsch

Tom
Wilkin

Debbie
Wilson

Jerry
Winterringer

Gerald
Wright

Ronnie
Wynn

My brother David and I in our school yearbook photos, 1971.

My brother James (Rahmaan) in Newcomerstown, 1971.

Frosh Strive for Perfection

N.H.S. - 30	John Glenn - - - 6
N.H.S. - 12	Coshocton - - - 0
N.H.S. - 16	Claymont - - - -0
N.H.S. - 0	Cambridge - - -14
N.H.S. - 16	Garaway - - - - 0
N.H.S. - 6	Ridgewood - - - 6
N.H.S. - 32	Meadowbrook - -0

FIRST ROW, L-R: Mike Dansby, David Trotter, Mike Belt, John Little, Steve Golden, Robby Duffy, Greg Hart, Terry McCrone. SECOND ROW, L-R: Ron Quillen, Dave Hill, Dave Parry, Jeff Danford, Ken Lewis, Larry Bouscher, Dave Mason, Lee Russell. THIRD ROW, L-R: Coach Wright, Terry Saylor, Bill McManus, Tom Wilkin, Jim Bradshaw, Gary Hawk, John Shaw, Max Moore, Steve Nay, Coach Ray McFadden.

No. 22 David Trotter, football team photo, 1971.

Reserve Football

FRONT: Manager D. Ervin, C. Couts, D. Tidrick, J. Baker, T. Jurin, T. Gadd, M. Baker, B. Mardis, W. Couts, G. Phillips, D. Hardesty, Coach Art. BACK: Manager K. Orant, J. Duff, D. Trotter, T. Saylor, B. McMannus, R. Quillen, L. Russel, D. Mason, C. Robinson.

Reserve football action

With this year's reserve record of 3-3-1, they guys on the squad should be looking forward to exciting varsity competition.

NCT 24	John Glenn 8	
NCT 22	Ridgewood 6	
NCT 6	Riverview 24	
NCT 14	Indian Valley South 14	
NCT 0	Tusc. C. C. 6	
NCT 0	Claymont 6	
NCT 16	Meadowbrook . . 14	

No. 86 David Trotter, football team photo, 1973.

seven

COLLEGE AND CAREER

AT ABOUT THE SAME TIME I was accepted into the university, a major tornado hit the town of Xenia, located four miles from Central State University, as well as the university itself. The storm demolished about half of the city and about 75 percent of the university campus. Close to thirty-five people died, including two or three on the campus. Considering the extensive destruction, it was unclear whether the school would remain open for classes.

A few weeks after the tornado, I called the university to see if it would be functioning in the fall. I was told that it would. Trailers would serve as classrooms and offices for buildings that had been destroyed or heavily damaged. Most of the residential buildings were still standing or functional.

For a state university that was already struggling somewhat, it was amazing that the institution was able to weather this literal storm. I was glad that it remained open. Had it closed, the furthering of my education would have been interrupted, to say the least. In fact, it was the determination of the students of my class at the time that was probably the deciding factor in the school remaining open. Quite a number of students who showed up on campus that fall took one look at the devastation and turned around and left. Luckily, enough freshman decided to stay to give us a sufficiently large class.

I arrived at Central State University that fall of 1974 in the company of my older brother James, who drove me down. With my old and out-of-style attire and meager possessions, I must have looked like Booker T. Washington when he first arrived at Hampton Institute. All of my possessions easily fit into two old gray suitcases. Some students arriving with their parents had small trailers packed with belongings.

The valuable possessions I had brought were good basic intelligence, decent educational prerequisites, and a strong determination to succeed. These were the things that were going to be the greatest predictors of my ultimate outcome, not stylish clothes, stereos, or televisions that other students had brought to furnish their dorm rooms.

The first thing I noticed upon entering the campus was the obvious evidence of the catastrophic storm. Several heavily damaged buildings had not been demolished yet. Dotting the campus were bare plots of land where structures had been, and numerous trailers were in evidence. The appearance of some reconstruction already beginning gave me and many other new arriving students a feeling of optimism.

Later on, after getting acclimated to the university, I met people who had been on campus when the tornado struck. They told how they desperately sought shelter under heavy furniture in their dorm rooms to escape the horror of the storm. The deafening roar of the storm as it unleashed its fury on the campus could clearly be heard. One student related to me how he and a few other people in a building survived only because they rode out the tornado under that heavy furniture.

The first few days we had orientation, and we took university placement tests to see how each freshman ranked compared to the others. I was pleased to find that on the verbal section I scored in the 95th percentile. In the mathematical portion of the test, I scored in the 65th percentile—not surprisingly, for math had never been my strongest suit. Though my scores were good overall, I was reminded by an adviser that many of the students I was competing against had graduated from lower socioeconomic school systems and were less academically prepared for college. In other words, he was suggesting that it might be beneficial for me to take advantage of any remedial assistance that was available, which I did when needed.

Registration was a nightmare. Long lines and anxious moments resulted when there were glitches in the registration process, which sometimes occurred when documentation for grants and admittance material that had been sent in couldn't be located. Due to the very limited financial means of my family, I was eligible to receive the maximum aid in the form of federal education grants and a couple of smaller state grants. This covered about 90 percent of my expenses. I made up the rest with a couple of small loans. I also signed up for a work-study job. This enabled me to obtain personal items I needed and a little spending money. Fortunately, all of my documents were in order, and I was able to complete registration and get my room assignment.

I was assigned a room with another student—with whom it was clear very early I was not going to get along. He did not like me because I was too "square" for him. He liked to smoke reefers, and I did not. I had nothing against marijuana, but it was not my cup of tea. Besides, it was probably not good for my heart.

One day he was lying on his bed, just looking at me. From his facial expression, I could sense his intense loathing of me. Suddenly, his feeling for me boiled over in one short, stinging verbal assault. He said, "You're a little boring, square motha-fuckin nerd that don't do shit." This shocked me speechless—although it was pretty clear a response would not have been productive anyway. It was obviously time to change roommates.

Had I known that my roommate would flunk out before the next quarter, I would have toughed it out and stayed in the room.

I met with my adviser and signed up for a slew of courses in line with my chosen major. Central State University in 1974 was on the quarter system, so the courses were broken down into smaller units. The classes I registered for were college algebra, English literature, French, psychology, states of matter, chemical bonding, and stoichiometry and the mole concept. This would be the first time in my life since first grade in West Virginia that I would have black teachers.

My academic routine was on track, but my social adjustment to campus life was more challenging. I was having trouble getting along with some of the other students, and I often felt as though I was the target of derision. This was probably because I did not play sports, and was not one of the "cool dudes." I became so discouraged due to my social difficulties that I considered dropping out.

I talked to my oldest brother, Joe, and he encouraged me to hang in there, telling me that those people targeting me were probably not serious students, and that many of them would probably flunk out before the end of the year. That often turned out to be the case. Others always seemed to be popping up, like never-ending zombies in a horror movie, trying to make things difficult for me, but I was determined that I would not let it dishearten me. I strengthened my resolve to finish school and not be distracted by the negativity. My shoulders must have been really strong, because I let tons of shit just roll off them.

I moved to another room, and my new roommate and I got along well. Steve Mealy, from Cincinnati, Ohio, and I are friends to this day. Steve was tall, thin, light-skinned. He had distinctive eyebrows that met like two opposing armies in battle, as well as a mustache that connected with a goatee—all of which made him resemble Wolf Man Jack with an afro. Sometimes Steve would imitate the Wolf Man, leaving me in stitches laughing.

One day, shortly after entering the university, I was on my way to the cafeteria when I noticed a man who looked familiar. He was tall, with a face that reminded me of a church steeple—a long forehead that was broad at the base but tapered off almost to a peak as it extended toward the top of his head. I thought to myself, I know I've seen this person somewhere. As I looked at him, I saw that he was looking at me. He probably was thinking that he had seen me somewhere, too.

He approached, and we introduced ourselves. I asked him where he was from, and he said, "Massillon." I now knew that was where I had seen him, but we had never met. His name was Ron Anderson, and he was what is referred to as a professional student. Ron was about thirty-eight or forty years old at the time I met him. He was very intelligent, and more opinionated than a Supreme Court judge. He could have graduated years ago if he'd wanted to, but he just liked going to school, being on campus, and helping new students. Ron was a residential adviser at the university, and he became a big factor in helping me get adjusted to life on campus. The fact that he was from Massillon as I was, and had a car, also meant that I had a way to get home for the major holidays. He rarely accepted my offer to help with the gas expenses for getting to and from home. That was the way he was: a happy-go-lucky type of guy—walking around whistling a tune, his long head, attached to his long, slim body, bobbing away—who seemed to revel in assisting people.

In a horrific twist of fate, Ron, along with his grandson, was killed in an auto accident in the summer of 2007. The car was broadsided by a Massillon fire truck, driven by a female cousin of his. The results of the accident investigation suggested that Ron had not heard the fire truck due to a severe hearing impairment. This made sense to me, because several months before, Ron, who did freelance carpentry and electrical work, had come over to my house to discuss some repairs I needed. He was obviously having difficulty hearing what I was saying, because I had to keep repeating myself. I will always remember Ron and the assistance he gave me in my first year at Central State.

My grades were nothing to jump up and cheer about the first year, but they could have been worse. Chemistry was pretty challenging, and it gave me some trouble. A couple of the chemistry units were pulling my GPA down. In comparison to other students I was not doing too badly, but I needed to have at least a B average in chemistry—it was like the cornerstone of my major in medical technology. I was beginning to wonder whether I should change my major to psychology.

Toward the end of the school year, I contemplated going to Washington, DC, to stay with one of my sisters and get a job for the summer. I looked forward to going; it would have been about six years since I had visited the "Chocolate City." DC obtained that nickname due to its distinction of having the highest percentage of black population of any major city in the country—at nearly 70 percent at the time. I stayed with Doris, who had moved to Washington in 1967 to study to be an IBM keypunch operator. When she discovered that that was not the career for her, she started working for the government as an assistant librarian.

In 1968, Doris was in the latter stages of pregnancy with her first child when Martin Luther King was assassinated, and riots broke out in DC as well as across the country. She had prepared to go to work, but our sister Dee, with whom she lived, warned her not to go. She went anyway. Around noon all government offices closed and the buses ceased running. She was stranded. A coworker took her as far as she could, so amid the chaos, anger, frustration, and destruction of the explosive rebellion in the city, she walked the rest of the way home, riddled with fear. While watching the funeral of Martin Luther King on television, she went into labor and was taken to the hospital, where she gave birth to a son. She named him Martin Anthony Trotter, in honor of the slain civil rights leader.

A couple of years later, she had another son, Charles Trotter, and two years after that she met a man by the name of Leon Brown. They married in 1972 and had a child, Rachier, together. Leon made it clear to Doris that he would care for and treat her other two children as his own. They were successful in raising three boys on DC's southeast side to be productive and law-abiding citizens.

Doris was happy to have her younger brothers or other relatives visit her anytime. I remember that sometimes we would arrive on her doorstep, unannounced, in the middle of the night. She was either ecstatic about our visit or she deserved an Academy Award for her acting ability. After coming to stay with her that summer, I got a job doing janitorial work at a place downtown called the International Bank. I would take the bus from near my sister's apartment to get there. I enjoyed it well enough. The work was not hard, and was similar to jobs I had when I was in junior and senior high school. I got along with the people I worked with. It was good to have the chance to make some money to buy clothes for school and to have a little chump change.

Besides this being the first summer I was not under my mother's roof and supervision, it was the summer I officially lost my virginity. On my job at the International Bank, I'd met a coworker named Lamont. Lamont was brown skinned and of average height and build. He was talkative and exuberant, and he had a penchant for playing practical jokes. We became pretty good work friends. Slyly smiling, he would often try to probe me regarding my level of sexual activity or lack thereof, as we went about our cleaning duties.

One day he just came right out and said, "You ain't getting no pussy, are you?"

I made a pathetic attempt to refute this, but my feeble denial made the truth as clear to him as if I had verbally admitted it.

Almost laughing at this point, he said, "Okay, meet me at the Shrimp Boat on East Capitol Street at five o'clock tomorrow." The next day was Saturday, and we had just gotten paid. "I am going to show you a little bit of the night life in the city," he continued.

We exchanged phone numbers.

The next day I called Lamont to confirm our rendezvous at the Shrimp Boat. We met at East Capitol Street and took the bus downtown to 15th and U Street. On the corner was a little bar. Although we were barely old enough to enter a bar, no one questioned our ages when we ordered a beer. At that time I rarely drank, so I merely repeated what Lamont said when I was asked what I wanted to drink. I said, "Give me a Miller's, too."

We sat there slowly sipping our beer, sporadically talking and enjoying the music playing on the jukebox. The Temptations' "Papa Was a Rolling Stone," Marvin Gaye's "Let's Get It On," Isaac Hayes's "Shaft," and an assortment of vintage Diana Ross and the Supremes' hits blared throughout the small bar.

Mellowed by the beer and the music, I was not too reluctant to make sustained eye contact with the scantily clad females Lamont alerted me to, tapping me on the shoulder and motioning with his head as three of them took a seat across the room from the bar. He said, "Oooh wee, OT, how would you like to get some of that?" With my eyes bulging out like I had a bad case of hyperthyroidism, and my mouth gaping wider than the Grand Canyon, it was obvious that I was locked into a state of enchantment over the three women, who radiated sexual heat that could melt the paint off the walls. Those were three smokin' hot black ladies!

Emboldened by liquid courage, we made our way over to where the women were sitting. Lamont introduced himself, and said, "This is Otis Trotter, from Ohio." I added, "Some people like to call me OT."

The three ladies' names were Candy, Starlet, and Ebony. Starlet, the tall, very dark one with fine features and the possessor of a soft, curly Afro, asked, "Where are you from in Ohio?"

I said, "Massillon."

"What larger city is Massillon closer to in Ohio?" she asked. "Is it near Columbus?"

"Actually, it's closer to Cleveland," I replied.

The other lady, Ebony, brown skinned, shorter than Starlet but voluptuously built, with the kind of booty you could sit a drink on, and with captivating eyes, interjected, "I have people in Cleveland."

I thought, Wow, this is the first time I've been out in DC, and the first people I meet have relatives close to where I live in Ohio. What a small world and how interconnected people are!

Candy was a light-skinned, petite young lady, her skin tone and facial features reflecting a beautiful blend of African, European, and Indian or Hispanic descent. She asked, "What are you guys up to?"

Lamont said, "Just trying to show OT a good time before he goes back to college in Ohio."

Candy said, "Y'all can start by getting us ladies a drink."

We gladly did, and got ourselves another round in the process.

Ebony was halfway done with her drink when the song "I'll Take You There" by the Staple Singers came on the jukebox. She exclaimed, "That's my song," and said, "Come on, OT, let's dance. I'll take you there."

We started dancing. She shook and moved her body sensuously, in perfect time to the music. Then she turned around and started backing her ample and shapely posterior toward my crotch, so I met it. She said, "Wait a minute, back up now, that's money."

The music stopped, and we went back to the table. Lamont leaned over, and said, "Man you can get that, but it's going to cost you a little money."

I said, "How much?"

He replied, "I don't know, but it shouldn't be too much."

"I hope not. I've worked too hard for this money," I said.

"Relax and live a little. You hold money so tight, you'd make a buffalo cry," he said, a statement that went right over my head at first. My eyes rolled around in their sockets about twenty times before my "ah ha" moment came. "You just got paid yesterday, so you should be able to handle it," he added. "You have to negotiate with her."

I looked around the room as I thought about it for a minute. Caught up in consuming the beer, the music, and dancing with the ladies, I was oblivious to how crowded the bar had become. Some people were looking at me with grins on their faces, as though they knew what was about to transpire. I tilted my head toward Ebony, cleared my throat, and tentatively asked her how much it would cost to get with her.

She said, "Twenty dollars."

This may sound rather inexpensive, but keep in mind that this was 1975. I agreed with the price, and she told me to follow her.

Lamont whispered to me, "I'll go with you, and be a lookout because you never know."

While the other two ladies stayed in the club, we walked out onto the dark street, lined on each side by row houses. The chill in the air was a profound contrast to the searing, stifling heat earlier in the day. I followed Ebony to some steps that descended to a basement apartment in one of the row houses. I could see the lights through the windows as we went down. Lamont remained up on the street, as though he knew this was not going to take long.

When we got down there, the apartment appeared to be a little efficiency type—a sleeping area, a tiny kitchen, and a small bathroom. Ebony wasted no time, quickly removing her clothes, revealing her delicious-looking goodies, and retrieving a condom from her purse, with the speed of a doctor preparing for emergency surgery. I needed no prompting to remove my clothes.

As she expertly slipped the condom on me, she asked me had I ever done this before.

I said, "No."

The truth was, I had never been anywhere near this far with a female except in fantasy. Heart issues during the peak of my teenage years interfered with my ability to develop the social skills that are important to establishing relationships with the opposite sex.

Just as Ebony had moved and gyrated in the bar, so she did here, but we were closer and lying rather than standing, and she was no longer repelling my advances. We could not have been any more intimate without completely melding with one another. After no more than seven minutes, it seemed that, as time suddenly stood still, I could hear rockets and bombs bursting in air and feel the sensation of floating back in time, into the womb, and then, with increasing warp speed, into the blood of my ancestral father as he walked the shores of the west coast of Africa. I was immediately jettisoned back to the present, emitting a primal scream, as I reached my peak.

After washing up and putting my clothes back on, I exited the apartment and jogged up the steps to the street, where Lamont was still waiting. He said, "Well, how does it feel to lose your virginity?"

I said, "Like dying, and going to heaven."

The objective of experiencing some of the night life of Northwest DC and losing my virginity had been accomplished. It was now approaching midnight. There was nothing else to do but head to the corner, and wait for the next bus heading toward East Capitol and Minnesota Avenue SE. We didn't go back to the bar. There was no need to. These were working women, and they were busy working on their next transaction. We were just money to them.

During the bus ride home, my euphoric state slowly degenerated into mild depression. I realized that even though I had lost my virginity, it had been through a business relationship and not a romantic one. Not to detract from any value my experience may have had, it had not provided the same self-validating quality that a healthy romantic relationship might have.

We reached our destination, and as we got off the bus, Lamont said, "I'll see you Monday at work."

"Okay, I'll see you," I said as he headed down Minnesota Avenue and I headed east on East Capitol Street toward 53rd Street SE.

I got to 53rd and made a right, walking briskly up the steep hill and thinking that before I'd had my first surgery at the age of eight, I would not have been able to negotiate a hill one-quarter the steepness of this one. I was still only about three years post-op from my latest surgeries. That I was able to function as well as I did was amazing.

I reached B Street and turned left, heading to Doris's house. It was now past 12:30 a.m. I was sure she was starting to worry, wondering where I was at that hour in a city with so many dangerous areas.

She would have no cause for worries that night, but on a night a little later in the summer any fears she might have had came to fruition.

I had been invited over to her place by a young lady I'd gotten to know. What I didn't know was that she was already the girlfriend of a man who was 6 feet 3 and weighed 215 pounds, and that he wanted to stake his claim on his territory—and do so violently. As I walked onto her property, the man walked up to me in an aggressive manner, and before I could defend myself, he had hit me in the jaw. I turned tail and scampered off like a wounded animal.

As I ran, I imagined him thumping his chest in conquest as though he were king of the forest. In reality, he was a cowardly lion for sucker-punching someone unprovoked, especially someone much smaller. I knew my jaw was broken because I could feel sections of it sliding against each other. Surprisingly, it did not hurt too much then. I suppose I was in shock. I made it back to my sister's house, told her what had happened, and she took me to the hospital.

Doctors there confirmed that my jaw was broken, and while they thought surgery might be needed to repair it, they decided to wait until the next day because they wanted me to have a cardiac evaluation.

After the evaluation, the doctors concluded that it would be safe to perform surgery under general anesthetic if needed to fix my jaw. They were able to repair it, however, without surgery. They wired it up, and it remained wired for about eight weeks.

One of the most impressive things about this experience was that it was the first time I had been treated by a predominantly African American medical staff. This helped reinforce my confidence in my ability to obtain a position somewhere in the medical field.

After I got out of the hospital, a detective came to the house to take a statement from me about what had happened. When he saw how small I was in comparison to the attacker, he said, jokingly, that he would have shot him. I'm sure the man was never brought to justice because I would only be in DC for another couple of weeks and had little desire to interrupt my education to make a special trip back to testify against him in court.

With school about to start shortly, I mentioned to the doctor that I was hesitant about going to school with my jaw wired shut. He brushed my apprehensions off, saying, "A fractured jaw is not going to interfere with reading a book and writing." I knew that, of course. What I didn't want was an additional element attracting attention to me. I'm glad I didn't postpone my education because of my jaw. I might have been thrown off track and never got back on. No telling what would have happened to me. For me, my education was the linchpin to a successful life.

I returned to Central State to start my sophomore year. I was even thinner than I had been before, weighing 110 pounds. I was so skinny I could barely cast a shadow. Many people thought I was sick until they saw my jaw was wired and realized it was broken. I had to get an excuse from the clinic to have my meals specially blended. I could hardly wait to get those wires off. It got old fast, having to slurp my meals through a straw like they were milkshakes.

Finally it was time to get the wires off. I went to an oral surgeon in nearby Fairborn to have them removed. It was a relief, but it was kind of weird at the same time. Having had those heavy wires on for such a long time, I had gotten used to the weight, and when they were removed, I had the strange sensation that part of my mouth was missing. Then I was out on Route 35 in Fairborn, feeling and looking, I am sure, like a ghastly phantom, trying to hitch a ride back to campus. Amazingly, some sympathetic soul picked me up.

I was happy to be able to eat normally and start regaining my fifteen or twenty lost pounds. However, since the amount of food allocated to each student's tray—except for members of athletic teams—was not enough to squelch my pent-up appetite, I took every chance I could, when I had extra money, to catch a ride into Xenia to indulge in a couple of Big Macs or fish sandwiches from McDonald's.

At the end of the quarter, I changed my major to psychology after continuing to face difficulty with the quantitative aspects of chemistry. My grades improved after changing my major. In fact, I was one of the top students in that major. I even became a tutor for some of the lower-level psychology courses.

Though immersed in my schoolwork, I nevertheless was conscious of the need to monitor my health. I was still going to Children's Hospital in Columbus every six months, even though I was about twenty-one at this time. (Children's would allow patients to be treated or followed up there until they were twenty-five.) The results of my examinations during this time were always good, but my blood pressure would sometimes raise concerns, since it tended to be a little above the desired range.

At the beginning of my junior year, I was assigned to a room with a person who was involved with the Mad Dogs, a kind of renegade or unsanctioned fraternity on campus. The ringleader of the group, who was an associate of my roommate, was a guy known as "Buck Buck." He had a thick neck, a rotund face, and a massive belly. Sometimes I would see him sitting in his room hunched over a hot plate, cooking up a hamburger or sausage or some other meat, while surrounded by his compatriots, drinking beer. He was like an African chief, proudly flaunting his prosperity, exemplified by his ample midsection.

I hung with them for a while, aloofly, until I came to the conclusion that they were not the kind of people I was comfortable with. Their class attendance was poor, and they never studied. I can't remember ever seeing them cracking a book or at the library doing research for a book report or term paper. When they did go to classes for tests, they would frequently try to cheat. I can recall a number of occasions when they attempted to elicit answers from me, saying, "Wizard"—my nickname—"what's the answer for number" 12, or 14, or 15. I gave answers a few times, but I didn't want to get caught helping them, so I just started ignoring them. Besides, it was their fault for not studying, and they were just slowing me down.

The group tried to get me to join them, but I was not interested. We were like water and oil. One possible reason they might have had for getting me to associate with them was to get money out of me. But there was no way I was going to give those losers what little extra money I had.

One day I was walking down the stairs on my way out of the dorm, when a couple of them stopped me and started asking me for money. When I said no, one of them tried to go in my pockets. I pushed him away and started walking briskly off. They followed me and continued to harass me. I rushed to the car that my sister Jessie had given me after she'd purchased another one, and retrieved the baseball bat I had stored on the backseat for an eventuality such as this. I warned them I would break their hands if they continued to bother me. They came toward me, and I started swinging. I hit at them with the bat, but they were able to take it away from me. I ran to my car to escape them, but before I was able to drive away, they cracked my windshield with the bat.

They reported me to the dean of the university, saying, "Y'all gotta get this crazy guy outta here!" and we all had to meet with the dean. They were expelled because they were on probation anyway.

I later met with the president of the university, and he actually thanked me for standing up for myself. He told me in a hushed tone, "I once broke a guitar case over a guy's head when he harassed me." He said that he would just dispose of the report on me after I graduated.

When I was a junior, I got involved with an organization called the All African People's Revolutionary Party (AAPRP). I can't even remember how I got connected with it—perhaps I read a sign or a pamphlet or I talked to someone who told me about the group. Somehow, I happened to meet a student by the name of Tyrone Griggs. He was the coordinator of the organization's chapter at the university.

Tyrone was a sophomore at the time, majoring in philosophy. He was a dark-skinned, soft-spoken young man, standing about 5 feet 8. The fact that his speech was on the slow side and his face expressionless at first seemed disharmonious with the sharp intellect you would expect of someone leading a chapter of an organization, but it did not take long for me to realize why he held the position. Tyrone was razor sharp, with superb organizational skills, and he had a great understanding of the intricacies of various political ideologies.

The AAPRP was founded by Dr. Kwame Nkrumah in Guinea-Conakry in 1968. Dr. Nkrumah produced a handbook outlining his political ideology, the central principle of which was "scientific socialism." The principle proposed a brand of socialism for African people in Africa and in the diaspora that introduced a new social synthesis that sought to implement scientific and technological advancement without destroying human values and causing the extreme social malefactions and deep divisions that are often associated with hypercapitalistic and hyperindustrial societies. After Dr. Nkrumah's death in 1972, Kwame Touré (Stokely Carmichael) took over the mantle of leadership in the party from the 1970s until his own death in 1998.

Tyrone carried Dr. Nkrumah's handbook wherever he went and referred to it often, as a preacher would the Bible.

Tyrone and some of the other members seemed to have a genuinely deep commitment to the organization, but I was involved mostly just to belong to something and to socialize with a group of positive people. But there was one major focus of the AAPRP that really excited me—apartheid in South Africa, a situation in the world that had captured a lot of attention in the 1970s. The aim of the AAPRP was to help build support for the elimination of that terrible system.

In the spring of 1977, I learned that the organization had planned an antiapartheid march in Washington, DC. I wanted to be a part of this, and I got two of my friends, Steve Mealy and Michael Mahan, to sign up to go, too. They were not members of the group, but the idea of going to Washington appealed to them. In addition to being part of the protest, I'm sure they were, as I was, also motivated by the hope of meeting up with some hot chicks in the "chocolate city." We were required to pay about twenty-five dollars each to go, and we would travel in one of the two buses that had been chartered to pick up students from Central State, Wright State, and the University of Dayton.

We left early on a Friday morning, arriving in Washington toward evening. We spent the night in some dorm rooms at Howard University. The next morning we all converged for the march. By the time we started marching, there were about five thousand of us, with more joining as the march proceeded. We marched about three or four miles to Malcolm X Park.

Tyrone, contrary to his usual low-key demeanor, was running up and down along the column of marchers, pumping the crowd up with the chant, "White man's hands off the black man's land." The marchers responded with the same chant. This "call and response" technique, which dates back to slavery and even before in Africa, was in effect all along the route, as the leaders from different chapters energized the throng of protesters in perfectly coordinated timing.

We finally got to the park. The place where my friends and I sat was far away from the stage where the speakers and performers were. The loudspeakers were not good quality, and the sound reverberated so that we felt we were in the Grand Canyon. I can't remember a thing that was said, but one thing caught my attention—the rather strange and shocking appearance of some of the performers. I could see these black people in the distance on the stage who had very long braided or twisted hair, and some had long beards. I had never seen blacks like this before, and I thought they looked very peculiar.

I asked Steve, "Who are they?"

Steve said, "They're Rastafarians."

I thought to myself, They need to cut that stuff off. Since then, of course, the Rastafarian style has become as common as tattoos.

After the march was over, I called my sister Voncille. She and all my other relatives in Washington knew I was going to be there for the march, and it had been agreed that my friends and I would spend the night with them. Voncille picked us up at Howard University and took us to Doris's place. Doris fed us a delicious home-cooked meal, and we enjoyed relaxing and chatting the rest of the evening.

We got up the next day and went back to Howard University to meet with the rest of the group, board the bus, and head back to Central State. As I got on the bus, I had the subtle feeling that a cold or flu was coming on, and on the ride back to campus I kept feeling sicker and sicker. By the time we got back, I had a full-blown case of the flu. To me the chill in the air, paired with the chill from the flu, made it feel like it was winter again without the snow, as I made it to my room.

But the winter of '77 is one of those times I will never forget. One February night, on a Friday, I believe, I was going to visit a friend who lived off campus in the country, near Wilmington. People who saw me getting into my car told me, "Didn't you hear about that monstrous snowstorm coming?" I said no, laughing at them because the weather seemed great. It felt warm for February, and there were no signs of any precipitation.

I went on my way, but before I could get two miles, the snow started coming down like crazy. Before long, my tires, which were admittedly threadbare, started slipping, and the car kept sliding off the road. I had to abandon it and walk back to campus. There was a chorus of laughter as I sheepishly entered the dorm. I felt like a complete fool. This turned out to be a historic snowstorm. Things were shut down for nearly a week. After about a week, a couple of friends and I went to dig out my car. Amazingly, it started right up. Things were getting back to normal, and the hiatus from academic work was over. The professors were forging ahead at lightning speed to catch up.

One of the friends who helped me dig out was Michael Mahan, who had accompanied me on the antiapartheid march in

Washington. Michael, tall and dark and with an uncanny likeness to Nat King Cole, was from Columbus. We had become pretty good friends, to the point that I accompanied him a few times when he went home to visit. His family, who were all very agreeable, lived in a nice working/middle-class neighborhood on the east side of Columbus. Their house, a neat brick and frame structure, was always orderly, clean, and nicely decorated. Their street was not far from Children's Hospital, where I'd had my surgeries years ago and was still going for my semiannual checkups.

Michael was quite intelligent, as demonstrated not only by the decent grades he earned but by his aptitude for efficient problem solving and by his skills as a chess player and player of the card game bid wiz. He also had a great ability to tell stories.

Over time, however, it became pretty clear that Michael had developed a serious problem with alcohol, which may have started in high school. Later on in college, he had an apartment off campus, where I would go visit him. Sometimes if we planned to go to a dance or something on campus, he would have to sit there and drink at least three or four beers before he was ready. It seemed as though he needed to drink too much before he was able to interact socially.

Over the years, he spiraled further and further out of control, eventually advancing to the use of crack cocaine. His addiction got to the point that I had to cease visiting him whenever I was in Columbus for checkups because he started asking me for money. I knew it was for drugs. In the early 1990s, Michael was living in a roach-infested apartment in a formerly stable area of Columbus that was now in a state of deterioration. His father, who had suffered a stroke, was living with him. I am sure Michael cared deeply about his father, but I got the sense that, while he was stressed out with having to care for him, Michael depended on the additional source of income he provided for the whole house. He would not have been able to afford the apartment with just the amount he earned from his job, when the amount of money he wasted on drugs was taken into account. It was sad that his father, who died a couple of years later, had to live out his last few years in this situation.

It was equally unfortunate to see a man with so much potential, and who had come from such a nice, stable middle-class family, drift into such a dysfunctional state. The last I heard, Michael has been homeless by choice for the last six years in Columbus. When you multiply his situation by the condition of hundreds of thousands of young black males of equal or greater intellectual ability, you can begin to comprehend the level of devastation that drugs and excess alcohol consumption has inflicted on the African American community.

I finished up my junior year with decent grades, and I was starting to think about the possibility of going to graduate school for clinical or physiological psychology. I did not work that summer. I just went home to Massillon for the break.

It was exciting to start my senior year, knowing that after this year I could get my degree and, hopefully, a good job if I did not go to graduate school. At the end of the first quarter, I took the Graduate Record Exam. I did okay on the verbal sections and the part testing psychological knowledge, but the scores were not high enough to get me into the schools I'd applied for, schools that were very selective. They took only the top applicants from a large applicant pool for the small number of spaces available. Graduate school for psychology would not be in my future.

The last semester of my senior year, I moved off campus to stay with my friend Steve, who now lived on a farm that belonged to his family near Wilmington, Ohio. It was agreed that we would split the cost of the oil for the heat, as well as the grocery bill. I liked this. It was good to get away from the noise and hassles from people in the dormitories.

Steve's family's farm had an interesting history, one that dates back to the time of Reconstruction. Steve's ancestors on his mother's side were part of a wave of escaped slaves that migrated to Ohio along one of the routes of the Underground Railroad that ran parallel to what is now Route 68. Route 68 runs north from Kentucky to Ohio as far as Springfield and beyond. I would suspect that a considerable number of the African American residents of the towns along this route—Xenia, Wilmington, Yellow Springs, Springfield—could trace their descent back to those slaves who were part of that wave of migration.

Steve's ancestors had to cross the Ohio River, which they did on flatboats. They worked on various farms for years, saving their money. The Quakers living in the area would have been a great asset, enabling Steve's ancestors to acquire land. The Quakers, known to be great sympathizers of and active in the abolitionist movement, were very instrumental in providing assistance to and protecting escaped slaves from bounty hunters.

Steve's ancestors obtained their land by having the Quakers bid on it on their behalf, since blacks were not allowed to participate in the land bidding or auction processes. When the Quakers won the bid, they signed the deed over to Steve's people. When this happened, many whites in the area were incensed, but nothing, legally, could be done. However, the family was not given the original deed until 1972, according to Steve. The deed was sent suddenly, after being discovered accidentally in the records, by someone working with the county auditor's office who knew the family. The history of this particular deed dates back to 1797, and it boasts signatures that include those of President John Adams and James McHenry, a physician during the Revolutionary War.

Steve's great-grandfather, known as Doc because he'd had the reputation of being good with sick horses, was the original family owner of the approximately seventy acres of land. The land was parceled up over time among different relatives and descendants. In the last several years, Steve told me, most of the family land has been sold.

Our life on the farm, however, did not involve any of the typical chores associated with farm life. I would not have agreed to stay there if I had been responsible for cultivating crops, milking cows, feeding hogs, or any such agrarian labor. I had not even been thrilled with helping my mom cultivate our little gardens in Newcomerstown. "I for damn sho' wasn't gone do no farming there."

Though we had a well outside, we did not have to rely on it for water. We did have the modern convenience of hot running water and an inside toilet. The water was, however, supplied by a well system, and there was a septic tank to handle sewage.

Some of Steve's relatives lived on the family farm land there. His aunt Alma Jean—the niece of his aunt Alma, who occasionally visited the farm from Akron—lived in a house about four hundred feet or so to the left with her daughter, Dee. His uncle Newt lived about eight hundred feet along a dirt road that went up a hill behind and to the left of his aunt's house. Newt's granddaughter, Kim, stayed with him.

We enjoyed going into Wilmington and partying with the local females—although my friends had to convince me to buy some new clothes and cut my hair first. My one friend Blaine from Cincinnati would say, "Wiz, I am going to take you to the 'Natti so you can buy some clothes and get your hair cut." Being a college student conferred special status upon us among the ladies. I am sure wearing stylish-looking clothes and sporting a nice haircut helped.

Soon the school year was coming to an end, and it was about time to take the final exams and turn in the term papers. I completed my term papers and turned them in. I finished all of my exams, and did very well on most of them, although I was a little worried about one.

After my last exam, I joined a couple of classmates at a little celebration. They were drinking all kinds of stuff. I normally did not drink too much, but that night I was so happy to be done with everything that I let it all hang out. I got pretty tipsy.

I was not too plastered, however to realize that I had to drive back to where I stayed, and could not just keep drinking and try to drive. I got in my car and left. If I had been stopped by the police, I would have been arrested for driving under the influence. Fortunately, I made it home uneventfully. The car I had at the time was a Fiat, and it had a stick shift. I had just recently purchased the car, but it seemed that night as though I could operate it as well or better than I could when I was sober. I was shifting those gears in perfect coordination as I negotiated the curves, hills, and valleys on that dark Route 42, with an alcohol-induced false sense of confidence.

My friend Steve's aunt Alma had been visiting the farm for a while. I liked when she came because she would cook for us. The food we cooked did not compare to the meals that she made. Aunt Alma could burn! In Ebonics, that means she could cook.

On this night that I came home intoxicated, at about eleven p.m., nobody was up at the farm—both Steve and Aunt Alma were asleep. But there was a plate of food on the counter. I was hungry, so I wolfed it down, grateful that they'd been so kind as to leave something out for me. The food did not taste as good as it did normally, but it satisfied my hunger. I went to bed shortly after eating. The next morning, I asked Steve about the food that had been left on the counter. I was just wondering if it had been meant for me. He started laughing, and said, "That food was for the cat!" I was speechless. At that point, it was too late—nothing could be done. The food was halfway through its intestinal journey.

Graduation was in the first week of June 1978. I was happy to be graduating. The week before had been pretty grueling. The use of NoDoz caffeine pills to keep me awake in the wee hours of the night, pecking away on my old prehistoric 1970s typewriter, had left me in a zombie-like state as I handed in my completed term papers.

I was still in that state on the day of my graduation, as I walked across the stage to accept my diploma. With my gaunt figure I was sure I looked like death on a cracker. I noticed one of my professors, the one who'd taught that course I'd been worried about, sitting with the group of faculty. My score on that final had not been too good, but in comparison with the average score of the group, it was not too bad. I had found out a few days before that my grade was a C+. When I saw him, I mouthed at him, from a distance, "Thank you!" He smiled back at me, but I swear he was thinking, Poor thing, get your degree and get outta here!

My mother, five of my sisters, and my brothers David and Rahmaan were there to support me when I graduated. When I met up with them outside, after I got my diploma, Rahmaan kept teasing me about how thin and starved I looked. I indicated that I knew I was thin, and I told him about the No Doze I'd been taking. I said, "Now that I'm done with school, I can concentrate on nourishing myself more adequately, and I won't be so emaciated." It was ironic that Rahmaan was ribbing me about being skin and bones; he's always been thinner than all of the brothers. I didn't really take him seriously. He often joked like that.

While introducing my family, saying my farewells to a few class associates, and taking pictures, we were approached by a small group of people who asked us if we were the Trotters from Vallscreek, West Virginia. After we responded in the affirmative, they indicated they were the Rogers. They were our next-door neighbors when we lived there. Here for a family friend's graduation, they had heard my name announced, and saw me during the graduation ceremony.

It had been about eighteen years since we had seen them. After my mother and older siblings talked with them for a while to catch up on what had been going on with each other's families, we took a couple of pictures, said our good-byes, and headed to the restaurant for a much-needed and deserved meal.

A good meal can literally bring a starving man quickly back to life, or, as my brother put it, "Yeah, that meal did you some good!" I think it revived me quicker than human blood restores Dracula.

After my family left, I went back to the farm and started packing my things in preparation for heading back to Massillon the next day. I had finished another chapter of my life, and now it was time for me to carve out a niche in the world of work. It was going to be a challenge to take that knowledge I had accumulated in a classroom setting and package it in a way that would maximize my ability to market myself in a competitive job environment, segments of which still largely favored whites.

It was good to be home after the previous hectic month, and I spent the first week relaxing. I had decided before I left Central State that I was going take some time to rest and decompress from the last few weeks of academic stress. After getting some much-needed beauty rest, days of gorging on my mother's cooking, and visiting friends and relatives, I started submitting resumes and applications to various companies and agencies in Stark County. In the meantime, someone I'd gone to high school with, Gilbert Brooks, told me about a position he'd had that was now open. He had resigned because he'd gotten a better position with a company in Houston, Texas. The position available was district manager with *The Independent,* a newspaper in Massillon. He suggested that I apply for it, and I did.

I got the job, but although "district manager" sounds impressive, it turned out to be a glorified paperboy position. I was the manager for a group of paperboys. When a paperboy was sick or did not show up to get his papers for some reason or missed some customers, the district manager would have to deliver them. The job did not pay well, but it was a job.

I lasted about three weeks on this job. I was fired, but I was relieved about it. My heart had not been in the job. I'd felt like an overeducated and overage paper carrier, which I was. I had been tempted on occasion to hide behind trees, run in back of houses, and duck behind cars to escape detection by acquaintances. The job had not been in line with what I'd studied in college, which was psychology, and I'd known I could not endure it for long.

Ironically, the one positive aspect of this job was what got me fired. While delivering papers, I met a couple of women several years older than I who expressed interest in me. This boosted my ego by four quantum levels, as I still had limited experience with women at the time.

One of the women was named Leona. One afternoon I had to deliver her paper, and we struck up a conversation, just as we had on previous occasions. But this day would be different. Our chatter stretched on longer than it should have, and I knew I should be making my way back to the office, but I was transfixed by the delectable treasures she revealed to me when she unbuttoned her blouse. They hung from her chest like generous and delicious pendulums of fruit. She invited me to explore them. They felt soft and warm as my hands methodically and gently massaged them. She reacted to my touches with deeper breathing and a mildly increased breathing rate. Her nipples took on a thornier and pointy contour, and felt more rigid.

I felt a little guilty about what I was doing, but it was difficult to stop or control the rising tide of nature in me, and I did not really want to stop. I wanted to ride that tide of sensuality to its climactic crest and experience the ecstasy as I descended from that peak. But it would not happen with her this day.

I noticed the clock on the wall said four-fifteen. That jarred me back to reality. I should have been back at the office at four. I suddenly stopped what I was doing and said, abruptly, "I got to go!"

As I made a hasty exit from the house, she said, "Come by Friday night around seven."

I said "Okay," and hurried away.

After a couple of times of such "socializing" and not getting back to the office in a timely manner, my supervisor approached me and said, "This is not working out," and I was fired. It stung for a minute, but I was freed to pursue jobs more compatible with my major in college.

After this I went several months without a job offer, and my mother and I were discouraged and concerned. Then, surprisingly,

I received a call from the Stark County Board of Mental Retardation and Developmental Disabilities, to whom I had sent a resume and submitted an application. They invited me to come in for an initial interview for the position of workshop instructor.

The day of the interview, I made sure that I dressed for the job and was well rested and alert. The interview went so well that I was scheduled for a second one, which would include role-playing an instructor/client interaction.

My performance was good in both parts of the interview, and I was notified several days later that I'd got the job. I was happy to have the opportunity to work at a job that was related to what I'd studied in college, and that paid well for the time.

The first day of work was quite shocking. I was not prepared for what I encountered when I was ushered into the classroom that first day. I can still remember the smells, the self-stimulatory or repetitive behaviors—head swinging, rocking, finger flicking, some of the people hitting themselves—and the very different physical features of some of the people in that room. I was suddenly faced with a group of eight individuals with profound developmental disabilities. I had said in the interview that I like challenges, but this was more of a challenge than I'd expected. My education at Central State had given me the theoretical basis for understanding the learning difficulties of this population, but it would take a while for me to become acclimated to the realities of my chosen profession.

My tasks would be to train these individuals to become more independent in terms of personal care—hand washing, eating, bathroom skills—using the appropriate behavioral training techniques. Secondarily, I was to train them to perform simple contract work.

I was also responsible for managing maladaptive behaviors, including self-stimulatory and aggressive behaviors. During my first couple of days of working, one of my clients kept leaving my classroom, which was in a separate room, and wandering about the workshop floor, where the higher-functioning individuals, separated by partitions, were focusing on contract work.

My assistant watched my area as I went to retrieve my client—a man about twenty-eight years old, 5 feet 10, and 190 pounds—from the workshop floor. He simply would not come back to where he belonged.

I asked one of the more senior staff members to assist me in getting the man back, but he said, "That's your job." So here I was—5 feet 6, 130 pounds, and with a history of heart surgery—faced with physically wrestling this large, noncompliant individual back to his proper area. Though sweating more than a boxer in the fifteenth round, I somehow managed it.

I had actually come across this man a few years before, when I'd been about nineteen years old. I remember walking down a street in Massillon and seeing him standing by a tree. He appeared to be a normal, nice-looking young African American man, but when I spoke to him he did not reply, and as I passed him, he suddenly lunged toward me, running with a profound limp and mumbling incoherently. I fled in fear. At that time, I'd had no experience in dealing with people with mental retardation—and I had no idea that one day I would be this man's teacher and caregiver.

Back then the staff I worked with had been trained to intervene physically when verbal coaxing failed to get an individual to respond to requests. Things have changed radically from that time. Physical management is never used unless it is to protect the individual from hurting himself or others. Nowadays a team approach, led by a behavioral manager adhering to state laws and protocols relating to appropriate and humane measures, is used to calm a distressed developmentally disabled individual.

After about a month, the shock of the smells, sounds, and peculiar behaviors had dissipated. I started to see my clients as individuals with unique personalities who needed compassionate assistance in developing skills that would lead to higher levels of functioning in the areas of basic personal care and vocation training. Within a year I was making substantial progress with some of the most challenging people in my group. Some made such good progress that they were moved to a higher-functioning area. Others became more independent in using the bathroom, tooth brushing, and eating. And to assist some of those who had really challenging issues with eye-hand coordination in doing certain production jobs, I had a knack for coming up with adaptive fixtures. I was even featured in *The Repository,* a Canton newspaper, one time about the work I did.

In my many years of service with individuals with developmental disabilities, I have encountered situations with clients who were so behaviorally challenged that I've been left emotionally and physically drained by the end of the day. Other clients have been so funny that they could have been characters in a sitcom, and some were a mix of comic relief and a pathetic reflection of societal ills.

I once worked with a man in his thirties by the name of Lawrence K. He exhibited a low level of intellectual functioning and frequent occurrences of aggressive outbursts. Lawrence was obsessive/compulsive about certain things. He had a preoccupation with small holes that he would notice in his clothing or someone else's.

Lawrence would start repeating over and over, while getting louder and louder, "That hole bother me, that hole bother me." He would then proceed to stick his hand in the hole in his clothing or that of others, making it even larger. His level of agitation would increase in direct proportion to the increase in the size of the holes he'd made. Before long, he would be in a full-blown aggressive-behavior meltdown, and the behavior manager would have to be called to assist with deescalating his behavior. At this point, chairs and tables may have been knocked over or he may have torn his clothing off or ripped the clothing of staff as we were attempting to restrain him and calm him down to prevent injury to himself and others.

Chris B., in his early thirties when I worked with him, would on occasion walk around saying, "Nigger, nigger, nigger, nigger," repeatedly, while looking at me and laughing louder and louder. He was obviously trying to get me to react, but I ignored him until his voice got so loud that it became a distraction to others. This was amusing in a way, but it was also a sad commentary on how racism has so permeated all layers of society that even people with severe mental disabilities have learned to utter racist epithets.

After working with the organization for about a year, I got my own apartment. I was finally completely on my own. It felt great to have a place to entertain friends, and to be able to come and go as I pleased. I had come a long way.

It was now about 1980, and the disco scene was still popular. With my rather lucrative job, I had the resources to do as any young single male then might have done—buy more stylish clothes and spend a little money at the disco clubs I frequented.

At this time, I was still kind of reserved—not completely a party animal, but able to connect socially with a few people. I never in general indulged too much in alcohol because, for one thing, I remembered my one drinking and driving episode. I was also concerned about the potentially adverse effects drinking may have had on my health. I could nurse two drinks all night long.

I enjoyed this period of my life between 1980 and the early part of 1981. The music then was the best. Memories of dancing, or doing my own "two step," in the clubs to music by Chaka Khan, Donna Summer, the Isley Brothers, Earth, Wind & Fire, Frankie Beverly and Maze, Michael Jackson, Stevie Wonder, and other popular artists of that period are forever locked in my mind.

eight

THE STRUGGLE CONTINUES

IN THE SPRING OF 1981, my blood pressure readings started to rise dangerously. I began to feel a little more fatigued in the evenings, after a long day's work. I am sure my doctor in Columbus knew that at some point I might have to consider the possibility of further surgery. Since I was working by then, and had good insurance, I guess he thought it was a good time to have my situation reevaluated. Twenty-five was the cutoff age for receiving treatment at Children's Hospital in Columbus, so at the age of twenty-six I was referred to the Ohio State University Hospital in Columbus. My doctor would be Charles Wooley. He and Dr. Hosier had collaborated on numerous clinical and medical studies.

In April 1981, I had heart tests completed at the sprawling Ohio State University Medical Center, and they confirmed what the clinical exams had suggested. Though the initial repair of the aortic coarctation in 1971 had worked well for a while, my vascular system had grown and developed quite a bit, so the previous repair was not able to handle the increased growth. As a consequence, excessive stress was being put on the left ventricle trying to push blood through a narrowed opening. This was reflected by high blood pressure readings and an enlarged heart. My heart was electrically stable, and the ejection fraction, or pump function, was okay. So my prognosis after having surgery should be favorable.

Several months after having the tests, I was scheduled for surgery. My surgeon's name was Dr. Kilman. (What a name for a surgeon!) My brother Rahmaan, formerly James, drove me the approximately 115 miles to the hospital in Columbus. My brother David accompanied us. After I was checked in, we chatted for a while, then they left. There was nothing more they could do, once I got settled in my room. I was a grown man, and I did not need them there to hold my hand. They had family and work responsibilities, and they needed to get back.

I was not as scared this time around. I had gone through these procedures so many times, and knew the routine so well, that I was ready to rattle off the answers to the questions of the doctors I knew would be coming soon to conduct their presurgical assessments. This episode was just another roadblock to overcome. My objective was to get back to my life, and not have to worry about an imminent stroke or episode of heart failure.

Not too long after my brothers left, I was deluged by several waves of doctors and medical students conducting their customary hands-on examinations. As usual, I got numerous visits from members of the hospital "vampire department," some of whom merely pricked my fingers to extract blood. Others among them, desiring a greater quantity, went for the veins. This required the use of a bigger needle, and more expertise.

It was always amusing to me when a nurse or technician had trouble getting the blood; they would most often blame it on some anatomical attribute of mine—"You got small veins," and so on. The truth is, some people are just not as good at this as others. My veins are just fine!

I spent the next day having a series of presurgical tests, and the shaving of my chest and groin completed my preliminary preparation. That done, I just lay there contemplating the impending surgery. I can't say I was consumed with anxiety about dying. The thing I worried about most, if at all, was how functional I would be if I survived. I didn't want to have a stroke during surgery or suffer cardiac arrest and flat-line, resulting in serious brain damage. I was terrified of waking up and being confined to a wheelchair, and having severe cognitive problems. To end up severely disabled and a burden on my family would have been the worst outcome to me.

Around six a.m. a nurse came in to start the IV, then another nurse gave me a sedative. Fifteen or twenty minutes later, I started feeling really woozy. Soon my mind was in a carefree state. I was not worried about anything at all. To be honest, this was a great experience. I can see how people become addicted to these drugs. I had no fear whatsoever. I'll bet that if a huge bear had come into the room, I probably would have said, "Come on, I'll fight you, bear!"

When I was being transported to the surgical area, I vaguely remember seeing my mother, brother ,and a friend of the family. I also remember waking up, in a dazed state, in that highly illuminated and sterile operating room with all of the high-tech machines and monitors surrounding me and the big bright surgical light above my head. I remember them telling me to count. Though my thinking was somewhat dulled at this point, I had the deliberate idea of trying to see how far I could count without being knocked out. I think I got to about seven, which was a great achievement. In the past I had never been able to get past three or four.

Before I knew it, I woke up in the ICU. I remember them asking me questions to assess my neurological status. They asked me who I was, and if I knew where I was, and questions like that. Here I am waking up from major heart surgery, and I'm thinking of responding to the question about did I know where I was with "Yeah, I'm on Mars." I must have decided that this wasn't the time to make wisecracks, so I answered the questions appropriately.

I found out later that I had been out for about a day and a half and had been in surgery for approximately twelve hours. They'd had to remove parts of two ribs, as had been done back in 1971 (after which the ribs grew back). This involves an incision running from about an inch below the left nipple and curved upward along the left scapula.

When I became more alert, and started to move around in the bed more, I had the sensation that part of my body was missing. I later found out that this was a reaction to the partial removal of ribs. I was in some pain, but it was nothing compared to what it was going to feel like after the anesthetic wore off in a few days.

The beehive of activity in the ICU diminished as the weekend approached. Patients were being transferred to regular rooms. As a result, not as many nurses were needed. There were only two or three patients, as compared to about ten at peak. By Friday night, it was just me and an elderly man on the other side of the room. It was so quiet, it was scary. I had crazy thoughts of a psychopath springing from behind the curtains, approaching me with a large knife, intent on performing his own special surgery.

Just one or two days earlier, there had been a constant chatter among nurses and doctors as they discussed vital signs and exchanged other medical information concerning the various patients. I could hear all kinds of noises in the ICU, from IV bags being changed to beds and furniture being moved around and doors being opened and closed. The incessant beeping of the heart monitors and the characteristic sound of ventilators were very audible. I greatly preferred this noisy activity over the eerie, foreboding quiet of that Friday night.

Around ten p.m., I fell asleep, awakening about four hours later, at two a.m. There was a very attractive blond nurse at my bedside. She was putting something in my IV.

In my now paranoid state of mind, I abruptly rose up, and I said, "What you doing?"

"I'm just putting some antacid in your tube," she said in a sweet, innocent voice. I was distrustful of this, and I focused on her like a laser. I was paranoid enough at this point to be convinced I was a guinea pig in some grand experiment conducted by a team of mad scientists, and she was one of their pretty assistants.

It didn't help my state to notice that the elderly man in the bed across from me was in an obvious state of delirium. He was thrashing and flailing about, and making incoherent noises. Before long, a small group of nurses and doctors had surrounded him and were administering physical restraints. Gradually he calmed down. I guess they had injected the man with a sedative to get him to relax.

After witnessing this, my state of paranoia intensified. With the head of my bed raised in an inclined position, I lay back in a hypervigilant state until dawn, saying to myself, I am not going to sleep! I constantly watched my heart monitor, and that of the old man, for any signs of suddenly dropping or speeding up. These people were not going to get me, I thought.

At about 4:30 a.m., I noticed two young black men come into the room wearing masks and green hospital gowns. They were carrying plastic bags that apparently had something in them. The young men were both about 5 feet 6, with medium brown skin and similar facial features. In my paranoia, all I could think was that they were responsible for collecting the organs that were extracted from human experimental specimens. And I was sure doctors were peeking through little openings in the shades hanging from the window of the ICU door, watching for the heart monitors to flat-line.

I lay there thinking, These are all evil people who are connected with a vast nefarious medical laboratory project—I've got to get out of here. I had visions of hobbling down the hallway while still connected to the intravenous pole, trying to negotiate the complex labyrinth of the institution to get help.

My awareness of the medical exploitation of blacks in the Tuskegee experiments in the 1930s, and the documented stories of grave robbers digging up black corpses to be used in medical schools in the late 1800s and early 1900s helped fuel my suspicions and state of paranoia.

Around six a.m. Saturday, more nurses and other staff started coming in, and the activity in the room started to pick up. I began to feel more secure. Later that morning Dr. Kilman came in and told me I might be transferred to a regular room that day. I was glad to hear this, and even gladder when, close to noon, he came in again and said, yes, I was going to go to a regular room. I told him I was happy to be leaving the ICU because it was making me paranoid. He indicated that he understood, and I got the feeling that this wasn't the first time he'd heard that.

About a day and a half after I was moved to the regular room, the effects of anesthesia started to wear off, rapidly. The pain increased in intensity, and before long I was crying out for pain medication. I had been pushing my button to summon the nurse, but they seemed to be slow in responding. I was groaning so much that my roommate called the nurse himself, telling them, "This man is in pain." They finally started giving me something for it. I suppose they'd had to wait for an order from the doctor. The medication helped ease the pain. It still hurt quite a bit, but at least it was more tolerable.

The bed I was in was outfitted with some metal framework. It had a bar running parallel to the length of the mattress. There was a chain about eighteen inches long that hung from it, right above my chest, and at the end of the chain was a circular hand grip. The function of this apparatus was to assist patients in repositioning their body when they became tired of lying in one position in the bed. In surgeries that involves a thoracotomy with some rib resection, it is excruciatingly painful to adjust your body without some kind of leverage.

Dr. Kilman came to talk to me the next day after I was moved to my new room. I asked him what procedure they'd used to fix my aorta. He explained that they had taken a synthetic Dacron graft and sutured one end to the ascending aorta. They then sutured the other end to the descending aorta. Since there was no longer a need to use my left subclavian artery to repair the aorta, it was reconnected to my left arm to give it more blood supply. I was now getting more efficient and direct blood flow to my left arm. When the left subclavian was used to repair my aorta, my left arm was getting blood flow, but it was via collateral circulation. My arm would tend to give out under unusual physical stress, however. I would no longer have that problem.

I was also pleased to find out that the vocal problems that I had suffered in previous surgeries did not seem to be as evident this time around. I had expressed concern about this risk before surgery and had been assured that they would be very aware of this during the surgery, and with the post-op use of the ventilator.

One thing that vexed the doctors while I was recovering from the surgery in the hospital was my persistent fever. Concerned that I might have an infection of the bypass graft, or somewhere else in the body, they carefully monitored for any signs of this. An infection in the blood was never detected, and the incision site continued to heal nicely. Finally, they surmised that I may have been reacting to some of the antibiotics I was being given. They stopped the antibiotics, and my fever went away.

After more than three weeks in the hospital, I was getting stronger and stronger. Times when I was not running a fever, I felt surges of energy. I could not do much with this energy in the hospital, so at times boredom would set in. One thing I did when bored was to comb out my hair and then braid it. It was amazing how much my hair seemed to have grown in the three weeks I had been there—I could only surmise that some of those chemicals I had consumed were responsible. One day when I knew I was going to get visitors, I took the braids down and combed my hair out so I'd look presentable when they came. This might sound kind of vain, but I always took pride in my appearance. When my visitors got there, they were surprised about how good and healthy I looked with my gigantic 1970s-style afro.

About two and a half weeks after surgery, a physical therapist came to my room. She showed me some exercises to do to prevent my right shoulder from drooping due to the partial rib resection on the left side of my chest. She also worked with me on a program I would be doing at home to gradually increase my cardiovascular fitness. I did well on these exercises, progressing by leaps and bounds. I must say, though, that at twenty-seven years of age, I was much younger than most of the patients there. The majority of patients were men in their late forties, fifties, and sixties, suffering from coronary heart disease. They looked at me with envy as I sailed through the routines.

I was released from the hospital after about thirty days. My brother Rahmaan came to pick me up. I had lost seven or eight pounds while in the hospital, but though I was thin, I felt excited, healthy, and energetic as I walked out of the hospital, politely refusing a ride in a wheelchair toward the exit. My determination to get home and continue my rehabilitation was undaunted, and my will to make a good recovery was strengthened. As a young man, it was my goal to maximize my cardiovascular fitness, and to minimize any effects of the partial rib removal.

The day after I was released, I started my rehabilitation program. I first started walking short distances. I would take my pulse and record it. The more I walked a certain distance, the easier it would become. This would be reflected by a slower pulse rate as my heart adapted to the physical stress. I increased these walking distances as my body increased its ability to handle more physical stress, and before long I was able to walk over two miles without any problems.

I also did arm-circle exercises, side bends, and pushups to strengthen my muscles. Months later I would get a set of weights and start light weight training. My conscientious performance of these exercises was successful in both preventing any significant asymmetry in my physique and improving my sense of well-being.

After about three weeks of recuperating at my mother's house, and eating her good food, I went back to my apartment. A few days after getting back, my friend Donald Furlow came over. He lived in one of the other apartment buildings in the complex.

Shortly after our family moved to Massillon, I'd met Donald in school. He had moved to Massillon from Columbus when his father got a top managerial job for a company in Massillon. Originally from Arkansas, Donald had a southern country voice, and that, along with his polite mannerisms, made him seem like a cool dude. We ended up being running partners for many years.

That night he nudged me to go out with him. I was a little reluctant because I had not yet been back for my follow-up with the doctor, to clear me for more activities. I did feel pretty strong and energetic, however, and besides, I was kind of bored, too. I decided that I would go out with him. I had a good time, and from then on, I started going out about twice a week without a problem.

My sick leave had just about run out, so it was critical for me to get back to work or I was going to be in real financial trouble. I was risking having the utilities shut off, losing my apartment, and dealing with creditors (including the medical ones who had just cut me up) in hot pursuit.

It took a couple of days to get acclimated to the work routine, but after that things went really smoothly, and I was able to finish my day with reserved energy.

My heart issues had basically been corrected, and I could look forward to many years of good health. I felt good, and by all objective measures, I was in fine shape. I had settled back into my normal work routine, and my performance evaluations were good. I was ready to enjoy life, and catch up on lost time.

It was the early 1980s, and Michael Jackson, Prince, and Lionel Richie were at their peak. Parachute pants, leather pants with zippers and studs, and Jheri curl hairstyles were all the rage—styles inspired by Hollywood and the modern R&B era. This was the decade of preoccupation with self (the "me" decade), when people were often concerned with their own material happiness and well-being. Hedonism was at an all-time high, and there was a definite uptick on the radar scale measuring social decadence. Drug abuse, criminal activity, HIV, and other sexually transmittable diseases were on a steep increase.

My own social decadence was definitely on the low end of the scale, but those were definitely exciting times for me. I was gainfully employed, and had money to get a decent car and obtain some of those "hip clothes" of the time. The weight-lifting program I was on was paying dividends in bulkier biceps and an expanded chest. And while my "Trotter ankles" were a challenge, being skinnier than twigs, they did not hinder me from being able to lift more weight with them than many men with ankles the size of Mason jars. I felt like I had a powerful physique, and was able to carry myself in a manner that discouraged victimization.

My hair was already fairly long, but when I got a Jheri curl, it doubled in length. I was one of the top Jheri curl kings in Stark County, and I played it to the hilt. Denied my fair share of female attention for too long, it was time to collect. Whenever I went out, I usually started out with a drink or two of gin and juice. By the time the drinks were hitting me good, the club would be starting to jump. In my mind, I felt like the "Mac Daddy" of the club, and I would be on the prowl. I probably looked and sounded like McGruff, the crime-fighting dog, but I was not trying to take a bite out of crime.

Over the course of the next eight or nine years, I developed relationships with a number of women, lasting varying lengths of time. I won't specify any number, but I would just say it was too many. This is not something, as I reflect back, that I am especially proud of, but at the time it was a boost to my self-perception. In retrospect, I realize that this was not a healthy thing. From the age of twenty-eight to thirty-five years I should have been settled enough to focus on trying to establish a more meaningful and long-term relationship. However, due to the health problems in my later teens, I did not have the opportunity to develop the social skills and confidence that most young men do. In a way, I was afflicted with social retardation.

Even under normal circumstances, teenagers' selection criteria for dating in some ways are more stringent than those for getting into Harvard University. So, if you have the physical disability I did, you are at a distinct disadvantage. Had it not been for a supportive and validating family, I may have been even more socially impaired.

The resulting relative awkwardness followed me into my college years, reinforced to a degree by the attitudes of some young women, still fixated at the high school level of preferring brawn over brains or selecting thugs and/or wannabe athletes over men just trying to establish a normally responsible and productive lifestyle. I could explore the multifaceted causes and the socioeconomic consequences of this phenomenon, but that would be way beyond the scope and the purpose of this book. I like to think that those who overlooked me in the past just failed to realize the diamond in the rough they could have had.

Fortunately, I did eventually, by my late twenties and early thirties, come to terms with my little insecurities and self-doubt. I stopped being concerned with how others felt about me. I started looking at myself in the mirror and recognizing all of the positive attributes I possessed, and I started to validate and value myself as I should. I am now comfortable in my own skin, can accept my imperfections, and even laugh at myself.

During my decade of hedonism, I managed to avoid two major bullets, getting someone pregnant and the dreaded HIV. Most of the time I practiced safe sex, but on the few occasions that I didn't, I contracted nonspecific urethritis. The fact that most of the women I had relationships with were on birth control may have explained how I avoided fathering a child during that time. (I did wonder for a period of time about my ability to produce children, so I had a test done to check it out. The results of the test indicated that my sperm count was adequate—my little soldiers were marching, with weapons fully loaded.)

If there was one thing I wish I could have changed about my life, it would have been to have had at least one child—and with a woman I'd married, because I think it is better for children to be raised by both parents together. I think I would have been a great father, with a wealth of knowledge and wisdom to share. But that did not happen, and it may have been for the best. Having a child with someone who would not have made a good mother, or with whom I was not compatible, could have meant disaster for the child, not to mention stress and tension for me. At that point in my life, though, I was not ready for children. Nevertheless, I am content, and I have found fulfillment in being a father figure from time to time and an uncle.

Around 1986, I got really concerned about the increasing AIDS risk, and more specifically, about reports of a significant increase in Stark County. I went to the county health department and had the test done. It took about two weeks to get the results, at which point I was contacted and told to come in to discuss them.

When I went to find out the verdict, I had a sense of foreboding as I made my way down the hallway toward the room where my fate would be decided. The man going over the results sat on one side of a table, and I sat on the other side. He talked slowly and deliberately, as though he was trying to build up suspense, the way they do on reality TV shows nowadays—and then what he said was, "Well . . . you are not even close."

By this time, my heart was beating a hundred miles a minute. I felt as though someone had snatched me from the guillotine at the last second, right before the blade was released.

I left the place feeling like I had a new lease on life. I had a fresh sense of commitment to a life of safe sex, feeling fortunate that I had escaped that bullet. My mission from here on out was going to be to observe a strict safe-sex policy one hundred percent of the time. And I did, at least for a while.

Eventually I got to the point where I felt I needed the stability of a more committed relationship.

Though I had a good job, I was not really accumulating savings. Through these serial relationships and a fairly debauched lifestyle, I was spending money as quickly as I made it. By that time, my early thirties, I should have been much more disciplined in my living and in the management of my money. They say hindsight is 20/20. That is so true, and if I knew then what I know now, I could have amassed decent savings and avoided a few social and financial pitfalls.

I had been dating a lady by the name of Dotsie off and on since 1987. In fact, I'd known her in high school, but at that time I'd felt like I had no chance of dating her. When I met up with her in 1987, she was coming out of an abusive marriage and I was starting to think about "slowing my roll."

After a couple of painful breakups, I proposed to her in 1990. I was thirty-six years old, and my thinking at that time was that I was not getting any younger, so I'd better take the relationship to the next level before it was too late. In retrospect, that was not a good reason to get married. Sometimes marriages turn out great no matter what the impetus is that propels the couple to get married; however, one should not get married just to feel like a whole person. You should already feel complete independent of marriage.

I was living then in the house I had purchased in 1988. It was next door to Dotsie's mom's house, where Dotsie also lived. I bought the house on impulse, without investing the amount of deliberation that I should have in such a major decision.

The realtor who was handling the house was an old work friend of mine. I saw him at the house and went to talk to him. He immediately tried to interest me in the house, letting me see the inside. I had been entertaining the idea of purchasing a property, but I had not conducted any preliminary research on what properties were out there or what was required as far as things like down payment, required income, credit scores were concerned. I had been a renter for years, and I thought that I should invest in a house. The condition of the house was very good, I thought, for an old house. The asking price was $21,000, which I felt was a good deal.

I found out later the house was worth less than what I paid for it. I should never have done the deal without doing more research.

The point of mentioning the house is to illustrate the dangers of real-estate impulse buying and the problem it presents when you are breaking up with someone and they live next door. For one thing, it makes it harder when you see the person with a new boyfriend or girlfriend. I would not advise anyone to purchase a house next door to where your girlfriend or boyfriend lives.

I got married to Dotsie on September 13, 1990, at the Friendship Missionary Baptist Church in Massillon the church we later joined. The minister who presided over the wedding was the Reverend Raymond Mason. My best man was my brother Joe. There were about 125 guests. It was a nice wedding, and I was basking in the euphoria of the moment, with the feeling that we were doing the right thing, and looking toward the future with great optimism.

Our relationship had been on a roller coaster, and I welcomed the stability that marriage promised.

The characteristics that had drawn me to Dotsie were her kindness, attractiveness, femininity, and willingness to laugh at my silly jokes. She had a smile and eyes that could put a man in a trance. Her laugh was as sweet as an angel singing in heaven, and her compassion toward others was remarkable.

Over the course of three years of marriage, this feeling of optimism and euphoria slowly gave way to the realization that we were incompatible and we lacked communication. In fact, I considered filing for divorce after about three years, but after speaking with my mother, I didn't go ahead with it. In an attempt to salvage the marriage, we decided to become more active in the church we had joined about a year before. Things got better for a while, but it would not last. After a long, turbulent roller-coaster ride, the marriage ended in divorce in April 2002.

What spelled the end for me was the morning I got up, and going downstairs to prepare for work, noticed that she had slept on the couch. The thing that bothered me was that she had a lit candle on the coffee table and the blanket covering her was inches away from the flame. An ashtray full of cigarette butts was sitting on the table, too. This really irritated me. She was risking both of our lives by doing this. It was the last straw.

Dotsie's doctors had warned her about smoking, and I resented being exposed to secondhand smoke. I'd had my share of heart issues, aggravated by an attack of viral cardiomyopathy, the last a couple of years before, requiring the implantation of a pacemaker/defibrillator. I did not need this further insult to my health, and shortly after this incident, steps were taken leading to our divorce.

The marriage, on the other hand, had had some good points. I have pleasant memories of going on vacations together, visiting her relatives in Mississippi and my relatives in Alabama, Pittsburgh, and Washington, DC. The trip to the Poconos to celebrate our fifth wedding anniversary was awesome. The hotel suite was beautiful, and the serenity and magnificence of the place, surrounded by nature, was absolutely divine. I can recall pleasant moments of just spending quality time at home, going to dinner or to the movies.

I missed the way Dotsie laughed at my corny jokes, and how she warmed my heart with her beautiful smile and bright eyes.

After finalizing my divorce in April 2002, Dotsie moved to Mississippi, where her mother had relocated. I did not have a burning desire to jump quickly into another marriage, but I was open to establishing a steady connection to someone. Starting a new romantic linkage can be fraught with apprehension and anxiety even under ordinary circumstances. When you have the extra baggage of potentially life-changing medical issues, the concern is greater. You have to consider when to disclose the information. Should I tell her now or should I wait until the relationship gets to the next level? You also wonder how the person will react to the information.

In 2003 I met Pamela Johnson. I was introduced to her by a friend, Sharon Wright, with whom I'd worked at the Stark County Board of Developmental Disabilities. Pamela turned out to be a wonderful woman.

It was evident after several dates that we really clicked. We liked many of the same things—movies, dining out, walks, live shows, family gatherings, reading, and even keeping up with current events. Pamela was independent, not looking for a man to rescue her. She was able to make it on her own.

The other thing that impressed me about her was the outstanding job she had done, and was doing, in raising her family of three sons and one daughter, which she did virtually on her own following her divorce. After about three years, we decided to live together.

In May of 2006, on a Saturday morning about nine o'clock, while we were in bed, I noticed a steady, audible tone being emitted from somewhere. I told Pamela that I thought it was from the pacemaker/defibrillator in my chest, but I wasn't sure. It had been about seven years since the device had been implanted, so I had been expecting the battery to run out pretty soon. In fact, I had been looking forward to the prospect of getting one of the newer-generation devices, which were smaller.

The episode did mean that the battery was running out, and I had that newer device implanted with Pamela by my side to support me through the procedure.

She's always been there to support me, not only during my own issues, but during those of my family, for example, when my sister Voncille was going through a critical illness. In 2006 Voncille nearly died from a bacterial meningitis episode. Losing her would have been very traumatic for me. We were close in age, tighter than O. J. Simpson's glove. We often laughed and talked on the phone for hours, confiding in and supporting each other. She had had both legs amputated due to the meningitis, but her mind and spirit were unaffected, and two years ago she got married to a great man named Melvin Greene.

My sister survived, but her close call, and the deaths of younger relatives, friends, and acquaintances, made me even more cognizant of my mortality. Death is something you can't ultimately escape. Everyone is going to die. It's a part of the cycle of nature. I've long resigned myself to its inevitability—not that I don't fear it, but I am not consumed by it.

This point was driven home even more starkly in 1999, when I had that episode of cardiomyopathy, which caused a potentially life-threatening heart rhythm problem.

Realizing how short and fleeting life can be makes you think about all the things you would like to experience and wonder if you will be able to do them before your number is up. Traveling to the "motherland," Africa, and a cross-country trip are two things on my informal "bucket list." I just hope I have time to do them both. The prospect of mortality also prompts you to gravitate toward a form of faith.

Friendship Missionary Baptist Church, in the wake of my mother's death, held true to the long tradition of black churches in stepping up to help their members, and in many cases nonmembers, through the grieving process. For this, I and my family were very grateful.

Feeling a "spiritual void," I had joined Friendship Missionary Baptist Church, the church that my mother and other family members belonged to, in 1993. I joined the usher board, and later on I became a tutor in a mentoring program called Project Lift. I assisted elementary and junior high school students with basic math.

While I was a member, I served as a master of ceremonies a couple of times for church programs. The brothers of the church tried to draft me to serve on the deacon board, but I did not feel I was ready for that. My commitment as a churchgoer was very high for years, consistently paying my dues and contributing generously to additional fundraisers. Though my wife's attendance had fallen off at some point, I continued to attend regularly for years.

Eventually it got to the point where I started feeling tired, burned out. Part of this may have been due to the developing viral myocarditis episode that I would experience soon. There also never seemed to be an end to fundraisers and appeals for more and more money from members, even when they had gone above and beyond what they'd pledged. The sermons started sounding the same to me, stale and boring. The only time I got excited was when the minister reached the climax of his sermon. I knew then that it would not be long before church was over and I could go eat. This is not meant as a criticism of the minister. He was doing his job, but I was just not into it.

Furthermore, I had become frustrated with trying to give a rational meaning to the stories in the Bible. What were these stories trying to say, and how could they be made relevant to the realities of the late 1990s? Around 2000 I gradually stopped going to church. I could no longer see a meaningful reason to go.

Historically, especially in African American life, the church functioned as a community center of social interaction and activism and as a civil rights organization, as well as promoting the spiritual, ethical, and emotional well-being of the people. But today I wonder if the church continues to serve these functions better than alternative nonchurch institutions.

In 1995 urban America was experiencing an explosion in crack cocaine and gang warfare and a continuing escalation in the AIDS epidemic, as well as the usual problems of chronic poverty, unemployment/underemployment, and familial instability. One of the leading voices in the African American community speaking out inspirationally and constructively about the pathologies affecting the black community was Louis Farrakhan. Though a controversial figure, and often criticized by the larger community for his embrace of Black Nationalism, Farrakhan appealed to millions of people in the inner city who felt that he understood their plight. Farrakhan also talked about the need for black men to stand up and act more responsibly, and for those who are responsible to participate in a mass demonstration to show the world that the majority of black men are not criminals, drug addicts, or derelicts.

One other key thing that Louis Farrakhan talked about was the need for the black community to become more economically powerful, that is, increasing the percentage of the profits collectively generated by businesses that are controlled by blacks. In general, these things appealed to me, and for that reason I joined hundreds of thousands of African American men and even men of other races in the Million Man March in Washington, DC.

After the march, I felt inspired to do what I could do to contribute to the economic enhancement of the black community. I started a small business called T.L.C. Lawn Care. This enabled dozens of men of all persuasions over the years to obtain some extra money doing landscape work. Therefore, in my small way, I did contribute to the economy of my community and to the general economic system.

My second cousin Marcus Simpson was the first person I employed to work with me. I really was trying to get a couple of his older brothers to help me, but his mother, Maxine Simpson, told me that Marcus was a very good worker, so I hired him, based on her recommendation.. He proved to be a very fast, efficient, and thorough worker. Years later, when I got out of the grass-cutting part of the business, I sold him some of my equipment and gave him my mowing customers.

We were out mowing one day when I unknowingly mowed over a yellow jackets' nest in the ground. All of a suddenly, a swarm of yellow jackets came out of the hole and started stinging me about the head and face. I immediately ran, swatting my face and head with my hands to get the yellow jackets off. My cousin did not know what the heck was wrong with me. I suppose for a minute he thought I was going crazy. When he found out what had happened, he made a thinly veiled effort to stifle his laughter. I know it was killing him to keep from bursting out completely.

We finished up with the work remaining there and proceeded to the next job. By the time we got there, my face and mouth were swelling. I didn't have any dangerous allergic reaction like my throat tightening up or breathing difficulties. It was just a disfiguring swelling. Looking and feeling like the Elephant Man, when we finished with this job I cut the day short and went home to tend to my situation.

Some members of my family had reservations about me getting involved in the rather physical demands of landscape work. The work did not seem to bother me, however, and my regular annual check-ups always came out positive. There was no apparent evidence that the work was putting an excess strain on my heart. My cardiologist at the time did not see any reason why I should not continue. She only suggested that I should not push myself beyond what felt comfortable to me. I always tried to have sufficient help when needed.

I felt fortunate that I was able to be so physically active. I'm sure that my family and others aware of my medical background were amazed that I would ever be able to be engaged in such strenuous work. I often thought my dad would have been proud that his boy with the "bad heart" at birth would one day get a truck and be the "hustler" that he was.

Between 2002 and 2007, a man by the name of Jerry Mitchell would work with me doing landscape and hauling jobs. Jerry was in his early to midsixties at the time. He was approximately 5 feet 8 and weighed about 150 pounds. Jerry was very trim and fit, having the energy of a man fifteen to twenty years younger, in spite of a bad cigarette habit. He had one very interesting physical characteristic—a somewhat diminutive, if well-proportioned, peanut-shaped head. Sometimes I would tease him by referring to him as Peanut Head.

His value to me on the job was immense. Unlike me, Jerry possessed pretty considerable mechanical skills and ability, and this came in handy on a number of occasions. I would often remark, after witnessing one of his astonishing mechanical feats, "You're a freaking African engineer!" In all seriousness, I think Jerry did have the ability to be a professional engineer.

One other thing about Jerry was that he was a scavenger. Whenever we'd do a hauling job, he was meticulous about sorting out junk that he thought had some value. I would just shake my head in annoyance. I just wanted to load up the stuff and go, and not be concerned with filtering through stuff. He was a real-ife Fred Sanford or Scatman Crothers. I use to razz him at times by humming the tune from the *Sanford and Son* show.

A few years later, I found out that Jerry's attention to sorting through junk was not merely a trivial or fruitless activity. It could pay real dividends. One day I did a hauling job by myself. What

I had to haul away was mostly scrap wood, but there were also a few pieces of metal—copper, aluminum, and some brass—about eighty pounds of metal total. I took the metal items to the recycling place and to my surprise I made about eighty dollars, which was pretty much clear profit.

I said, "Hot damn," then called Jerry up and said, "I'm in the junk business now."

He laughed and said, "See, you thought I was crazy, didn't you?"

Ever since then, I stopped making fun of Jerry's scavenging.

My brother-in-law Isaiah Jackson was someone else who possessed an entrepreneurial spirit. While sitting at the table in his small kitchen or while pecking at his computer, navigating the *Nigerian Sun News* online, Isaiah would talk extensively about life in his native country of Nigeria. His eyes would widen with excitement, seeming to double in size, as he spoke in a deep Nigerian accent about the customs and cultures of the major tribes of Nigeria such as the Igbo, Hausa, and Yoruba.

Isaiah was a member of the Yoruba tribe, but he would always say that the Igbo were at the top of the economic food chain: "If a person was doctor, engineer, professor, big business owner, most likely they are Igbo." Before he became disabled, he would travel to Nigeria at least twice a year, taking at least two or three gigantic suitcases stuffed with goods hard to get in Nigeria to sell. On his return trip the suitcases would be stuffed with things made in Africa, especially African attire and sculptures, to sell.

A natural-born entrepreneur, Isaiah had established a number of businesses in the past. One of his most successful ventures was a small restaurant in Canton called World's Famous Sandwiches in the early 1970s. Although promising, the business folded after a year or so because he had trouble maintaining dependable and trustworthy workers.

While we had repeated discussions about my accompanying him on one of his excursions to Nigeria, as we sipped beer or a glass of wine, this never became a reality. Maybe it was just "whiskey talk" anyway. As Isaiah got sicker, the prospects of this happening dimmed. It could not be crossed off my bucket list.

In the early spring of 2000, my brother Joe called me with a proposition. He wanted to know if I would help him drive his car back from Palo Alto. He would be out there for a year on a research sabbatical related to one of his books, *The African-American Experience,* at the Center for Advanced Study in the Behavioral Sciences at Stanford University in California.

The prospect of driving cross-country was appealing to me. I had always fantasized about doing it, but I'd never gotten the opportunity. Joe would fly me out there, and then, after spending a couple of days while he and his wife tied up some loose ends, we would drive back. A moving company would transport the bulk of their possessions, so we did not have to tow a trailer.

This was a deal that I could not pass up. It also provided an opportunity for me to cross another thing off my list. My only concern was the possibility of my defibrillator going off during that long road trip. I was not concerned so much about myself, but I did not want to endanger other people's safety. There's a possibility that, if it goes off while you are driving, you can lose control of the vehicle from the jolt, and risk the lives of others in the car. I felt it would probably be okay, but you never know. I did not want to scare Joe by discussing these concerns with him.

I thought about whether to do the trip for a few days, then decided that I would. I had experienced only a couple of instances where the device went off. Furthermore, I was on medication to control the racing of my heart, and I'd had no incidents of discharges from the system since starting the medication.

I called Joe and told him that I would do it, and he arranged for me to take a flight there in a few months.

In early July, I flew into the San Francisco airport, where he and his wife picked me up. I stayed in a room they'd reserved for me in a motel next door to the building where they'd been living in a tiny apartment. In a couple of days, they had packed up all of the things they would be having shipped and the things that they would carry in the car.

Joe, in his effort to maximize the opportunity to sightsee on our trip back East, had included in the itinerary a drive through Lake Tahoe. We had also planned for a night stay in Reno, to visit one of the casinos and try our luck at some of the games of chance. That night I was not successful at winning any money, but fortunately I did not lose too much either, only ending up in the hole about forty dollars. I pretty much stuck to the nickel, dime, and quarter slot machines, with a few dollar and five-dollar games thrown in.

The next day, we decided we would play a little bit before getting back on the road. My brother, noticing that I was continuing to play those small-wager slot machines, suggested that maybe I should start playing the ten- and twenty-dollar slots. I was not getting anywhere with the nickel-and-dime strategy, and switching up seemed to work. I started winning more than I was losing, although I had not really hit it big at this point.

I continued walking around the casino, trying to decide what beautiful, sparkling, and colorful machine I was going to play next. The sounds of bells, whistles, the jingling of change being ejected from the machines, and the loud, incessant chatter of hypnotized gamblers were dizzying.

Finally, I saw this machine, glowing with wild clown colors and pretty multicolored blinking lights. The eyes of the queens and jokers pictured on the machine seemed to draw me toward it. I decided to put in a twenty-dollar bill. Adjusting myself comfortably on the stool, I pulled the lever firmly. Suddenly, bells and whistles went off and the machine's lights started blinking wildly. Money was ejected from the machine for what seemed like forever. I was sitting there smiling like an idiot. I knew I'd won something, but I didn't how much. People all around me were gazing at me in envy.

My brother said, "Man, you hit big!" and suggested that we just cash out and leave while we were ahead.

I won about $450 after subtracting my losses. I did cash out, and we went back to the hotel, packed our things, and got out of Dodge.

We got on the interstate and headed East, realizing that we had a long trip ahead of us. Thank God for the air conditioning, for it was hot enough to fry an egg on the hood of the car that day. Our goal was to cover at least six hundred miles for the second leg of the trip, and we did, traversing great stretches of that vast, hot, barren territory. During our travel, I tried to imagine how those traveling West by covered wagon in the 1800s were able to survive that scorching heat. It was amazing to behold the natural massive rock formations in the distance and realize the vast dearth of any green vegetation. Most of what I saw was just barren, dry, sand-colored earth. The lack of traffic, coupled with the straight, boring highway and the lack of visual stimuli, constituted a perfect recipe for self-hypnosis. We had to force ourselves to stay alert.

We stopped in Salt Lake City, and after touring the city a little, we got back on the highway and continued on, driving for another hundred miles or so before quitting for the night in Evanston, Wyoming.

Much of the territory we covered the next day was pretty desolate, devoid of the hustle and bustle we'd encountered passing through cities and towns. Around five p.m., my sister-in-law, LaRue, started calling hotels in cities ahead of us to reserve a couple of rooms for us for that night. She had trouble getting her cell phone to work because apparently, even in those days of growing cell phone popularity, very few cell phone towers existed in those isolated areas of the Great Plains. We just kept driving in hopes that she would be able to get some connection on her phone. Before we knew it, nighttime had come, with no motel in sight. We did eventually come upon a gas station that was open around ten p.m. in North Platte, Nebraska, but still no motel. We filled up the tank and kept right on going.

We proceeded toward our destination on Route 80 East, with Joe driving. It was clear that we were in for an all-night session of marathon driving. It was pitch black except for our headlights and those of cars approaching us very intermittently from the opposite direction, and quiet, a condition conducive to sleep. I was wide awake. But I knew my brother, and I was well aware that around ten or eleven p.m., he was prone to falling asleep without a moment's notice.

I kept a vigilant eye on him, watching for signs like frequent eye blinking or head drooping, and before long, I started noticing some signs.

I said, "Joe, you need a break?"

He laughed sheepishly, that little silly laugh you emit when you're caught doing something you shouldn't. I took over and drove for another 175 miles, and then we alternated driving the rest of the night. We were not home yet, but it felt good to at least be in the Midwest.

It was about eight a.m. when we arrived in Davenport, Iowa, a few miles from the Illinois border. Upon seeing the Welcome to

Illinois sign, I said to LaRue sitting in the back seat, "Well, we're in your home state. How far is this from Zion?"—Zion being her hometown.

She said, "We're a long ways from there, probably about two hundred miles or so."

Remembering something about LaRue's ancestors playing a significant part in the settlement of Zion came to mind. I asked her about this, and she told me she was the granddaughter of Naomi Williamson Marshall of Zion, whose parents had helped settle and develop the town in the early 1900s.

Larue recalls warm memories of growing up in Zion as a fourth-generation descendant. Her grandmother always referred to her as Legs, because on holidays and during the summer, LaRue would spend her time running "Marshall errands," delivering meals to the old, sick, and shut-in members of their community. Mrs. Marshall also worked with a variety of groups, including theatrical groups, which influenced LaRue's decision to pursue a teaching career in theater and English.

The East Moline sign jolted me back to the present. We got off the highway in East Moline and went to get gas and something to eat. It just so happened that the very day that we were in East Moline, the John Deere Golf Classic was being held, and the town was in a very festive mood. We went over to the golfing site and checked out a little of the action, then, around noon, exhausted from the previous twenty-four hours of activity, we checked into a motel and retired early.

We arrived back in Ohio around ten-thirty the following night. I could now claim to have traveled cross country, and could cross this off my bucket list.

In June 2010 my three brothers—Joe, Rahmaan, and David—along with my nephew, Carson, and I went on a retreat to Bluestone State Park, about sixty miles from Vallscreek, where we used to live in West Virginia. I sponsored this as a birthday gift to my oldest brother, Joe. Being the chairman of the History Department of Carnegie Mellon in Pittsburgh as well as a professor, and handling numerous other responsibilities, he had little time to really focus on an event like this, so I did it for him. He had always wanted to have an outing like this with his brothers.

It was very significant that my nephew Carson accompanied us on this retreat. He is a great representative of that generational link to the Trotter family's connection to West Virginia and Alabama. Though Carson came from humble beginnings, without the benefit of his father in his life, he managed to succeed in life in spite of it, graduating from the University of Cincinnati with a degree in communications. Now at the age of forty-one, Carson has a rewarding position with a major company.

That Trotter legacy of reaching for a higher level than your predecessors is reflected through the achievements of Carson's two daughters, Kersha Deibel Trotter and Alexis Grimes Trotter. Carson contradicts the stereotype that African American males are not involved in the lives of their children. He has been involved in their lives since their births. Both daughters have or are working on advanced degrees.

Though Carson and his current wife, Tanya, do not have any children together, they have been mutually supportive of each other's. This family embodies the qualities of compassion and concern for others, ambition, intelligence, and perseverance in the face of injustice and hardship—attributes possessed by their parents, grandparents and great-grandparents that have been transmitted through the generations.

On the second day of the retreat, we went down to Vallscreek. This place is so isolated from the main highway system you have to take a series of rural roads, cross over into Virginia, go around a big mountain, and go north on Route 16 to get here.

I pity those who live there if they get seriously ill or have any kind of major trauma, for they would be hours away from a significant medical center. They would need to be medevaced to get advanced medical care. I think of the situation with my father. Even if a modern trauma center had existed in that region of West Virginia when he was shot, it would have made no difference because we were so remotely located. It's a miracle that any of us children survived in that isolated and materially destitute place.

It had been years since I had been there, and my youngest brother, David, had never been back since we left in 1961. At one time, the population of this place was about eight hundred, but now there are probably fewer than two hundred people combined in the upper and lower camps. It is so tiny and off the beaten track that it is no longer listed on any West Virginia maps.

We went to see the old one-room school house, and the church we'd attended. They both have been abandoned, and pretty much over taken by vegetation, woods, and the critters living there.

To get where we used to live, you have to drive over a little wooden bridge that spans a shallow creek. The road we lived on is still a dirt road. Five or six houses on the road are still standing. The rest of them, including the one we lived in, are gone. The only thing left that suggests houses were once there are fragments of concrete pillars that the small wood-frame houses sat on.

Surprisingly, we ran into one of our old neighbors, Rex Crawford. He had moved away to New Jersey years ago, but later in life he returned, preferring the peaceful, serene setting of the hills of West Virginia to the hustle and bustle of urban life. It was amazing to see him, and to be walking the same dirt road that we'd run and played on so many years before.

We went across the wooden bridge back to the other side of the creek and took some more pictures. I looked across the creek at those few remaining houses. I could hear the whistling of the wind in my ear as it blew down the big hills behind me through the trees, and the calming sound of the water running in the creek as I stood there on the bank looking into the distance. Faint echoes of the gleeful voices of children playing in the dusty roads and the spirited chatter and laughter of adults, unfettered by often desperate poverty and the daily grind to just survive, filled my mind's ear. These were reverberations from a more vibrant community in the distant past. These auditory footprints have become part of the collective cosmic noise. Cruising through time and space at 768 miles per hour, echoes of dead relatives from four or five decades ago have traveled hundreds of millions of miles.

My cousin and the brother of Pete Foster, Howard Foster, once walked these lands. He died in Alexandria, Virginia, in 1994. We were about the same age. Neither Howard's nor my childhood was a walk in the park. Mine was difficult economically and medically, but his was emotionally difficult in addition to being economically challenging. His mother and father separated when he was five years old. His mother, Cora Lee Foster, left her husband, my mother's brother, Luther Foster, and moved to Youngstown, Ohio. My uncle Luther, an unemployed coal miner, left Vallscreek in search of work and settled in Alexandria, Virginia. Howard was left with his teenage brother, Pete, to take care of him. Most teenage boys do not have the maturity to take care of small children, so Howard ended up being neglected.

My mother, sensitive to Howard's plight, tried to help as best she could, but she was already stretched to the limit with her own children. Ultimately, Howard joined his father in Virginia. When his father remarried a few years later, Howard's living with them caused tensions between him and his wife, and eventually Howard went to live with his uncle, Thamon Foster, in Massillon.

Howard was intelligent and had a good sense of humor, but it seemed that friction accompanied him everywhere he went. I think he never really felt accepted. Howard dropped out of school around the tenth grade in Massillon, and he moved back to Alexandria. Over the next couple of decades, his life tumbled out of control, with deepening alcoholism, marital problems, and uncontrolled diabetes. Although he never got into serious trouble with the law, his life came to a tragic end when he was found dead on a deserted street in Alexandria.

My cousin, Maxine Simpson, the daughter of Thamon Foster, my mother's brother, died in 1998. She was preceded in death by her brother, Will Foster, who was murdered in 1984 in Detroit. Maxine spent her first few years of life in Vallscreek also, until her family moved to Massillon. Maxine loved life and family. She was funny, had the gift of gab, and loved to gossip. With the help of her mother, my aunt Innie, Maxine managed to raise all six of her children after divorcing her husband, Andy Simpson. Aunt Innie died in 2013, at the age of 92. Her husband, Thamon, preceded her in death in 1981.

In 2000 my niece Geneva died from an illness she had battled for several years. Geneva had a heart of gold, a very keen intellect, and the ability to do great things. It's too bad the world never benefited from the full realization of that potential.

Eleven years later her sister Thelma, whom we called Poochie, passed away. Only forty-seven, she died from a stroke caused by undertreated hypertension. Thelma and Geneva were the daughters of my sister Dee, who had previously lost a newborn son and a three-month-old daughter, Karen, about forty-four years ago. She has experienced far more tragedies than any human being should have to endure.

In March 1995 my mother passed away. This event would forever change the tone of the Trotter family dynamics.

My mother had been suffering with kidney failure for five or six years, due to a long history with diabetes. The last three or four years of her life, she lived at the Hanover House Nursing Home in Massillon. Before she went to the nursing home, I was the one who usually took her for her appointments and assumed the role as contact person and intermediary between the doctors and the family. It was ironic how the roles played by my mother and I had flipped over the decades. I was now, to a degree, her caretaker, as opposed to her caring for me. I was my mother's "local yokel," at her beck and call before and after she went to the nursing home.

My one regret is that I wasn't living then where I live now. It would have been nice if Mom could have spent her last years before she got really ill with family. I lived in a two-story house back then, with all the bedrooms upstairs, and it would not have been suitable for her. Now I live in a new ranch house with two bathrooms on the main living floor, which would have been ideal.

I can't erase from my mind that picture of her face as a dark cloud of sadness spread across it, so dark that it partially eclipsed the sun shining through the living room window of her house as she was preparing to leave for the nursing home. Sitting in her wheelchair, she was clutching the little Ziploc bags full of sugar, flour, and salt she had desperately and inexplicably packed.

I asked her why she'd done it.

She said, "I might want to make something."

It was clear to me that she was just trying to hold on to something tangible associated with her roles of mother, grandmother, and family host.

On her seventieth birthday, before she got really sick, her children gave her a big birthday party. All of us attended, and everyone had the opportunity to give his or her own testimonial about the love they had for Mom, and how much she meant to them. We wanted her to receive her flowers while she was alive.

Just as we loved our mother, she deeply loved all of her children, and was committed to keeping us as safe and healthy as possible during our development. She wanted all of us to have successful lives. Our mother's child-rearing methods were strict, rooted in that deep southern tradition that subscribes to the notion "you spare the rod, you spoil the child." Some of my siblings felt they'd borne the brunt of our mother's chastisement. This may have been true, and might explain why she said a few weeks before her death, "If it's anything I might have said or did that any one of my children has hard feelings about, I'm sorry."

When she said this, I was the only one there. She knew she didn't have much longer to live, and she was trying to resolve any possible grievances her children might have had with her. But after everybody said their good-byes near the time of her death, I am confident that she was assured that none of us harbored any bad feelings, allowing her to pass peacefully.

On the day leading up to the night of my mother's death, she seemed to perk up when she got a visit from a couple of ladies from the church. She communicated with them as coherently as ever, maintaining eye contact and a strong voice, and displaying no obvious distress.

After her visitors left, she lay back and just gazed at the ceiling. I asked her what she was looking at, and she said, "I want to go up there."

I said, "Up where?"

She replied, "With Josh, Thamon, Zack, Washington, and Raymond."

Raymond? Who was Raymond? I said, "You just have five brothers, the four that have passed and Luther." Zack and Washington we heard about, but never met. Zack, whom she said I resembled, died at the age of twenty-five. Washington, the oldest brother, left Alabama in his twenties, and was not heard from again.

She just smiled and said, "You're always trying to analyze me." She continued, "I had a brother that died when he was two or three, named Raymond."

I had actually been relieved that her suffering was coming to an end, but when she took her last breath that night, the realization that her voice would be silenced forever hit me hard, and I became distraught. I kept reminding myself that she had not wanted her suffering to go on. She had made me promise her a couple of months before that I would not continue medical interventions that were just prolonging her misery.

During the grieving process, emotions often are up and down. On the day of the funeral, I was in good spirits, considering the situation, as I prepared for the funeral while enjoying the mutual support of family members, many from out of town whom I had not seen in a while. My emotions took a steep dive, however, as we filed by the casket to view our mother's body. Lying there was the woman who had birthed me, nurtured, comforted, and validated me, imparted values to me that had successfully carried me through life, and who had loved me unconditionally—as she had done for her thirteen other children and her grandchildren.

Our brother-in-law, Ralph Harris, delivered our mother's eulogy. Ralph, who passed away in 2012, and my sister Josie had been divorced since the early 1970s, but the ending of their marriage did not change the way we felt about him or how we interacted with him.

As clear as a pristine brook, I remember Ralph saying, "It is easy to preach her funeral because she has lived her life by the Christian principles she has professed."

This was so true. My mother had the compassion of a Mother Teresa toward others, and would share whatever she had with those in need. By making herself a living example, along with requiring us to attend Sunday school regularly, she inculcated those values in us.

One of the ministers, Reverend Arrington, spoke about the importance of the family maintaining closeness after the death of the parents. He cautioned that often family cohesion suffers when the bonding force provided by a parent is weakened upon the death of that parent. It is therefore critical, he said, that the surviving family members make a concerted effort to keep those family connections strong. The family's functions of strengthening the spirit, providing a sense of belonging, keeping one grounded, and providing needed material and moral support are crucial to enhancing the well-being of an individual. A person without healthy family connections is like a lost ship in the all-too-often hostile waters of the world, devoid of empathy. Fortunately, our family has sustained those bonds.

While I sat in the church listening to the eulogy and the words of other speakers, my mind reflected back to years past in New-comerstown. I thought about how our mother regularly tried to encourage us. I could hear her voice, strong and clear, still colored, though faintly, with the accent of an African American woman from Alabama, even after years of living in the North. She never seemed to be upset with her children's academic performance as long as it was at least a C average, even if she felt they were capable of doing better. Maybe from her perspective of growing up in the South, just making it to high school was an accomplishment in itself, or on the other hand, perhaps she just simply didn't want to risk discouraging us.

I remember her inspecting my grade cards, with their abundance of Cs, in junior high school. Her usual response would be, "Well, you're on the level," followed with a remark about the many average people who ended up doing great things.

Her favorite example was Dwight D. Eisenhower. She would say, "Eisenhower got average grades in school, and he became a great general and the president of the United States." She would go on to say, "You can do whatever you want if you put your mind to it."

That's how she was, always encouraging and trying to inspire hope when one felt hopeless and insecure. One thing she would say, based on the scriptures, to uplift one weighed down by the burdens of life was "The race is not given to the swift, but to those who endure to the end." I remember her saying to me, when I expressed worry about dropping dead suddenly or simply dying at a very young age, "It's not the sickest that die the quickest."

As I sat there in the church, I thought of being in her kitchen as a child in Newcomerstown, my appetite stimulated by the mouth-watering aroma of beans, cornbread, and government beef, wafting so strong I could taste it. I could not wait to dive into that delicious food, especially on those cold, late fall evenings. It was so soothing to the soul to feast on those meals in that warm kitchen. I remember looking out the kitchen window, the glass beaded with condensation, and seeing birds flying back and forth over the trash can at the back of the yard, scavenging for sustenance, and an occasional dog rummaging through the trash around the can in search of food in that frigid prewinter weather. I felt warm and safe inside, anticipating the dessert of rice pudding or bread pudding that was to come shortly. At that moment, even with the drywall bulging in the ceiling from the leaky bathtub drain under the floor above, I felt like I was dining in a palace.

During the funeral service, I would be aroused periodically from my mental wanderings into the past by the sudden change in a speaker's voice or by the jarring effect of an uptick in music from the organ, only to lapse back into random deep thoughts and memories of my mother. I thought about how she'd made the decision to dedicate her life to raising her children on her own, and not parceling us up, after our father's death.

My mother's world was her children. She loved us deeply, but we were still a burden, not because she lacked the will to care for us, but because the needs and requirements of the twelve children remaining at home after my father was killed were so great. The economic and emotional hardships borne by one individual to care for so many would have caused a weaker person to throw in the towel. My mother had no spouse to lean on for support, and forget having sufficient "me time," when she could take time for herself.

Sitting there thinking about the tremendous struggle it must have been for her to raise all of her children and years later deal with significant medical issues, my heart ached for the suffering that my mother had endured throughout her life. I also felt some guilt for the freedom we children had had to make certain choices and come and go as we pleased. She could not do those things, but through her sacrifices, we could.

My guilt was extinguished when I remembered how she felt about the decisions she'd made regarding raising her children. I know she was pleased with the way we'd turned out and felt her sacrifice had been well worth it. She was glad that our lives overall are much easier than hers was. I think all parents want their offsprings' lives to be just as good as or better than theirs.

I was jolted from my deep meditation by the change in the tone of the service, which signaled the winding down of the funeral. The choir started singing "Like a Tree Standing by the Water," a refrain that was repeated over and over. No matter how much I resisted, the flood of tears now could not be stopped. That was one of the songs my mother would often sing as she went about her daily routine, and it reminded me of how much of herself she had given to the family. For me, because of my health issues, she had gone a few extra miles.

The minister motioned to the pallbearers—my three brothers, two nephews, and me—to carry the casket to the waiting hearse. We walked down the middle aisle of the church, modest only in size, with its red plush carpeting, gleamingly polished wooden pews, cathedral ceiling, and majestic choir stall. We walked in sync through the opened double doors from the sanctuary, out into the hallway between the fellowship hall and the sanctuary, making a left turn. Thirty feet ahead was another opened double door, which led to the hearse standing outside.

After putting the casket in the hearse, I felt my grief starting to ease, marking, to me, the start of the healing process. Following the short burial service, however, a feeling of profound sadness and guilt overcame me as we walked solemnly back to our cars. I had the feeling that we were abandoning my mother, to be entombed in a cold grave forever. The depressing thought I'd had of never hearing her voice again returned in full force.

Memories and echoes from the past once more flooded my mind. Those Saturday nights in Newcomerstown, when my brother and I would be playing in the street or in a neighbor's yard with a ton of other children, when I could hear my mother saying, "Otis and David, get in here! Y'all know you supposed to be in the house when the streetlights come on!" Or the times she would try to do something special for her children even on a meager budget, compromising other things that were probably more critical to provide us with a rare treat, like ordering a pizza from Armando's on Cherry Road, the street we lived on in Massillon.

I thought about trips back and forth to Children's Hospital for appointments, graduations she'd attended, the various holidays over the years with her as host and center of the family, and her presence at church and school programs to support her children. There is no shortage of positive memories to substantiate the fact that our mother loved and cared deeply about us, as we did her.

We and other families in Vallscreek hadn't had much, but we'd had family unity and the values of cooperation and compassion and concern for others. The fact that my brothers, my nephew, and I were able to get together and go on this harmonious retreat where our life started reflects for me the value of family unity.

This family cohesion was displayed in an even more profound way Memorial Day of 2012. This holiday turned out to be a somewhat impromptu family reunion, conceived by my sister Voncille, and dubbed the Trotter 14 Reunion. It was planned and executed in no more than two and a half months. All fourteen children attended, along with many nieces, nephews, and grandchildren. To quote Voncille, "Joe Trotter Sr. and Thelma Trotter must have watched from above and bragged around heaven for all to see," as we all came together in love as a family.

Yes, the Trotter family continues to press on into the future. The seeds of positive values that were planted by Joe Trotter Sr. and Thelma Trotter so long ago continue to grow into valuable fruit, as exemplified in the character and accomplishments of their progeny. Joe Senior's children younger than I and other descendants don't know how he looked or have any recollection of him. I can recall him, but my own view of him is as faint as if I were legally blind. Nevertheless, we learned of his greatness, courage, compassion, love of family, and humor from our mothers, siblings, fathers, uncles, and aunts. The memory of our mother and the faceless memory of our father will be passed down through the generations for perpetuity.

At the reunion, I reflected back on all of the challenges that I had been presented with. I realized that, separate from the experience of my family, my life was and is a miracle within itself. Beyond the medical issues, there were impediments related to race and socioeconomics. Just coming from rural West Virginia by itself and adjusting to life in a new state was a challenge. To transcend these barriers, and to reach even the modest heights that I have, could not have been predicted by even the most optimistic, knowing my situation as a child. It seemed as if the stars lined up just right at the different stages of my life—like days when you are running late and the sequence of the lights just turn green right at the second you get to them, allowing you to just keep moving. Medical developments, sociopolitical changes, and family situations always seemed to shift to an orientation that was advantageous to my survival.

Sometimes I have wondered if I was a pawn in a game played by God, presenting me with challenges and then manipulating situations where I could avoid pitfalls. But what would be the challenge of creating a world where the outcomes of individuals' lives were totally controlled? To not allow a person any input in determining his or her ultimate course, you create a puppet. Often things, good and not so good, happen by chance. You have to find a way to capitalize on the good, and seek ways to overcome the problems.

At each stage of my life as a child, as a teenager, and as an adult, when confronted with medical crises, other difficulties, or disappointments, I have met the issues with confidence and the determination that I would get past them and continue on with a productive life. It was not easy, and there were times when despondency threatened, but I was able to summon that inner strength and stiffen the spine inherited from my mother and father, the spine that served them well in weathering the storms of racial oppression of the Jim Crow South.

I have not overcome these difficulties through my efforts only. Having an extraordinarily loving and supportive family to help me along the way cannot be underestimated. Armed with the confidence, positive attitude, and perseverance gained from my family helped me to succeed as an adult. I feel blessed to have survived to live in a country that has morphed into one that more closely resembles the ideals of its creed. When Barack Obama was elected as the first African American president, he implied that only in America was his story possible. I feel that this was probably true for my situation as well. The dreams of my mother, my family, and me to overcome the obstacles I faced to arrive at where I am today were probably only possible in this country.

When I was a child, I had no idea that I would one day go to college and earn a bachelor's degree. I just hoped that I would survive until a cure for my heart condition was developed. After the success of my first surgery, the prospect of a much longer life was created, but I still did not see myself living beyond my early forties. When I did become more hopeful, I began to make a more concerted effort to prepare myself for the pursuit of a higher education, and through sheer determination, grit, and will, sometimes in the face of harassment, persecution, and attempts to crush my spirit, I achieved my goal when I was awarded my bachelor's degree in psychology from Central State University. I now had a chance to obtain a decent job, and greatly improve my standard of living.

My job as a workshop instructor with the Stark County Developmental Disability beginning in 1979 provided me with an economic foundation, leading to the purchasing of my first home in 1988, my current residence in 2007, and a couple of rental properties in 2009. Being a landlord and having run a landscape business would have seemed like things of fiction during my youth, when I was just concerned about living until the next year.

It's an amazing coincidence that the community where I started life, Vallscreek, and the community I live in now, Highland Creek, share similarities in their names. Other than the names, the communities are hugely different. Highland Creek is a solid, middle-class community of new-construction homes—suburban, multiethnic, and multiracial. Highland Creek is a community that personifies the achievement of the American dream. Even though Highland Creek is much more affluent than Vallscreek, the values of family unity, interfamily relations, compassion for others, and concern for the welfare of the youth existed at least as much in Vallscreek as in Highland Creek.

There is little about the Highland Creek area that would have suggested its past history, which I learned about, to my surprise, during a casual reading of the Canton newspaper *The Repository*. I encountered a story about a black Canton woman, Gerry Radcliffe, who was researching the history of a vanished Ohio town called Aultman, about a quarter of a mile from Highland Creek, which once had a predominantly black population of a thousand. Workers had been recruited by the National Fireproofing Company from Appalachian states such as Tennessee and Kentucky, starting in the early 1920s. The company made clay conduit blocks for underground telephone lines.

This community of unique round houses had been constructed by the company for its employees using its rounded ceramic tiles, with the result that they looked like enormous cookie jars, with conelike tops. The community thrived until the late 1950s or early 1960s, when the company was purchased by Fuqua Industries of Atlanta. Shortly thereafter, that company became bankrupt, and it went out of business when purchasers of their products shifted to plastic conduits because they were cheaper and easier to make.

The residents of the community were proud, highly adaptable, and industrious people, who refused to let the loss of their livelihood crush their spirits. They found employment with brickyards or other businesses in other localities in Stark County and beyond—but what this meant was that a previously thriving community was disbanded. After a thorough search of nearby woods and brush, I was able to find red brick remnants of the houses, the first two or three feet of portions of the walls of several houses, still intact, and multiple discrete, small piles of red brick rubble. But a casual observer driving through, would have no idea that it was once a thriving community.

Like Vallscreek and Newcomerstown, Aultman was another example of the thousands of African American communities created by blacks migrating from the South and elsewhere in search of a better life.

It's been about fifty-two years since I left Vallscreek. I have lived in Newcomerstown and Massillon and have visited many cities and towns in this country, but there's something unique about that Vallscreek brand, forged by the experiences, good and bad, of my parents in the Deep South and reinforced in southern West Virginia. This label is indelibly stamped on my soul, conferring upon me strength of character, tenacity, confidence, courage, compassion for others, and a sense of humor in the face of adversity.

That famous saying, "A rolling stone gathers no moss," is only too true. You have to keep moving; otherwise, you'll be overtaken by the elements. The same applies to a car left on the street and not driven—it will eventually succumb to dust and rust. I try to remain engaged and active. I retired four years ago, but I went back to work as a provider for the Ohio Department of Developmental Disabilities, providing transportation services and facilitating recreational and socialization activities for individuals, as well as transporting the Amish. Benjamin Franklin once said, "In this world nothing can be said to be certain, except death and taxes." I say, give me more taxes. As far as death, I ain't got time for that.

My sister Doris's senior picture, 1967.

My brother David and I at my graduation from Central State, June 1978.

My sister Dee, back in Vallscreek to attend the 1991 Excelsior High School Reunion in War, West Virginia.

A group of former students and others at the Excelsior High School Reunion, Homecoming, around 1997. *Front:* My sister Voncille (did not attend Excelsior). *Back:* My sisters Dee (graduate) and Josie (graduate), me, my sisters Eva (graduate) and Isalene (completed her junior year there, but graduated from Newcomerstown High School), and Isaiah Jackson, Isalene's husband. This school became War Junior High School after segregation began to be phased out.

My mother at seventy.

My brother Joe and his wife, LaRue, when he received his named chair at
Carnegie Mellon University.

My fiancée, Pamela, and I at the Black West Virginians' recognition dinner, Charleston, 2010.

Voncille and Melvin's wedding, June 17, 2011.

Trotter 14 reunion, 2012.